A Feminist Compa...
Methods in Psychol

Series: Feminist Companions to Psychology
Series Editors: Sarah Riley, Rose Capdevila, & Hannah Frith

Other titles in the series:

A Feminist Companion to Social Psychology
by Madeleine Pownall and Wendy Stainton Rogers

A Feminist Companion to Research Methods in Psychology

Hannah Frith and Rose Capdevila

Open University Press

Open University Press
McGraw Hill
Unit 4,
Foundation Park
Roxborough Way
Maidenhead
SL6 3UD

email: emea_uk_ireland@mheducation.com
world wide web: www.openup.co.uk

First edition published 2022

A catalogue record of this book is available from the British Library

ISBN-13: 9780335250134
ISBN-10: 0335250130
eISBN: 9780335250141

Library of Congress Cataloging-in-Publication Data
CIP data applied for

Typeset by Transforma Pvt. Ltd., Chennai, India

Praise page

"This is an outstandingly accessible, persuasive and entertaining critical feminist engagement that demonstrates its politics in its pedagogy. It is both feminist psychology and feminist critique of psychology, and – as the authors, who are themselves key figures in the field – make clear, you don't have to be feminist to read and benefit this book, because it's what we all need to know anyway to do inclusive and social justice-oriented social science. This is essential reading for all undergraduate and applied psychology courses."

Professor Erica Burman, University of Manchester, UK,
editor of Feminists and Psychological Practice and
co-author of Challenging women: psychology's exclusions,
feminist possibilities

"This book provides a wonderful, gently provocative, critical companion to the standard psychological curriculum! By centring research, the questions that are (and aren't) asked, and how they are asked, Frith and Capdevila reveal the complex, messy, political reality that swirls behind the smoke-and-mirrors façade of scientifically neutral knowledge production in psychology. This is a book for any student who has wondered where they are in psychological research, or indeed anyone hasn't wondered – because they are there – and hasn't questioned who and what is being left out, and with what consequences."

Professor Virginia Braun, School of Psychology,
Waipapa Taumata Rau/The University of Auckland, NZ

"The scope of this text is impressive, demonstrating the continued importance of feminist informed approaches as a valuable means to think critically about research methods in psychology. Using customary examples from within the discipline, Frith and Capdevila invite the reader to probe the methodological principles of reputable studies on memory, gender differences and social behaviour and more; to reach beyond traditionally proposed social categories and theories, and to question time-honoured assumptions underpinning conventional psychological evidence. If you are interested in lived experience and meaning making, or want to think more creatively about psychology, this text is utterly invaluable."

Paula Reavey, Professor of Psychology and Mental Health,
London South Bank University, UK

"A gem of a book! Frith and Capdevila engagingly explore the 'whys' rather than the 'hows' of feminist approaches to psychological research methods. Important critical lenses of place, power, social justice, ethics, representation and intersectionality, and reflexivity are introduced and re-visited. Their tone conveys feminisms plural, is friendly, and the book appropriately advocates for theoretical and methodology pluralism. Reading this is guaranteed to challenge (in a good way) and improve the critical thinking skills of students. I wish an accessible and well-crafted feminist guide such as this had been around when I was a psychology undergraduate!"

Elizabeth Peel, Professor of Communication and Social Interaction at Loughborough University, UK, and co-author of the textbook Lesbian, Gay, Bisexual, Trans, Intersex, and Queer Psychology

"In the book 'A Feminist Companion to Research Methods', Hannah Frith and Rose Capdevila provide an excellent overview of how to become a feminist researcher. In the book they clearly justify the need to engage with feminist concerns. A key strength of the book is the outlining of six different lens through which to critically evaluate and conduct research. Using classic and contemporary research, they illustrate difficult concepts in an engaging and easy to understand manner. I was particularly impressed by the coverage of a range of core psychological approaches to research taking a sympathetic style in their examination of these. The book is suitable for those new to research and yet still provides something for the more experienced researcher and additionally it is useful resource for teaching research methods. The final chapter moves to a consideration of conducting your own feminist research and throughout the book there are useful summaries and signposts for further exploration of your own. Reading this book, I felt that I was in 'safe hands' and will be adding it to my own reading lists."

Dr Sarah Seymour-Smith, Associate Professor, Psychology, Nottingham Trent University, UK

Contents

Series Preface

About the *Feminist Companion* Series

Series Editors: Sarah Riley, Rose Capdevila, and Hannah Frith

As Series Editors we can each remember pivotal moments during our undergraduate psychology studies when we were exposed to feminist research and theorising. These moments have shaped our own identities as feminists, our approach to teaching, learning and research in psychology, and our engagements with psychology as a discipline. There are some fantastic feminist psychology lecturers and mentors. For those of us who are fortunate to be taught by them, these are experiences that we never forget.

Hannah

For me, this came in the form of my second-year undergraduate module on research methods in psychology. On the first day of this module, in bounced my teacher (Celia Kitzinger) brimming with energy and enthusiasm, and bursting with exciting ideas about research. I was brought up short by a double whammy of learning about qualitative research for the first time and realising (with some surprise) that research might involve talking with, learning from, and respectfully listening to people. Hearing the voices of women, talking about issues important to women's lives for the first time, lit a fire in me.

Rose

Reading feminist literature was an integral part of my undergraduate degree in politics. There were loads of stats and stories that could tell you the world wasn't fair, no convincing needed. However, the real revelation came when I attended a departmental talk shortly after starting my PhD in Psychology. Usually these talks revolved around experiments, controlling variables and producing statistical analyses. However, the speaker that week (Christine Griffin) didn't do this. She talked about her research with young, working-class women; how they were constructed – both inside and outside of academia – as 'troubled' when they behaved in certain ways, and how this was used to manage them. The speaker described how, by using qualitative methods, researchers could explore the world in ways that valued experience and relationships, rather than converting them into variables to be measured and controlled. I had never thought of things in that way, and it opened up a whole new approach to making sense of world. Much reading followed.

Sarah

My story is slightly different. I had some great teachers and supervisors at undergraduate level, but none were explicitly feminist, other than a course on gender which was cancelled the year I could have done it while the lecturer was on sabbatical. In my research project though, I was supported to do feminist experimental research, but my greatest feminist education came from my friends Emma and Terry, who were studying Philosophy, Women's Studies and Russian Studies, and who taught me the art of thinking, arguing, and drinking. There were also important books that gave me language for understanding my world; it felt like they explained what I already knew, but hadn't had the words to describe.

In our stories, we offer a range of experiences. Face-to-face with visionary feminist psychologists or peer taught – we had people with us on our feminist journey. But not everybody does. Although feminist research and theorising has grown enormously over the many years since we were undergraduates (continuing a trend which began way before then), it remains marginalised in most undergraduate curricula and teachers can be unsure about how to integrate feminism into their classes. At the same time, feminist activism outside of academia is flourishing; Everyday Sexism, SlutWalks, #MeToo, Everyone's Invited, and the Million Women March are just a few examples. Curricula which fail to include feminist scholarship risk failing to engage students who want to see the psychology they study reflecting what is important in their lives.

The *Feminist Companions to Psychology* series was born out of a desire to address these gaps. It draws on the historic strengths of Open University Press of taking complex concepts and presenting them in a clear and accessible way, and aims to provide resources to support staff who are looking to incorporate the latest feminist thinking into their existing modules.

We wanted to develop short, snappy, pedagogically informed books which would sit alongside – as well as complement, complicate, and contest – psychology textbooks and courses. We wanted to support teachers and mentors in psychology by providing short, accessible books which speak to the British Psychological Society's curriculum areas (starting with the core areas of social, cognitive, developmental, biological, personality and individual differences, and research methods). We wanted to engage undergraduate psychologists in academic work which might speak to their values, their activism, or help them make sense of their experiences. We also think psychology undergraduates are missing out! Feminist psychology is a diverse, multifaceted field of work creating cutting edge, energising psychology that challenges all of us to think and act in new ways. It's important that we share it with the next generation of psychology students. This series is a celebration of the fun, fierce, fabulous, and wonderful things that feminism has to offer to psychology.

About *A Feminist Companion to Research Methods in Psychology*

Series Editors: Sarah Riley, Rose Capdevila, and Hannah Frith

In this provocative and fast-paced book, Hannah and Rose guide you through a whistle-stop tour of research methods in psychology showing you how feminists have taken up, used, and transformed tools and techniques, as well as creating exciting new methods, in the service of gender equality. Jumping between key moments in the development of feminist psychology, and between classic and contemporary studies in psychology, you are invited to consider how the questions researchers ask, and the methods they use to generate answers, are powerful tools. Demonstrating the ways that these tools can, and definitely have (!), been used to oppress, belittle, and limit opportunities for women (and others), and showcasing how feminist research can open up liberatory possibilities, this book aims to inspire the readers to engage their anger and creativity to put research methods to work in securing social justice for all. Inviting readers to scrutinise research practices through six different feminist lenses – place, power, social justice, ethics, representation and intersectionality, and reflexivity – this book will sharpen students' critical and analytical skills providing a set of concepts and language which they can take with them through their exploration of the many fascinating aspects of being human which psychologists study. This book examines the core British Psychological Society curriculum in research methods through a feminist lens, providing an accessible resource for educators who are looking to spark students' critical thinking and teach methods through topics which will speak to their concerns with social justice.

Welcome to *A Feminist Companion to Research Methods in Psychology*, a journey into the creative and critical possibilities of producing knowledge.

Preface

Psychology is a diverse discipline, held together loosely with a common interest in the systematic study of minds and behaviour. This makes research methods core for psychologists. Some see this as a problem, they argue that we're obsessed with methods and students rarely to choose to study psychology for their love of research methods. But told the right way, the story of research methods in psychology is fascinating. Hannah and Rose are such storytellers, experts in the field, they take you through the British Psychology Society curriculum on research methods in a way that no one else has.

Clear and accessible, Hannah and Rose examine classic and contemporary studies across the discipline exploring the kinds of questions psychologists ask and how they try to answer them systematically. Their feminist lens illuminates a range of topics, these include, exploring what experimental studies of memory tell us about objectivity; the pathologizing of women in personality disorder research; the difficulties of doing research on children without reproducing mother blaming; the way measures for altruism are biased towards male behaviour; and how brain differences research – from chromosomes, to genes, to neuroscience – is being shaped by feminist scholars.

Introducing students to different epistemological approaches to research (positivist, phenomenological, social constructionist, etc.), they show how feminist research has used all of these approaches to challenge existing paradigms and generate new forms of knowledge. The book helps students develop critical and analytical skills by encouraging a questioning approach to understanding how psychological knowledge is produced. It also offers alternative, feminist informed approaches to: framing research questions, adopting data collection techniques and analysing and interpreting data. As such, this book is a unique resource not just for students but also faculty who are looking to incorporate the latest feminist thinking into their research methods teaching. Welcome to a 'Feminist Companion to Psychological Research Methods' we hope you enjoy the ride.

Acknowledgements

From Hannah

Thanks to the community of feminist researchers who continue to inspire and excite me to keep doing the sweaty work involved in asking difficult questions, exposing gender oppression and injustice, and imagining different futures together. Special thanks to Rose Capdevila for plotting this book together and pushing it over the finish line despite the chaos of everyday life in a pandemic, and to Sarah Riley (fellow series editor) who has an excellent combination of incisive critique and humorous observation. This includes the work of all those involved in the Psychology of Women and Equalities Section of the British Psychological Society, which welcomed me in when I gave my very first presentation of my undergraduate research at an annual conference in the 1980s. This organisation holds open a crucial space for feminist psychology within the institutional structures which shape British psychology, and together with the journal *Feminism & Psychology* provides opportunities for rigorous and thrilling scholarship as well as community and comradeship.

Thanks also to Richard for endless cups of tea and reminding me to switch off the computer and take a break, my super-sisters (Nancy and Melanie) who provide much-needed dollops of glamour and belly laughs, my mum Susan who encourages me to be creative and of the importance of greenery, Tom for cheekiness, Josh for paddleboarding, and to all the other people in my life who nurture me and make me laugh.

From Rose

Not to be too repetitive but, like Hannah, I want to thank all of the feminist researchers who have encouraged and supported me with their ideas and their kindness in many different spaces primarily around the Psychology of Women & Equalities Section of the British Psychological Society. POWES has always offered the safe and productive, yet intellectually challenging, space that is invaluable for anyone in our field. A POWES Conference is also where I first met Hannah Frith who has been a joy and inspiration to work with in the very challenging context of a global pandemic. Similarly, thanks to Sarah Riley, co-editor of this series for her perceptive and sometimes irreverent comments as well as her spirit and insight. It's a pleasure co-editing with these two eloquent feminists. I have appreciated all of the feedback we've received at different stages of this process and am particularly grateful to Danai Dima for her helpful comments on the biological psychology chapter. I would also thank my friend and colleague Lisa Lazard with whom so much of the 'sweaty work' of feminist research has been carried out over many years, cans of Coke, cups of tea, and glasses of wine. My thanks too to Claire Cooper, who on numerous occasions held the fort so I could turn my attention to this book. On a personal note, I must thank my partner David, who picked up so much of the slack of managing family life and my fab children, Jess and Julia (and intermittent housemate Georgie) for just being there to temper my wobbles along the way. I am so very lucky to be surrounded by these really wonderful people.

From both of us

Thanks to our reviewers who were so positive and supportive of this endeavour, both the book itself and the series as a whole. Thanks to the lovely team at Open University Press (Beth Summers and Hannah Jones), but perhaps especially to Clara Heathcock whose passion and determination to bring (academic) feminism to an undergraduate psychology readership ensured that the Feminist Companions series, and this book, are now an excellent resource for aspiring feminist psychologists.

Introduction

Both Rose and Hannah have been teaching research methods for many years and we are also active researchers – we love it! From our experience of teaching research methods to undergraduate students, we know that this is often not your favourite topic. Students who come to university to study psychology often want to find out more about people – what makes people tick – rather than to learn about statistics, matched pair designs, and sampling (don't worry if you don't fully understand these terms, you get the point!). In fact, many of you may find research methods boring and difficult. We think this is because all too often research methods are seen as neutral tools to be picked up and used in any context. We think it is important to examine how research methods are used by psychologists to answer the questions that inspire and intrigue them, to understand how methods shape what we know (and don't know as psychologists), and how the psychological knowledge we produce impacts on individuals and societies. As this is a Feminist Companion to research methods in psychology, we will not be considering in detail the technicalities of how to design research, or the intricacies of specific data collection or analysis techniques. Rather, we will explore some of the ways in which feminists approach research methods. In other words, this is not a *how to* book, it's more of a *why to* book.

This book is about research methods. Chapter 1 invites you to consider research as intimately connected to issues of power, inequality, and social justice. This is why for feminists – and others – really being able to understand research methods is about much more than knowing which statistical test to conduct with which data (although getting this right is important). However, research is about much more than these technical issues. In Chapter 2, we think together about the importance of asking questions as a cornerstone of conducting research, and about how *which* questions we ask (and *which* we don't) has far-reaching consequences for people, communities, and societies. We also explore some of the different ways psychologists think that research questions can be answered. Chapter 3 outlines five feminist lenses through which research can be scrutinised. These lenses will help you to think about what research questions you want to ask, as well as what research methods and techniques you should use to answer them. Collectively, these three chapters hope to engage you in feminist ways of thinking, which will help you to develop your feminist consciousness and sharpen your critical analysis skills. This will help you to think about your own values and position in relation to: *Why do research? What is research for? Who does research benefit?*

As this book is designed to be a companion to your undergraduate studies, we often zip back and forward in time to consider both 'classic' studies in psychology as well as contemporary research. This is deliberate. As a companion, we could not hope to give you comprehensive and thorough grounding in the other core areas of psychology (cognitive, personality and individual differences, biological, developmental, social, conceptual and historical issues – we come back to this last one later). For this reason, in Chapters 4–8 we focus on a particular topic within these areas – memory, sex differences in personality traits and abilities, biological sex, attachment in childhood, and helping behaviour (or altruism) – so that we can explore the methods used to research these key topics in some detail. We also often start each of the chapters with a well-known example of research within each sub-discipline. This serves as a springboard for discussing methods and the role that methods play in critical debates within these areas. The final core subject areas of a psychology undergraduate degree, 'conceptual and historical issues in psychology', is integrated throughout the book rather than being the focus of a specific chapter. This is because these conceptual and historical issues are integral to understanding how ideas about what 'counts' as knowledge, how knowledge should be produced, which research methods produce the most useful knowledge, and how these ideas have changed over time is the core focus of this book.

Mapping this Companion against QAA and BPS curricula

This Companion is designed to accompany the British Psychological Society's core undergraduate curriculum (2019), as informed by the Quality Assurance Agency's Subject Benchmark Statement for Psychology. Here, we provide a detailed breakdown of how the topics, theories, and debates covered in this Companion map onto the requirements for teaching and learning about research methods in psychology as outlined by the QAA (Table 1).

Mapping this Companion to the QAA topics in Research Methods

The Quality Assurance Agency for Higher Education (QAA) publishes a Subject Benchmark Statement for Psychology that defines what a graduate in the subject can be expected to know, do, and understand at the end of their studies (section 4.4):

i.   apply multiple perspectives to psychological issues, recognising that psychology involves a range of research methods, theories, evidence and applications

ii. integrate ideas and findings across the multiple perspectives in psychology and recognise distinctive psychological approaches to relevant issues

iii. identify and evaluate patterns in behaviour, psychological functioning and experience

iv. generate and explore hypotheses and research questions drawing on relevant theory and research

v. carry out empirical studies involving a variety of methods of data collection, including experiments, observation, questionnaires, interviews and focus groups

vi. analyse, present and evaluate quantitative and qualitative data and evaluate research findings

vii. employ evidence-based reasoning and examine practical, theoretical and ethical issues associated with the range of methodologies

viii. use a variety of psychological tools, including specialist software, laboratory equipment and psychometric instruments

ix. apply psychological knowledge ethically and safely to real world problems

x. critically evaluate psychological theory and research.

So, you can see why you have a busy few years learning about psychology! There are lots of different skills and knowledge you are expected to be able to demonstrate at the end of your studies. Many of these skills are embedded within the content across the whole of the book. For example, the ability to 'apply multiple perspectives to psychological issues' is the culmination of the range of 'research methods, theories, evidence and applications' presented across all the different chapters in the book. In Table 1, we outline just some of the ways the BPS curriculum and QAA benchmark statements map onto the content of specific chapters. Of course, the only way to *really* gain these skills is to put your learning into practice by conducting your own research. This is the focus of Chapter 9.

Table 1: Mapping this Companion to the QAA and BPS topics in Research Methods

Chapter	BPS Core Curriculum Area	QAA Statement	What this Feminist Companion has to offer
1	Conceptual & Historical Issues	Apply multiple perspectives to psychological issues, recognising that psychology involves a range of research methods, theories, evidence, and applications	Introduces feminism as a valuable perspective from which to explore psychological issues
		Apply psychological knowledge ethically and safely to real-world problems	Explores the relationship between knowledge and power and how psychological knowledge oppresses women (and others)

Table 1: *(Continued)*

Chapter	BPS Core Curriculum Area	QAA Statement	What this Feminist Companion has to offer
2	Conceptual & Historical Issues	Generate and explore hypotheses and research questions drawing on relevant theory and research	Introduces students to the importance of asking questions and how the questions we ask are shaped by our own values and social location. Examples of research questions and/or hypotheses are given throughout the book
		Critically evaluate psychological theory and research	Outlines six critical lenses through which to examine psychological research: place, power, social justice, ethics, representation, and intersectionality
3	Conceptual & Historical Issues	Integrate ideas and findings across the multiple perspectives in psychology and recognise distinctive psychological approaches to relevant issues	Introduces readers to distinct epistemological approaches in psychology and four main paradigms: positivism, critical/ transformative, interpretivist/ phenomenological, and social constructionist
4	Cognitive Conceptual & Historical Issues	Carry out empirical studies involving a variety of methods of data collection, including experiments, observation, questionnaires, interviews, and focus groups	Introduces experiments as a research method and also media analysis and analysis of naturally occurring conversations

Table 1: (*Continued*)

Chapter	BPS Core Curriculum Area	QAA Statement	What this Feminist Companion has to offer
		Apply psychological knowledge ethically and safely to real-world problems	Considers the ethical issues surrounding the application of memory experiments to the issue of memories of childhood sexual abuse
		Apply multiple perspectives to psychological issues, recognising that psychology involves a range of research methods, theories, evidence, and applications	Contrasts positive and social constructionist approaches to researching memory in the context of child abuse
5	Personality & Individual Differences Conceptual & Historical Issues	Use a variety of psychological tools, including specialist software, laboratory equipment, and psychometric instruments	Demonstrates how questionnaires and psychometric tests are developed Introduces meta-analysis as a method of aggregating data
		Apply multiple perspectives to psychological issues, recognising that psychology involves a range of research methods, theories, evidence, and applications	Explores how some feminist research uses tests/questionnaires, whilst the use of such methods has also been critiqued by feminists
6	Biological Conceptual & Historical Issues	Use a variety of psychological tools, including specialist software, laboratory equipment, and psychometric instruments	Explores the use of fMRI technology in neuropsychology in relation to 'sex differences' research
		Employ evidence-based reasoning and examine practical, theoretical, and ethical issues associated with the range of methodologies	Examines how the results of fMRI have been interpreted and some of the theoretical and ethical issues raised by this

Table 1: (*Continued*)

Chapter	BPS Core Curriculum Area	QAA Statement	What this Feminist Companion has to offer
7	Developmental Conceptual & Historical Issues	Carry out empirical studies involving a variety of methods of data collection, including experiments, observation, questionnaires, interviews, and focus groups	Introduces observational and ethnographic methods
		Critically evaluate psychological theory and research	Examines attachment theory and the 'Strange Situation' observational method used in developmental psychology from a feminist perspective
8	Social Conceptual & Historical Issues	Carry out empirical studies involving a variety of methods of data collection, including experiments, observation, questionnaires, interviews, and focus groups	Introduces field experiments, intervention studies, interviews, and participatory action research as different methods for examining helping behaviour
		Apply psychological knowledge ethically and safely to real-world problems	Explores the application of research to bystander intervention in the context of sexual violence
9	Conceptual & Historical Issues	Use a variety of psychological tools, including specialist software, laboratory equipment, and psychometric instruments	Considers the ways in which new technologies are shaping and changing research methods in psychology
		Apply psychological knowledge ethically and safely to real-world problems	Introduces the importance of decolonising research and research methods

Boxes

Throughout the Companion, you will come across information aside from the main text in boxes. These boxes are a chance for us to share with you some additional insights or issues that might not always be central to our key work in the chapter, but which we think will be interesting and will help you to develop your feminism consciousness.

See and hear for yourself

To see feminism and feminist research 'in action', we use 'See and hear for yourself' exercises to share films, videos, interviews, TED-talks, and other resources where you can see some of feminist research methods' most impressive and inspirational women, or hear about key moments in feminist history.

Summaries

We know that there is sometimes a lot of information for you to take in, and lots of new ideas to chew over, so we have included a summary box for each section within a chapter, and an overall summary at the end of each chapter. As well as giving you the key 'take home' messages within each chapter, these can help you to check your learning, and can be helpful when it comes to revising what you've learnt at the end of the Companion.

Glossary

Research methods in psychology sometimes require the use of technical words and phrases which need translating into everyday talk. Similarly, feminist theory and research draws upon a rich and complex history of ideas both within and beyond psychology which may be unfamiliar to you. Therefore, we sometimes use words and phrases that require a little more definition and explanation. Where we can, we explain these terms as we go along, but to avoid interrupting ourselves too much, we have created a glossary of terms which you will find at the end of the book. Whenever you see a word that is both ***bold and italic***, you will find it in the Glossary.

1 Five reasons you need a Feminist Companion to Research Methods in Psychology

Learning objectives

Study of this chapter should enable you to:

- Recognise how the (research) questions we ask powerfully shape what knowledge is available for making sense of ourselves and our worlds.
- Identify how different ideas about feminist scholarship, activism, and popular culture have emerged over time.
- Understand what feminist thinking can offer to the study of research methods in psychology.
- Become comfortable with the idea of *sweaty work* and asking questions *from the margins*.

Asking questions, creating knowledge

This book is about asking questions – about asking difficult, tricky, challenging questions – questions which critically explore *what* we know about the world, and *how* we come to know it. If research is, in essence, gathering information in order to gain understanding of something, then asking questions is absolutely central to research. This book will help you to think about what questions to ask and how to ask them. Turning our ideas into a ***research question*** or ***hypothesis*** is a pivotal moment in the research process. *What* questions we do or don't ask (including those which we do/don't pose in questionnaires or ask in interviews) inescapably shapes what we find out or the knowledge we create. You can only the get answers to the questions you ask, right! But *how* we create knowledge – the research methods, tools, techniques, and processes – also has a powerful influence on what we know. Asking questions is both a central aspect of the research process itself, *and* an important skill which you can use to interrogate knowledge that is already 'out there'.

A Feminist Companion asks questions 'from the margins'. This is a phrase used by author and social activist bell hooks (1984) to describe Black women's location at the edges of society, and to challenge the dominant perspective of white, middle-class, and professional women within the feminist movement. Asking questions 'from the margins' means asking questions from the perspectives of, and in collaboration with, those who are often invisible or misrepresented in psychology. It also means asking questions from the perspective of those who are often the 'objects' of psychological research – those living with experience of mental illness, children and young people, older people and the elderly, and those subject to prejudice and discrimination (i.e. the objects of 'abnormal' psychology, developmental and lifespan psychology, and social psychology respectively). Psychology as a discipline, including psychological theory, research, and practice, often claims to be an objective science. However, it inevitably reflects wider society, including the inequalities and injustices (e.g. racism, sexism, ageism, disablism, heterosexism, genderism, classism), as well as the attempts to transform, challenge, change, and disrupt such inequalities.

Asking questions invites you to engage your curiosity, to take notice of the world around you, and to be rigorously sceptical about psychological knowledge. Some of the best (most productive, most exciting, most influential) questions have been rooted in the everyday experiences of psychologists. For instance, how can we remember things? Why do people help each other or hurt each other? How do children learn? Are men and women really different, and if so, why? Historically, due partly to unequal access to education and employment, the psychologists posing these questions were white, middle-class men and, inevitably, the discipline of psychology was shaped by the interests, values, and perspectives of this group. Reflecting the civil unrest of the 1960s and 1970s (gay liberation movement, second-wave feminism, civil rights, etc.), criticism of this bias intensified and this was reproduced in key texts. Here are some examples:

- Naomi Weisstein's (1971) classic paper 'Psychology constructs the female' made visible the ways in which male bias shaped the representation of women as psychologically different to and, notably, less than men.
- Robert V. Guthrie's hugely influential book *Even the Rat Was White: A Historical View of Psychology* (1976/2004) exposed racism in psychology, arguing that the discipline perpetuated ideas about Black inferiority.
- Celia Kitzinger's *The Social Construction of Lesbianism* (1987) revealed the ways psychology pathologises sexual minorities.

Of course, bias is not unique to psychology, nor has it disappeared over time. Caroline Criado Perez's (2019) recent book *Invisible Women: Exposing Data Bias in a World Designed for Men* demonstrates how data that excludes women is used to inform policy and practice across a range of contexts from government and medical research to technology, workplaces, urban planning, and the media. In this book, we ask you to consider how you ask questions and we invite you to ask questions from a feminist perspective. We think you will find it interesting and, sometimes, surprising.

According to influential philosopher and social theorist Michel Foucault: "Two words sum up everything: power and knowledge" (1981, p. 293). In this book, we call on you to explore how knowledge shapes, and is shaped by, power. And, in turn, how knowledge shapes identities, practices, institutions, and policies. Knowledge and information are powerful mechanisms for social change – this is what makes research so exciting and keeps us engaged in doing, reading, arguing about, and sharing research with others. If our goal as psychologists is to create new knowledge with which to support equalities and challenge injustice, then research methods are our essential tool for producing robust evidence and good quality knowledge about the world. This is perhaps even more important in the current socio-political climate where 'fake news' pops up in our news feeds, and scientific knowledge about everything from climate change to social injustice, to the global COVID pandemic is both increasingly visible and increasingly questioned or overruled by political expediencies. If posing questions is the springboard for producing knowledge about the world, and knowledge is intimately connected to power, then the methods, tools, and techniques we use to generate knowledge are vital. So, as well as paying attention to *what* we know, we also need to look carefully at *how* we know it.

SECTION SUMMARY

- Asking questions is a central part of the research process. What questions we ask, as psychology researchers, is influenced by who we are (our identities) and the contexts in which we live.
- The questions asked by psychology as a discipline have often reflected the limited perspective of white, middle-class men living in Western contexts (like the UK, North America, and Australia).
- Knowledge and information are powerful tools for social control and also for social change.
- As research questions are the foundation for creating knowledge, feminists see the questions that researchers do or don't ask as very important.

What is feminism?

Feminism is troublesome – it will not go away. In her book *How to Live a Feminist Life*, Sara Ahmed invites us to hold onto "the promise of that word, to think what it means to live that life by claiming that word as your own: being a feminist, becoming a feminist, speaking as a feminist" (2016, p. 1). Here, we invite you to do the same, but we also explore some of the obstacles which get in the way. So, what *is* feminism? bell hooks describes feminism as "the movement to end sexism, sexual exploitation and sexual oppression" (2000, p. 33); it is a collective political movement that seeks change. As such, feminism puts an understanding of gender inequality at the heart of political ***activism***, academic theorising, everyday experience, and empirical research. Feminism is not one thing – there is much diversity within feminist movements and groupings which sit under the collective umbrella of feminism. Feminism has adapted flexibly to changing historical and cultural contexts and to the ways in which gender inequality is shaped in such contexts. These shifts can be characterised as waves – periods in which feminist activism and visibility swells, and periods in which it is diminished or repressed.

Making waves in/with feminism

Describing feminist histories (like all histories) is never value free. Histories are a version of events which are shaped by power and privilege, where some key moments and people are brought to the fore, whilst other stories are neglected or later reclaimed as 'hidden histories'. So, the history of feminist movements in the English-speaking world tend to dominate international narratives because they are more widely documented, both academically and in the media, and because of the cultural violence of *colonialism*. Moreover, UK feminisms are often overshadowed by stories from the US, and both are dominated by stories about straight, middle-class, white women. Understanding that histories are linked to power may give you some insight into why we feel it is important to give you a historical map of developments within UK feminism in this chapter. The importance of understanding psychological theory and research in historical context is also acknowledged by the inclusion of Conceptual and Historical Issues in Psychology as a core area of the BPS curriculum. Ideas emerge in specific social, cultural, political, and economic contexts, they are a response to the accepted wisdom that came before and will shape the thinking that follows. Asking 'where did this knowledge come from?' and 'why did this knowledge get created at this moment in time?' are powerful questions which help us to thinking critically about knowledge and how it is produced.

One way in which feminism has been widely conceptualised has been as different *waves*, each building on the strengths and responding to the critiques of those which preceded it. Although criticised for suggesting a coherent, linear march of progress, this metaphor does provide a useful way of illustrating key touchstones in feminist scholarship, activism, and culture. Feminism is often characterised as moving in four waves:

- the *first* wave fought for suffrage and property rights;
- the *second* wave focused on the workplace, sexuality, and reproductive rights;
- the *third* wave championed issues of diversity and inclusivity, challenging understandings of what constitutes gender; and
- the *fourth* wave represents the emergence of #hashtag feminism communicated through social media and in popular culture; recognition of the complexity of identities and experiences (as simultaneously gendered, raced, classed, sexualised, embodied), and the rising popularity of issue-based political activism (eco-feminism)

Not only are these waves characterised by different forms of activism centred on different key issues, but importantly, they are also underpinned by changes in thinking and theorising about how to produce knowledge and what methods to use – we say more about this in the next chapter. For now, we briefly outline these four feminist waves of activism and scholarship.

First-wave feminism (late nineteenth and early twentieth century)

The first wave of feminism refers to a sustained movement in the West to achieve political equality for women – although of course feminists existed before this time. As well as the right to vote, the movement also focused on equal opportunities to education and employment, and the right to own property. In the US, the suffrage movement had an uneasy relationship with the abolitionist movement fighting to end slavery. While Black women (like Sojourner Truth, Maria Stewart, and Frances E.W. Harper) fought for an end to slavery and the right to vote for all people, only some of the white, middle-class educated women who dominated the suffrage movement fought for both causes. Although a legal change granted women the right to vote in 1920, in practice the introduction of obstacles like taxes, tests, and long queues to register prevented many Black women from exercising their right to vote. Over a century later, legal and illegal efforts to prevent Black and/or working-class people from exercising their right to vote (known as voter suppression) remain a very live concern in contemporary US culture.

In the UK, the right to vote was linked to property ownership, which effectively limited the rights of women and Black men to vote. Liberal suffragists (like Millicent Fawcett) peacefully campaigned for votes for middle-class, property-owning women. In contrast, militant suffragettes (like Emmeline Pankhurst), campaigning for votes for all women, favoured direct action like chaining themselves to railings, disrupting public meetings, and damaging public property. In 1918, the right to vote was granted to (some) women over 30 and was later extended to *all women* aged over 21 in 1928, mirroring the rights of men. Pankhurst, who went on hunger strike each of the eleven times she was jailed, tragically died shortly before the 1928 Act was passed in Parliament.

See and hear for yourself

The life of Emmeline Pankhurst was dramatised in the 2015 film *Suffragette* (2015, Dir. Sarah Gavron). Following its release, the film was criticised for 'whitewashing' Black women out of history. Prominent Indian women were active in the British women's suffrage movement (including Princess Sophia Duleep Singh, Madam Bhikaji Cama, and Mrs. Lolita Roy) not least because this coincided with the call for Indian independence from British colonial rule. See Sumita Mukherjee's excellent book *Indian Suffragettes: Female Identities and Transnational Networks* (2018).

This focus on extending the same rights enjoyed by men to women was reflected in the study of psychology. Psychology as a discipline was working hard to establish itself as a rigorous science by championing the use of rigorous experimental methods to make discoveries about psychological phenomena. Dominated by male psychologists, the white educated man was presented as the norm against which everyone else is judged. Arguments that women were naturally more mentally feeble than men were commonly used to justify their exclusion from education and civic participation. Since women still had limited access to education and employment, there were few women psychologists at this time. Nonetheless, early female psychologists like Helen Thompson Woolley used experimental methods to study sex differences in the mental traits of men and women in order to challenge assumptions about the inferiority of women and the idea that such deficiencies were biologically based (Thompson, 1903). You can see from this example that concerns about ensuring that women were treated equally informed both feminist scholarship and activism and that both had a role to play in creating social change. At the same time, it is fair to say that the rights of *all* women were not prioritised equally.

Second-wave feminism (1960s and 1970s)

Second-wave feminism, also known as women's lib, emerged following women's engagement in a wider range of occupations as part of the war effort coupled with growing political concern with 'human rights'. Second-wave feminists continued to fight for women's right to participate *fully* in civic life, including receiving equal pay for the same work, to access male-dominated professions (like science or engineering), and to be able to study these subjects in school, or the right to access other economic services liking having a mortgage or bank loan. Did you know, that until 1970 a woman in the UK could only secure a mortgage if she had the signature of a male guarantor (perhaps this would have been the case for some of your older female relatives – go ask them!).

> **See and hear for yourself**
> An example of feminist activism around pay was the 1968 strike for equal pay by sewing machinists at the Ford factory in Dagenham, which was depicted in the film *Made in Dagenham* (2010, Dir: Nigel Cole).

What was distinctive about second-wave feminism, was that it set about dismantling social and cultural expectations about women – like the idea that women should accept limited roles only as wives and mothers or could be treated as sex objects. As well as fighting for equality in the law, second-wave feminism also challenged people's beliefs about what women (and men) were able to do and be. This included a searing critique of women's domestic life and the representation of women in the media:

- inequality in marriage (women being seen as the 'property' of men and/or dependent on men to access services);
- the extent of sexual and domestic violence experienced by women and girls – including within marriage (it wasn't until 1992 that rape within marriage became a crime in the UK) and the family;
- the economic benefits and personal costs of women's caring responsibilities (the 'wages for housework' campaign and support for subsidised childcare attempted to release women from financial dependency);
- women's greater control over their bodies through the introduction of the contraceptive pill (1961) and increased access to abortion (the Abortion Act 1967);
- the limited and stereotypical representation of women in the media (as wives and mothers) and the sexualisation of women in mainstream media and in pornography.

Feminist research in psychology focused on documenting the realities of women's lives and asking (research) questions about issues that were important to women. Feminists adopted and developed *qualitative methods* to enable women to describe the realities of their lives and experiences in their own words. Research also began to focus on the importance of social context for understanding women's lives – how the symbolic world (images, discourses, beliefs) about women exerted a powerful influence on women's lives. It began to examine how attitudes and beliefs about women were responsible for discrimination and oppression. For example, exploring how erroneous beliefs about what a 'typical' rape looks like (an attack by a stranger, at night, in public spaces) prevents women recognising experiences which do not fit this picture (date rape, rape within marriage) *as* rape. Or, how this and other rape 'myths' (e.g. 'women lie about rape because they regret having sex', 'women provoke men to rape by wearing revealing clothes', or 'if someone is drunk it is their own fault if they get raped') place responsibility onto the woman victim/survivor of abuse rather than the perpetrator and how this, in turn, can influence the way decisions are made about prosecuting, convicting, and sentencing sexual offenders within the criminal justice system.

See and hear for yourself

This was also the time when feminists within psychology began to organise, to argue for the importance of studying women's lives, and to establish this as a legitimate and meaningful area of study and a form of collective action in itself. The US-based Association for Women in Psychology, for example, was established in 1969 in response. The Association for Women in Psychology was convened because the American Psychological Association failed to respond to the issues raised by the new women's liberation movement such as employment discrimination, sexual harassment, and lack of research and theory on women. You can see and hear more about the development of this organisation by watching the following AWP Herstory video: https://www. awpsych.org/awp_herstory.php. Unbelievably, the Psychology of Women Section of the British Psychological Society was not established until 1988, although feminist psychologists had been arguing for this for many years.

Third-wave feminism (approximately 1990–2010)

Despite substantial gains for women's equality, the feminist movement experienced some serious tensions, and third-wave feminism emerged as a response to these tensions. While second-wave feminism aimed to unite people in the fight for women's equality, some began to question who was and was not included in the movement and challenged feminism to take intersectionality seriously. Responding to this, third-wave feminists wanted to establish a version of feminism that was transnational and globally focused; a diverse, inclusive movement explicitly concerned with intersections of gender, class, ethnicity, sexuality, nationality, and other inequalities. This was also reflected in research, as researchers began to explore intersectionality identities and experiences, often adopting qualitative methods to do so. To give some examples of intersectional research:

- Researchers who interviewed women smokers and ex-smokers in Australia found that their experiences of smoking-related stigma were shaped by their multiply intersecting identities as smokers (marked as disgusting, immoral, or an addict), women (ugly and unfeminine), working class (a sign of poverty or poor education), and mothers (irresponsible or uncaring), as well as their cultural background (e.g. the particular expectations of Chinese women) (Triandafilidis et al., 2017).
- Interviews with 20 South Asian heritage, Muslim, female leaders, managers, and supervisors in the UK demonstrated the multi-layered issues and challenges they face in pursuit of employment and leadership positions in relation to their gender ('Six months into the job all I got was "women cannot do this job" and I was never taken seriously'), as well as ethnicity and religion ('Senior colleagues would make inappropriate remarks, such as "oh it's Ramadan, I hope you don't pull any sickies"') (Tariq & Syed, 2017).

As feminist theory became more established in academia, a schism between academia and activism widened, often with academics questioning gender while activists relied on it as a rallying call for action. Third-wave feminists also prompted a reconsideration of some of the key arguments of second-wave feminism. For example, second-wave feminists were highly critical of the 'beauty myth' (Wolf, 1990) as ensuring that women were valued only for their appearance. Third-wave feminists explored beauty practices as a site of pleasure. Similarly, whilst second-wave feminists positioned pornography as uniformly harmful, by adopting an intersectional approach third-wave feminists argued that for sexual minorities, pornography could be pleasurable, joyful, and affirming, and could subvert normative ideas about what sex should look like. Rather than seeing pornography as universally harmful, third-wave feminists encouraged us to ask: what kind of pornography?, produced by whom?, featuring what kind of sex? Dubbed a 'sex positive' approach, this generated research about sexual practices, activities, and identities.

From the 1990s in the US, and the early 2000s in the UK, there was a resurgence of political activity and activists explicitly adopting and adapting feminism as a way of expressing shared goals and motivations. The third-wave mounted resistance to the prominent post-feminist discourse which saw feminism as outdated, women's social and economic equality as largely achieved, and women as empowered through individual 'choice'. Sometimes characterised as largely academic or theoretical, third-wave feminism also signalled a distancing from the white middle-class feminism of the second wave, embracing postcolonial and postmodern thinking. While postcolonial thinking explores the influence of colonialism, slavery, migration, suppression and resistance, difference, race, gender, and place in shaping people's lives, postmodernists consider how knowledge is used to maintain the political and economic power of elites. This attention to other ways of knowing was important for researchers who started to think about different ways of producing knowledge that was more inclusive.

Fourth-wave feminism (2011 onwards)

Since around 2012, we have witnessed a resurgence of feminisms which are, in many ways, defined by technology. This fourth wave has been marked by a renewed interest in feminism in popular culture (Rivers, 2017). This is reflected in everything from high street clothing with feminist slogans and secondary school feminist clubs, to hashtag feminisms involving social media campaigns that reach hundreds of millions of users. For example, the *Everyday Sexism Project* by Laura Bates, as the name suggests, aims to call attention to everyday instances of sexism. Similarly, the #MeToo and #TimesUp campaigns, to end sexual harassment and sexual assault, signal the importance of social media as a platform for feminists to 'shout back' in response to sexism and misogyny (Turley & Fisher, 2018). Concurrently, fourth-wave feminism has arguably been characterised by 'celebrity feminism' represented by superstars such as Ariana Grande, Beyoncé, Miley Cyrus, Emma Watson, Angelina Jolie, and Laverne Cox. This popularity of feminism in the public sphere is unprecedented and is partly a response to the erroneous postfeminist positioning of feminism as no longer necessary as a collective form of social activism in popular discourse. Fourth-wave feminism reasserts the pressing need for feminist activism.

Although one aspect of fourth-wave feminism is its popularity, a more controversial and influential element has been its critique of gender as essential and **binary** (in other words, that gender is a fixed, biological characteristic of the individual and is strictly divided into the 'opposite' sexes – male *or* female). Fourth-wave feminism sees gender as fluid. This is resonant with its championing of intersectionality and queer theory. Intersectionality theory (Crenshaw, 1989) tries to explain how people's life experience is shaped not only by gender, but also race, class, sexuality, (dis)ability, age, and so on. The experience of being a Black working-class woman is different from being a white working woman, or a Black working-class man. Intersectionality invites feminists to be mindful of how these multiple intersections (places where two or more things meet – say, gender and sexuality) shape inequality and provide opportunities for political alliances. So, feminist and disability activists might work together to secure reproductive and sexual rights for disabled people. While intersectionality foregrounds the joining together or overlapping of social positions, queer theory examines the oppressive power of dominant unwritten rules (known as norms) that we live by. This includes unwritten rules which say that heterosexuality is the default, preferred, or normal sexual orientation. This 'heteronormativity' assumes both a gender binary (that there are only two distinct sexes) and that sex should happen between two people of the 'opposite' sex. Queer theory actively subverts these norms by disrupting gender and sexual binaries and by celebrating the variety and fluidity of different sexual and gender identities (gay, lesbian, bi-, pan-, asexual, or kinky sexualities, as well as folk who identify as non-binary, gender queer, or gender fluid).

Of course, the metaphor of feminist waves is an oversimplification – all these forms of feminist thinking and activism are relevant in the contemporary context (for example, equal pay has not yet been achieved and women still have greater responsibility for unpaid work), and the metaphor has been developed to describe an Anglo-American history of feminism. In the light of these different shifts and changes in feminist movements, and growing attention to how feminism is shaped by local, national, and global contexts, it is perhaps more accurate than ever to refer to feminisms, rather than a singular and united feminism, and to celebrate the cacophony of feminist voices and perspectives.

Do I need to be a feminist to read this book?

You do not need to identify as a feminist to enjoy this book, learn about psychological research, or think about what's missing from the books you already have. You may consider being a feminist to be an integral part of your identity and way of being in the world. You may identify as feminist but might not have thought too deeply about what this means. Many folk (women, men, transgender, gender queer, and non-binary) do not explicitly identify as feminist despite believing firmly in gender equality. You may be sceptical about whether feminism has anything to offer you (in which case we appreciate your open-mindedness in choosing to read this book). But, as feminism is a *collective* movement for change, it is important to better understand the structural and individual factors which might influence people's willingness to engage with feminism.

Feminism is a political movement for social change – specifically, one which aims to expose sexism, misogyny, and gender discrimination and work towards gender equality. As not everyone shares these goals, or indeed, may benefit from maintaining the patriarchal status quo, each rising 'wave' of feminist popularity and activism has come with a backlash. The backlash to second-wave feminism, for example, focused on dismissing feminists as ugly (hairy, fat, and unfeminine), politically extreme (as bra-burning man-haters), and lesbians. The current context is no exception. Just as feminist civic engagement is thriving with visible collective activism (#MeToo, #TimesUp, and women's marches), the resurgence of feminist communities, debates, and theories online, and enlivened academic interest (Aune & Holyoak, 2018), so too have we witnessed a rise in hate, ridicule, harassment, and contempt for women. Campaigner Caroline

Criado-Perez was subjected to extensive, extreme abuse after calling for women's representation on banknotes (Thompson, 2017). Feminist media critic Anita Sarkeesian, who documents sexist portrayals of women in video games, faced sexist harassment that included rape and death threats and hacking of her webpages and social media. And the abuse of American politician Alexandra Ocasio-Cortez by Republican Representative Ted Yoho gave her the opportunity to give a widely televised speech in which she condemned his behaviour and violent language and condemned systemic sexual behaviour and male privilege. A British study documented the increase in online abuse, harassment, threats, trolling, stalking, and defamation directed at women espousing feminist views (Lewis et al., 2017). Yet, this abuse is not only directed at visible, prominent, and noticeable women who actively identify as feminist. Women in the public eye are commonly victimised (for example, politicians being trolled on Twitter; Watson, 2019), as are many women who engage in public forums. It is important to notice and study this backlash. Since it is specifically designed to threaten, intimidate, and silence feminism, it is perhaps easy to see why some people feel discouraged about identifying as a feminist or with feminist activism or scholarship.

A second institutional barrier to engaging with feminism is the pervasiveness of **neoliberalism** which shapes policy and practice in the UK, and inevitably infuses our own thinking, behaviour, and identities. This neoliberal thinking places economic competition and individual responsibility at the centre of human activity. Individuals are depicted as consumers who have individual responsibility to exercise choices through buying, selling, or deploying (or not) other resources like time, energy, skills, and knowledge as efficiently as possible to achieve success. To give an example, neoliberalism perpetuates the idea that we can all be healthy if we eat correctly and exercise regularly (things that are positioned as within our own control and our own responsibility), overlooking health disparities resulting from structural inequalities in housing conditions, poverty, levels of pollution, or access to health services. Likewise, the idea that the world is a meritocracy, and the wealthy deserve their riches because they have earned them through hard work and clever choices, illustrates neoliberal ideas about individual responsibility and merit whilst overlooking the advantages gained through private education, inherited wealth, class, or global/national/regional economic disparities. On the flip side, poverty and other inequalities are blamed on individual failings (poor motivation, lack of willpower, laziness, and so on). This focus on individual self-improvement and competition can undermine people's ability to see connections between their own experience and those of others, and to identify structural inequalities. Feminist researchers study how neoliberalism operates and its impact on our sense of ourselves, demonstrating how it implicates women differently in terms of what and how they are expected to work on themselves and their bodies to achieve a successful life. In their book on postfeminism and health, for example, Sarah Riley, Adrienne Evans, and Martine Robson (2018) draw on discourse analysis to demonstrate how women are presented as *both* inherently flawed (as needing to be more healthy, thinner, or fit) *and* able to transform themselves into 'perfect' women through self-help, dieting and exercise, and pregnancy advice. These narratives, along with backlash discourses, can influence women's (and men's) views about the relevancy of feminism, feminists, and feminist activism. Feminist research helps to show how these processes operate.

Finally, although anyone who is concerned about social injustice, including gender inequality, can identify as a feminist and can benefit from learning about feminist theory and research, there are specific reasons why some people might find it difficult to identify as feminists. As we have seen in the discussion of the four waves of feminism, when some voices have become dominant and others muted within feminism, at times feminism has not always felt like a welcoming or relevant space for people of colour or for gender and sexual minorities. Moreover, some men do not identify as *feminist* because they do not identify as *female*, and they believe that feminism is the exclusive domain of women. For example, while the backlash associated with feminism may explain why some men are reluctant to identify as feminists, the unique position of men within the feminist movement may also be important. Specifically, although the role of men within the feminist movement has been contested, both in academic writing and popular media, increasingly feminist scholars and activists argue that inclusion of men in the feminist movement is essential for increasing the weight of collective action and for disrupting problematic cultural gender roles from within (see, for example, Flood, 2011 on engaging men in activism to end violence against women). Men are encouraged to see feminism as disrupting and reducing men's privileges, where feminist gains become men's losses (think of news headlines which blame feminism for problems like boys' failure in schools, unemployment among men, and well, just about everything really!). Yet, feminism has helped to change many men's lives for the better too – including campaigning for parental leave to include fathers, the recognition of sexual assault of men and boys in legal definitions of sexual violence, the right for men to access stereotypically 'female' professions (like nursing or psychology), prison reform and the humane treatment of prisoners (most of whom are men), and challenging stereotypes about men and masculinity to name but a few.

SECTION SUMMARY

- For some of you, feminism may already feel an important part of who you are while for others, feminism might feel quite alien.
- Embracing or rejecting feminism is not simply a matter of individual choice. Social and political forces (like neoliberalism and postfeminist claims about feminism being defunct) shape how feminism is represented and understood.
- Whenever feminism is talked about a lot, or when women make social economic or political gains towards greater equality, there is often a backlash.

Whether or not you personally identify as a feminist however, there are good reasons to engage with a feminist companion to research methods such as this.

Five reasons you need a feminist companion to research methods in psychology

Comprehensiveness

Feminist research and feminist researchers have been at the forefront of challenging, developing, and transforming psychological research practice and psychology as a discipline for as long as psychology has been in existence. Yet, feminist contributions to methods are often not included in the undergraduate curriculum, or their inclusion often depends on having excellent feminist tutors (of which there are, unfortunately, not enough). In the mid- 1990s, almost a century after early feminist critiques of research in psychology, Rebecca Campbell and Pamela Schram (1995) wanted to see whether feminist developments in research methods were routinely included in methods textbooks in psychology and the social sciences. Disappointingly, although there was some evidence that these books avoided the very worst sexist bias (i.e. avoiding using 'he' to refer to all people), there was still little discussion of feminist challenges to psychological research. More recent analyses of the impact of feminism on psychology have found a enormous growth in the number of published articles reporting research on women and gender (Eagly et al., 2012). Yet, some of the core feminist challenges to methodology were still receiving 'negligible attention' in the most popular psychology methods textbooks (Eagly & Riger, 2014, p. 698). Textbooks are powerful tools for communicating the central assumptions, methodologies, and achievements of a discipline and for showcasing what kind of knowledge is most valued. Although these publications are often presented as objective and value-neutral, they reflect the judgements that authors, editors, and publishers make when choosing content and language to represent their field to a relatively naïve audience (Marecek, 1993). This *Feminist Companion to Research Methods in Psychology* is an important counter to the omissions present in many of the existing textbooks used in undergraduate psychology courses, and is designed to help you to recognise what is missing from these books as well as to provide information about effective and well-established alternatives.

Criticality

Thinking through a feminist lens will help you to develop your critical thinking and analytical skills. These are essential for producing high quality research – and therefore knowledge – but are also crucial to your academic skills and your ability to be successful as a student. British feminist scholar Sara Ahmed (2016) talks about the importance of '*sweaty work*' – the work of challenging, critiquing, looking beyond the published word, to feel uncomfortable about knowledge that is produced, and to acknowledge and sit with this discomfort in order to identify its source. In this book, we invite you to engage with us in this sweaty work. We invite you to bring yourself, your experiences, and your own knowledge about what it means to be human into dialogue with the discipline of psychology and the methods used to generate understanding of human experience. Thinking critically means evaluating whether the knowledge that is produced by psychologists is attuned to your own experience and ways of knowing the world. If not, sweaty work may mean finding ways to challenge established or emerging knowledge. Alternatively, it might mean confronting your own assumptions, privileges, or blind-spots and recognising the limits of your own experiences. A focus on feminism and feminist research methods will help you to attend to issues of *power* and *ethics*. This includes recognising the power of psychology as a discipline, considering unequal relationships between researchers and participants, asking questions about who is doing research and who research is designed to benefit. Sweaty work might also mean considering who and what is missing or underrepresented in research, and considering how research can challenge, transform, or solidify the social inequalities which shape our societies.

Representation

In 1971, psychologist Naomi Weisstein wrote, "Psychology has nothing to say about what women are really like, what they need and what they want, especially because psychology does not know" (p. 197). It is fifty years since Weisstein's searing attack on psychological knowledge was published, and although feminist psychology and feminist approaches to research have blossomed since then, this is not always reflected in mainstream psychological texts or research literatures. One element of Weisstein's critique was that psychology was dominated by primarily white, middle-class men who conducted research with mostly white, middle-class male research participants. Women have been active in psychology since its inception. They now exceed men numerically in the discipline as academics, researchers, and practitioners. Yet women are not yet equally valued or rewarded for their contributions as measured by things like citations, journal editorships, and prizes (Eagly & Riger, 2014). Analyses of psychology textbooks, for example, show that the female pioneers who have shaped the discipline of psychology are still often absent (Alvarez et al., 2020). Likewise, although the frequency of all-male samples appears to have declined, this is still evident in some areas of psychology – notably biomedical research and neuroscience (Eagly & Riger, 2014).

Representativeness is not only about making sure that women are included as participants in research, and about recognition of women's contribution to shaping the discipline, it is also about asking different questions. Starting from the perspective of those on the margins, feminist research puts producing knowledge about aspects of life which are directly relevant to women at the forefront – including sexual exploitation and violence, parenting and childrearing, and women's working lives and conditions. Feminist research puts these areas on the agenda for psychology, raises them up as important and worthy of study, and takes the lives of women seriously as a focus for research. Given the invisibility of women, feminism, and feminist research in most psychology texts, this *Feminist Companion to Research Methods in Psychology* seeks to offer you a more representative picture of research than you will find in your standard undergraduate psychology course in the UK.

Inclusivity

Feminist research is not only about women – indeed, part of the sweaty work of feminism has been to unpack and problematise what the term 'woman' means and to expand our vocabulary for talking about gender and gender identities. Feminist research applies to research on all psychological topics and all people who might be involved in research (researchers, participants, and audiences for research). Feminist research is about understanding psychological research through the lens of gender and how this intersects with other aspects of identity and social inequalities. Being inclusive means doing research that addresses issues which really matter to people, and which ultimately improves their lives. It means accessing and representing their views and experiences and treating people with respect and dignity. Being inclusive also means involving all people and communities in research – although in practice, for feminists, this often means finding ways to include people who are often marginalised, excluded, or silenced in society. Being inclusive also means working collaboratively with communities and people to produce research which meaningfully engages with issues that are important to them. In this *Feminist Companion to Research Methods in Psychology* we aim to ensure that you have a more inclusive understanding of key issues in research by making visible the issues relevant to people and groups which are often excluded in psychology.

Relevance

Feminist research focuses not just on the research setting, but how this can impact the world, including how it affects different groups in different ways. Feminist research often goes hand-in-hand with feminist activism – a desire to change the world often through collective action. The practical use of psychological research, the use of research to transform lives and change practices is central to feminist concerns. A key aim of this *Feminist Companion to Research Methods in Psychology* is to illustrate how research (albeit not alone) can prompt these changes and share our passion and enthusiasm for seeing research into practice. It is the possibility for change that keeps us motivated to undertake research.

CHAPTER SUMMARY

- Feminism is concerned with gender equality; research (and the methods used to create this research) are tools for exposing gender-based discrimination and inequality and for moving towards gender equity.
- Feminist research is about asking challenging questions from the margins.
- Feminism shifts and responds to the different social, cultural, economic, geographical, and political contexts in which it is put to work.
- Feminist thinking research will help you to gain a more comprehensive, critical, representative, inclusive, and relevant understanding of research methods to apply to your own research projects.

2 Thinking like a feminist (or thinking through a feminist lens)

Learning objectives

Study of this chapter should enable you to:

- Think critically about the role of questions and problems in psychological research.
- Consider the impact of looking at research methods in psychology through different lenses.
- Understand the implications of thinking through a feminist lens.

What's the problem?

In the previous chapter, we discussed different ways in which feminism has been understood and practised, drawing on the sometimes contentious but widespread notion of 'waves'. While these narratives are always approximate and developing, one of the reasons we thought this approach would be useful is that it highlights the multiplicity of feminism or, more appropriately, feminisms, while making visible how these are interwoven. While not all feminists think the same (more on this later in the book), there are resonances and affinities that hold these differing positions together. One of those things, as we argued in Chapter 1, is that all feminists start from the perspective of those on the margins – and those margins are pretty wide given that sexist inequalities include people even in otherwise powerful positions. Based on this position, we talked about the importance of asking questions and how what questions we ask affects what knowledge we can (and, importantly, cannot) create. What this means is that questions are unavoidably situated and embedded in the political. As Foucault (1980) told us, not only is knowledge power but power is also knowledge. Questions can signpost what we believe is important and what is not, what deserves our attention and what does not, and, critically, what is a problem and what is not. Until very recently, for instance, wolf whistling or cat calling at teenage girls in the street was seen as a bit of fun and even flattery. Certainly not something to be concerned about. However, when feminists asked, *is this a form of street harassment?*, it was constituted as a problem, opening it up to investigation by both researchers and activists (Logan, 2015).

So, when we design a research question, we are letting people know what we think the 'problem' is. If we take a feminist approach, we want to problematise behaviour that is sexist or discriminatory. However, we also need to challenge how a problem is being defined and what assumptions underpin that definition. Let's consider research on autism spectrum disorder (ASD). While we would agree that society can be challenging for those with an ASD diagnosis, much of the literature positions children with this diagnosis as a problem. The focus of the research then becomes solving this problem. It could be argued, however, that there are other ways of making sense of this experience. For instance, world renowned environmental activist Greta Thunberg has stated publicly that she considers her ASD as a superpower rather than a limitation. For Greta, the fact that she isn't really bothered by what other people think of her, that she can focus on a problem without getting distracted, and that she has no trouble speaking her mind has been an asset for her as an activist because she is less easily discouraged from advocating for environmentalism. More and more people diagnosed with ASD have been making similar arguments and have come together to form what is often referred to as the Neurodiversity movement, which is having an impact on the research into ASD (Leadbitter et al., 2021).

We see this pattern in many areas of research. For instance, 'single mothers' are too often presented as a symbol of failure in our society and researchers are asked to find a 'solution' to this 'problem'. However, how much does this reflect our culture rather than our experience? When we problematise 'single mothers', we are implying that they are, in some way, deficient in their mothering – particularly if they are also young. Yet, research that explicitly questions this assumption has found that this is not the case (e.g. Kirkman et al., 2001; Yardley, 2008). What this example brings to light is how women's behaviour is made the focus of societal surveillance. Rarely in these discussions does the question of absent fathers come up. Why do we so easily problematise the woman who stays with the children and takes on their care?

What we hope to demonstrate with these examples is that by asking some questions and not others, we are also saying what we think constitutes a problem and needs explanation and what can go unobserved, unnoticed, and unexplained – which historically has been widespread sexist and discriminatory behaviour.

SECTION SUMMARY

- While not all feminists think the same, all feminist perspectives are from the margins.
- Drawing on the work of Foucault, we have argued that the power to define a problem means the power to decide what is knowledge.
- It is important to pay attention to which issues are deemed to be problems and which are not while also paying attention to what assumptions are being made in making these decisions.

What's the question?

As this book is about feminist research methods, we can begin by exploring how we decide on the questions we ask and, thus, the knowledge we produce. In order to do this, we will need to consider what is referred to as **epistemology**. Epistemology, simply put, is the study of knowledge. However, it is also commonly used to refer to particular theories of knowledge. As we have argued, all knowledge must be understood in context and it is useful to think about what we see when we look at things from different locations. As Wiggington and Lafrance have argued, "How one engages in research necessarily flows from one's epistemological commitments at the time of inquiry" (2019, p. 10).

In this chapter, we're suggesting that we can think about these different ways of looking as different lenses that you can look through to focus on different aspects of the object or scene you want to know more about. For instance, a zoom lens can focus on something far off in the distance and a magnifying glass will let us see things that are close up. Similarly, different coloured lenses let through different kinds of light, as in the saying 'looking at the world through rose coloured glasses'. In this book, we will consider the effects of looking at the world through six different lenses:

- The lens of place
- The lens of power
- The lens of social justice
- The lens of ethics
- The lens of representation and intersectionality
- The lens of reflexivity

What is interesting about these lenses is that, traditionally, psychologists, and many other researchers, have behaved as if they were not there – as if we are observing the world in an objective and direct way (this is called positivism and we discuss this in more depth in Chapter 3). Feminists have, along with many other marginalised groups, questioned this assumption. This is often what we mean when we talk about *research* that is 'feminist'.

SECTION SUMMARY

- We have argued that all knowledge should be understood in context.
- Traditionally, psychology has generally behaved as if it can observe the world directly and objectively.
- Feminists, along with other groups from the margins, have questioned this assumption.

Looking through the lens of place

The first lens that we will look at is the lens of *place*. What do we mean by this? Some of the things we might consider is how location impacts on research questions. How does it influence design? How does place affect the analysis and how we make sense of findings? As we have discussed, problems are often defined by the values of a specific society. One obvious example is what is considered appropriate behaviour between men and women. As we've suggested, not that long ago, most women would just ignore men who wolf whistled them, patted their behind, or made sexist jokes in their presence. They would feel uncomfortable but not able to label the behaviour as sexual harassment (Lazard, 2020). In a matter of a few years, however, this situation has changed.

Now reread the paragraph above and think about how we've talked about this change. What are we really saying? Are we talking about all women everywhere? We think you will agree this is not the case. In some places, this behaviour has not been acceptable for a very long time; in others, it still passes without comment. This is what we're talking about when we say that knowledge is located. Depending on the lens we use, in our case from an academic setting in the south of England, it certainly feels like things have changed. However, it is critical to good research design that researchers explore their location in relation to the research itself and consider how it might impact the production of knowledge.

At this point, we would like to introduce a term coined by Joseph Henrich, Steven Heine, and Ara Norenzayan in 2010 that has become particularly popular in some academic circles in the last decade or so: WEIRD. WEIRD is a term used by researchers to refer to populations that are from countries that are predominantly White, Educated, Industrialised, Rich, and Democratic. The acronym is also appropriate, the authors argue, because the people who inhabit these countries are 'weird' in the colloquial sense, in that they are not very representative of the world's population as a whole. Yet, much of what is held to be 'psychological knowledge' in your textbooks is based on research that uses this population and, in particular, undergraduates in US universities (and a few European and Antipodean ones) as participants. The assumption here is, of course, that the drivers of human behaviour are constant wherever you go. However, there is growing evidence that this is not the case (Henrich et al., 2010; Henrich, 2020). In fact, Henrich et al. argue that people from WEIRD societies are probably some of the least representative of all.

There are some really basic differences from place to place even in functions like visual perception. For instance, in your studies you may have come across the Müller-Lyer illusion. This is the line with arrows at either end pointing in different directions (Figure 2.1). In the original study, widely reported in undergraduate textbooks, most participants indicated that they perceived the line with the arrows pointing inward to be longer than the one with the arrows

Figure 2.1: The Müller-Lyer illusion whereby participants judged the bottom line to be longer than the top one although they are measurably the same length.

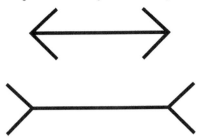

pointing outward. As early as 1966, though, cross-cultural studies indicated that this phenomenon was not consistent. In some cultures, participants easily identified the lines as being the same length (Segall et al., 1966). However, cognitive theories about human perception have been based on the original place specific findings.

While you might think times have changed, many prestigious journals publish papers all the time that make this same assumption. In spite of all the evidence indicating the issues associated with this approach, the number of psychological studies that take place in areas outside the G7 (Canada, France, Germany, Italy, Japan, the United Kingdom, and the United States) is still limited (Masuda et al., 2020). In 2021, the *British Journal of Social Psychology* published an article about how the hiring of leaders in the workplace is gendered. Who did they use as participants? In one of the studies the participants were all UK undergraduate students that completed the study in partial fulfilment of course requirements and had limited, if any, experience of hiring and firing practices in the world of work (Pireddu et al., 2022). It is worth thinking about what the implications might be here for those who might want to make use of the findings from this study.

The assumption that this small number of countries represent everyone extends to the news, art, music, literature, history, and most of the other fields that contribute to our culture. We only see the subset of it that prioritises WEIRD countries. For instance, in the previous chapter, we warned you that the dominant storied version of feminism that relies on the 'waves' metaphor is contested. This is because, while it is a commonly shared history in the UK, it is only really relevant to those in Anglo-American societies. Academics working in different contexts, particularly those who do not work primarily in English, struggle to have their research published in the most prestigious journals. This means that lots of what we 'know' about psychology isn't very representative of the work that is going on. As new research builds on the currently published work, this magnifies the bias. The lens of place, however, allows us to consider the research and ask, what difference does place make?

SECTION SUMMARY

- We have argued that problems are often defined by the values of a specific society.
- Data from WEIRD (White, Educated, Industrialised, Rich, and Democratic) societies are used for most psychological research, but they are not very representative of the world as a whole.
- Even basic cognitive experiments that are the foundations of psychological theory do not produce consistent findings across different locations.
- In spite of many critiques, these place-based practices still continue in mainstream psychology.
- Much of what we 'know' in psychology isn't very representative of the world at large.

Looking through the lens of power

The next epistemological lens we will explore is the lens of power. Scholars have been theorising and trying to understand how power works for millennia. Psychology has mostly ignored the issue of power – it is, after all, a very messy business, both conceptually and practically. Rather than take on the whole debate, in this section, we'll just be focusing on a few examples to illustrate some of the issues that feminists have raised because, in many ways, a recognition of the role of power has shaped feminist engagements with psychology. According to Celia Kitzinger, psychology as a discipline was "deeply implicated in the maintenance and reproduction of power relationships which it persistently refuses to make explicit" (1991, p. 111). We would argue that this continues to be the case as long as psychological research claims to be objective and apolitical. This is the reason, many feminists have argued, that power has rarely been addressed in psychological research, and when it is, it is usually as simplified variables. For feminism, the problem with this exclusion of power from traditional approaches is, of course, that feminism challenges these existing power relations.

So, the first thing we might want to ask ourselves is what do we see when we look at psychological research through the lens of power? How can power affect the findings of a study? Feminist psychologists have for decades mapped out how existing societal power relations are embedded in the research process. This is evident from the very start of the research process, as we have discussed, through the power to define the problem. However, power is relevant to every stage of the research process: the decision on what methods to use, on where to conduct the study and with whom, as well as how you interpret the findings. If these decisions are in harmony with the status quo, then the study will reinforce the existing distribution of power. In order to make use of this lens, when looking at any study we should ask who stands to benefit from the research. For instance, psychology has spent a lot of energy trying to make workers more productive and soldiers better fighters rather than making them better union activists or pacifists. Not so long ago, the American Psychological Society (APA) became entangled in a controversy around the involvement of psychologists in the 'enhanced interrogations' of suspected terrorists in Guantanamo Bay (most of us thought of it as torture).

See and hear for yourself

If you'd like to read more about this shameful episode in the history of the APA, you can find a database of all the statements issued by the APA on the subject. Compare those before and after 2007 at https://www.apa.org/news/press/statements/interrogations.

You might want to contrast this with the statements made in 2006 and 2008 by the Society for the Psychological Study of Social Issues (SPSSI) – itself a subsection of the APA – that lobbied relentlessly for a change of policy in the APA at the time:

https://www.spssi.org/index.cfm?fuseaction=Page.ViewPage&PageID=1460
https://www.spssi.org/index.cfm?fuseaction=Page.ViewPage&PageID=1088

The lens of power also allows us to focus notions of 'empowerment'. We read a lot in the media about how women, particularly young women, have been empowered over the last few decades but what do they mean by this? In what ways have they been 'empowered'? A number of feminist authors (e.g. Rutherford, 2018) have argued that while promising independence and control, what is available is actually a very limited form of power – often centred on the power of the consumer. Take, for example, the way social media promises the user control of their image. In the early years of the internet, there was a hope that this would be an unregulated egalitarian space were identity play (presenting yourself as someone different to your everyday in person self) was possible and things like gender, age, ethnicity, and disability, amongst others, became irrelevant. As we all know, this did not quite turn out to be the case.

Although the internet and social media have made access to information much easier, the environment is socially regulated in very normative ways – particularly in the case of young women. Research looking at the types of selfies that women post found that these tend to be much more gender-stereotypical than those in magazine advertisements (Döring et al., 2016). It's worth thinking about why that might be. Research asking that question has indicated that young women and girls, in particular, are subject to *pathologisation*, social concern, and disapproval (Senft & Baym, 2015; Warfield, 2014). That is to say, they are often criticised for being narcissistic and inauthentic. (In fact, young women are criticised for just about everything they do and like – their posting, their clothes, the way they talk, the music they listen to, the films they watch, the books they read, and so on – see Box 2.1.) However, research by Lisa Lazard and Rose Capdevila (2021) – yep, Rose is one of the authors of this book – frames the problem differently by asking a different methodological question, one that takes young women seriously rather than disempowering them. We asked them to tell us what they thought they and others were doing when they posted selfies. We found that, on the one hand, while narcissism did play some part, it was more about trying to create relationships and connecting with other people. Authenticity, on the other hand, was understood very differently. Participants in our study were trying to say something true or real about themselves, to influence not how they looked but how they were seen. So while they used the technology with expertise and artistry, to curate themselves, their identity, in a particular way (something mostly overlooked in the mainstream literature), this was not an attempt to deceive but rather to relate to others. In this case, asking a different question, one that isn't guided by condescending societal assumptions about young women, but rather asks them about their experience, allowed us to make sense of this practice from a different, less judgemental, perspective.

Box 2.1: The problem with young women

There is a growing discomfort among feminists and others about the way society continues to treat young women in terms of both gender and generation. Here are two young women speaking to this issue. The first is a TED talk from Katie Emanuel talking about her experience as a young woman, while the second is a poem by young Scottish author Erin May Kelly about the strength of women.

Why do we hate young women?
In defence of teenage girls by Katie Emanuel
https://www.youtube.com/watch?v=M4anrceML8I

The Strength of Women | Little Girls Don't Stay Little Forever
A poem by Erin May Kelly
https://www.youtube.com/watch?v=pL9NYwsWfjE

This brings us to an important issue made visible through a lens of power: how we identify and work with those who are not powerful in research – those that might be considered vulnerable. Psychology has traditionally dealt with this through the lens of ethics (see below for more discussion of this). However, if we understand power to be *relational* – that is, as something that plays out through relationships – we need to be very attentive when we define people as vulnerable and how they self-identify. For instance, those who have experienced sexual assault may think of themselves as survivors and reject the assumption of vulnerability that comes with the label of victim.

For instance, a poster we came across from the Women's March in Sydney, Australia reads:

How many women are killed by men every year?

How many women are raped by men every year?

How many women are assaulted by men every year?

It then crosses out the latter part of the sentence to read:

How many men kill women every year?

How many men rape women every year?

How many men assault women every year?

And finally,

Stop making the conversation about violence against women passive.

This brings our attention to fact that the conversation about violence against women is often presented as passive by actively focusing on the victim rather than the perpetrator.

The argument presented in that poster is similar to the one voiced in the 'Take back the night' marches, held internationally from the 1970s to 2021. In these protests, women argued that the onus of keeping women safe should not fall on the women themselves but rather on those who threaten them. This was a response to policymakers and researchers who asked the wrong questions when asking how women can stay safe. In the wake of the 2021 murder of Sarah Everard by an active police office in the UK, a group of representatives from the Psychology of Women and Equalities Section (POWES) of the British Psychological Society wrote a report to the government about their approach to Violence Against Women and Girls.

See and hear for yourself

Here is an article from *The Conversation* about the Sarah Everard murder and the government's plan to make women feel more safe: https://theconversation. com/sarah-everard-murder-the-problem-with-the-governments-plan-to-make-women-feel-safer-169072

You can also read a blog post about the POWES response to the UK government's consultation on their Violence Against Women and Girls Strategy 2021–2024 here: https://powesbps.wordpress.com/blog-posts/

SECTION SUMMARY

- We've discussed how, historically, the discipline of psychology has rarely recognised or theorised the role of power in research methods.
- We have argued that a consideration of power is relevant to every stage of the research process.
- A good question to ask is, 'Who stands to benefit from this research?'
- Taking participants' experience seriously can help address power imbalances and results in better research and more useful findings.

Looking through the lens of social justice

One of the ways in which we can address issues around the imbalance of power in research is through considerations of *social justice*. What is social justice and what does it have to do with research? The Oxford English Dictionary defines social justice as "justice in terms of the distribution of wealth, opportunities, and privileges within a society" (OED, n.d.). For psychology, these considerations can be looked at in at least two ways: how we do our research and what kind of research we do. Melba Vasquez, in her presidential address to the American Psychological Association (APA), the largest organisation of psychologists in the world, argued that it is the responsibility of psychologists to "be proactive in addressing critical social problems, especially those to which our research speaks" (2012, p. 338). What does that mean? For Vasquez, this means that, as psychologists it is our responsibility to work towards a fairer and kinder society. You will know from your studies in psychology that many of the topics addressed by the discipline have precisely this goal, such as research into aggression, education, poverty, prejudice and discrimination, public health, violence, and others. In recent years, the British Psychological Society has set an annual Senate Policy Campaign that aims to influence government policy on issues such as tackling poverty and increasing play time in schools. In the US, the APA has a division dedicated to the Society for the Psychological Study of Social Issues, which brings together psychologists with a shared interest in research on the critical problems of today's world in order to affect policy. So you could argue that psychology has a clear investment in social justice and influencing government to this end. However, when, in the 1980s, a group of early career feminist psychologist petitioned the BPS to create a section to represent their research, they were told that this was 'too political' (Burman, 2011; Wilkinson & Burns, 1990). When the section was finally approved, after a number of failed attempts, it was named the Psychology of Women Section.

The argument about what is and isn't political is, of course, at the heart of feminist thinking. The feminist slogan that 'the personal is political' (Hanisch, 1969) speaks to the fact that for women, and indeed all members of marginalised groups, their personal experiences are heavily impacted by wider societal and political structures. For instance, the lack of affordable day care means that mothers, particularly those who are not affluent, are limited in what they can do and achieve if they have young children.

How are psychological research methods implicated in this? Well, once again, we come back to the kind of question we are asking. If as a society we want to know if we should be investing in day care, we could design a research study with the following *hypothesis*: 'Do preschool children do better if they are cared for by their mothers or if they attend day care?' We could design a *matched pair study*, measure success in terms of a number of *variables* such as sociability, speech development, attachment, etc. Or, we could do a *longitudinal* study that looks at something like educational attainment or affluence in later life. These studies could compare outcomes for these children, conduct some *inferential statistics*, and tell you how each group performed.

Seems straightforward enough. However, let's step back and examine this question using a social justice lens that takes into account 'the distribution of wealth, opportunities, and privileges within a society'. That is, instead of a narrow focus on the child's outcomes according to this one variable, whether they attend day care or not, we consider the broader implications of the situation. In the study we have imagined above, there is no consideration of the mother's needs or requirement, nor those of the family, the community, or the broader society. It is not that this question is not relevant, it is simply that it fails to engage with the broader implications of such a decision. For many women, whether they work or not is not a choice. Perhaps they cannot afford to stay home or they may have responsibilities that take them out of the home, or they have health concerns which means they need support themselves. What are the implications of psychological research that is set up to answer questions in this very limited way that excludes those with limited access to societal resources? A social justice lens would advocate for an approach that explores the possibilities for facilitating the best outcomes, rather than assuming that every individual had limitless choice and is not subject to the impact of societal and political pressures. Whereas a focus on equality is sometimes taken as the need to treat everyone the same, the lens of social justice recognises that people often do not start from the same place and may need different kinds of resources (access to free childcare, financial support, better healthcare, etc.) to facilitate better outcomes for themselves and their children.

What we would suggest is that a lens of social justice allows you to stand back and look at the implication of psychological research in terms of who has access to what and how different groups might be differently impacted by the way we do our research.

SECTION SUMMARY

- In this section, we talked about the relationship between psychological research and social justice and argued that psychology has a clear investment in this agenda.
- Many of the professional societies that psychologists belong to are explicitly invested in societal issues and work to influence governmental decision-making based on psychological knowledge.
- We returned to the importance of questions in the kind of research we conduct and findings we produce.
- A social justice lens allows you to look at how our research impacts different groups.

Looking through the lens of ethics

As part of any methods training in psychology, students are taught about the importance of **ethics** to the research process. What do we mean by this? One way of thinking about ethics is as the principles that determine right and wrong behaviour. In psychological research, for instance, ethics most often refers to the codes and principles that researchers should adhere to. You will likely have been taught that the British Psychological Society bases its *Code of Ethics and Conduct* (BPS, 2021b) on four ethical Principles: respect, competence, responsibility, and integrity. That sounds fine, but what does it mean in practice? How do we know what is right and wrong? How do we make sure our research is ethical? On a very practical level, this often means filling in a form where you explain how and why your study is ethical and having it approved by a representative of the university – one of your lecturers or an ethics committee. However, what if we think beyond that limited framework?

Ethics don't just appear out of nowhere. They are intimately intertwined with our cultural values. That's why research that was considered to be perfectly acceptable some time ago (think Harlow's Maternal Deprivation research, Milgram's Obedience Experiments, Zimbardo's Prison Study) are completely unacceptable today (thank goodness!). As a society our values have changed and with them the way we think of ethics. So what can feminism offer to this discussion? According to Brabeck and Ting, feminist approaches provide a means for "determining what one ought to do and deciding on a course of action in the face of competing ethical principles" (2000, p. 18). Let's look, for instance, at some classic research in developmental psychology.

In the late 1950s, developmental psychologist Lawrence Kohlberg proposed a theory of moral development that suggests that there were three levels of moral reasoning (pre-conventional, conventional, and post-conventional) and that they were hierarchically organised – that is to say, that you go through these in order, with a higher stage representing a more complex and developed understanding than the one that precedes it. Kohlberg developed his theory based on a storytelling technique in which he told the participants a story which ended with a moral dilemma (see box) and asked them what they thought the character in the story should do and why.

Box 2.2: Heinz and the expensive medicine

Heinz's wife is ill and needs some expensive medicine that will save her life. Heinz and his wife can't afford the medicine and they know the chemist is aware he is overcharging. Should Heinz steal the medicine to save his wife?

What Kohlberg was interested in was not really what people would do but what explanation they would provide for their choice. He used these answers to build his theory of moral development.

If you are interested in learning more about this, you might enjoy listening to this episode of BBC Radio series Mind Changers on Kohlberg: https://www.bbc.co.uk/programmes/b008drfq

---

Carol Gilligan, however, a feminist psychologist who was Kohlberg's research assistant, argued that Kohlberg's work was flawed and not **generalisable** to women and girls. What evidence did she have for this? First of all, Kohlberg's research was based on studies that had been conducted exclusively with male participants – something that was widespread at the time and the basis of far too much theorising in developmental psychology. Second, Kohlberg's stages of moral development prioritised what Gilligan referred to as a 'masculine voice'. This voice relied on an 'ethic of justice', that relied on logic and was individualistic. For Gilligan, a feminine voice that used an 'ethic of care' was more likely to emphasise the importance of relationships and taking care of others. The problem was that, if you used this 'ethic of care' rather than an 'ethic of justice' using Kohlberg's model, women appear to have inferior moral development.

See and hear for yourself
You can read more about Gilligan's work on the Psychology's Feminist Voices website, which also includes filmed interviews with her about her work. See https://feministvoices.com/profiles/carol-gilligan

So far we've argued that ethics can vary but they are intertwined with our values – what we think is important and what less so. Looking through the lens of ethics, we can see that assumptions made in our research methods can make it impossible for us to see how our experience of different phenomena can be shaped by gender as well as other markers of difference.

SECTION SUMMARY

- Ethics in psychological research is more than just filling in a form to show you are complying with the guidelines.
- Cultural values are critical to how we understand ethics.
- How we make sense of what is right and wrong can vary according to what ethical lens we might be looking through. Gilligan, for instance, argued that men tended to rely on an ethic of justice while women often used an ethic of care.

Looking through the lens of representation and intersectionality

Lafrance and Wigginton (2019) have argued that *representation* and *intersectionality* are at the very heart of critical feminist scholarship. Why might they say this? You will be familiar with the way in which mainstream psychology uses an 'objective voice' – one that is neutral and unrelated to issues of value, power, or politics. Traditionally, those taking part in psychological research were often referred to as 'subjects'. More recently, it has become far more common to use the term 'participants' or 'respondents', and sometimes terms like '*co-researcher*' are used to make clear the importance of everyone involved. The lens of representation forces us to think about how we are making sense of other people's lives and if we are doing it in a way that is responsible and respectful. This issue becomes particularly relevant when you conduct research with participants who are different to you.

Kitzinger and Wilkinson (1997) explored how feminist research aims to represent the experiences of those it studies. It is not straightforward. Of course, as we've discussed, women's experiences have historically been ignored, dismissed, or even ridiculed, whilst those of white, middle-aged, middle-class, straight, able-bodied men have been *universalised* – that is, used as representing everyone. So it is important to provide a space for women and others in the literature. However, the attempt to represent these experiences risks a different kind of universalising – the universalising of the experience of white, middle-class, able-bodied, straight Anglo-American women. This is where intersectionality comes into play. As we discussed in Chapter 1, intersectional approaches acknowledge how people's life experience is shaped not only by gender, but also race, class, sexuality, (dis)ability, age, and other markers of difference. Although there are experiences that are shared by women, the experience of one woman will always be qualitatively different from that of another, not just due to their personal circumstances, but importantly also due to the multiple intersections of disadvantage that they might have suffered or privileges they may have enjoyed. This is important to the research process. Most feminist researchers will contend that the research relationship is just that – a relationship. We need to acknowledge this to be able to do our work successfully.

We would agree that the issue of representation and intersectionality is, as Lafrance and Wigginton suggest, at the heart of feminist scholarship and particularly, we would argue, feminist research. This lens allows us to see that relationships with, but also within, psychological research can have an impact on what claims we can make. When you break down the space between the researcher and the researched, that relationship becomes key to how you make sense of the findings, so the next and final lens we will explore, is that of *reflexivity* – arguably one of the most emblematic elements of feminist social science research.

SECTION SUMMARY

- The question of representation becomes particularly important when you are conducting research with participants who are different to you.
- Historically, psychology often treated the experience of one small group of people as if they represented everyone. This still happens much more often that it should.
- When doing research, we need to consider the different markers of difference that shape people's lives. Intersectional approaches focus on the 'intersection' of the disadvantages and privileges that we may each be subject to because of our membership of certain groups and not others.
- This lens focuses on the relationships between things.

Looking through the lens of reflexivity

Reflexivity is a particular kind of lens because rather than look outward it, in a sense, looks inward. Lazard and McAvoy conceptualise reflexivity as a form of critical thinking, stating that "the point of reflexivity is to scaffold critical thinking in order to make visible some of the connections between research questions and research conclusions" (2020, p. 160). Thinking about *why* – from all the possible questions you could ask – you are asking *this* particular question, through each element of the process, to how you write the final research report. In a sense, then, this whole book looks at research through the lens of reflexivity, as we are always asking why this way and not that.

In her classic paper on 'The role of reflexivity in feminist psychology' (1988), Sue Wilkinson sets out three forms of reflexivity. We could actually think of these as three separate lenses which look on the researcher from three different focal points. *Personal reflexivity* is when the researcher examines their own identities, values, and life experiences to consider how these have shaped the research topic, methods, and interpretations of their study. To give an example, Victoria Defrancisco, Jennifer Kuderer, and April Chatham-Carpenter (2007) talk about how reflecting on their own experience shifted the way that they chose to research women and self-esteem. They were originally interested in this topic because of their own struggles with self-esteem and anorexia. However, once the study began, they came across an article on autoethnography.

This approach draws directly on the researchers' experiences and after reading it Victoria wrote: "This is what we should have done in the first place with the self-esteem research ... This time we should begin with our own stories" (2007, p. 238).

There were insights to be gained, the authors realised, by placing these experiences centre-stage in the research. They decided to invite a small group of women to join with them in the "very intimate and challenging experience" of writing their life stories with self-esteem, sharing them with each other, and discussing these stories as a group (2007, p. 238). This process was, at times, anxiety-provoking, embarrassing, and freeing as these women shared their fears and experiences. It also led to new insights as they came to realise that their low self-esteem did not reflect a personal weakness but was systemic and related to social expectations of women, the struggle to balance multiple roles, and the demands of perfectionism. As you can probably see, this kind of research involves a very different commitment from the researcher. As Defrancisco et al. note, the insights gained by using this method arose out of the "inherent risk-taking involved in making ourselves vulnerable to self-explorations of self-esteem and the method of sharing ourselves with others" (2007, p. 237). It can be uncomfortable and sweaty work to invest so much of ourselves in the research, but after all, we are often asking our research participants to share difficult, intimate, and challenging aspects of themselves and their experiences with us. Looking through the lens of reflexivity doesn't inevitably mean changing your methods in the same way as these researchers, but it does mean thinking about ourselves (our identities, assumptions, values, experiences, and skills) and exploring how this shapes the questions we ask, the methods we use, how we engage with our participants, and the knowledge we produce.

A second form of reflexivity proposed by Wilkinson, which is particularly compelling, is that of **disciplinary reflexivity**. This is about the discipline itself and how it operates and is supported by the institutions and structures of academia. For instance, the value of 'proper science' and 'objectivity' that mainstream psychology adheres to has implications for what is and isn't considered to be legitimate psychological knowledge. We must ask what are the criteria of acceptance being applied to ideas in psychology and who decides on these criteria of acceptance? In the early days of psychology, the variability hypothesis, the idea that males display more variability in different traits in particular intellectual ability, was used to argue that women were less intelligent than men. Interestingly, there was no accounting in these studies for the social or environmental factors that might affect these findings. For feminist psychology, this means that we need to consider how women's experiences are excluded by these approaches to the discipline. The key takeaway point here is that we must reflect on all these aspects of knowledge production, not just for the sake of finding fault but so that we can consider how these work to produce findings, and eventually knowledge, in a particular way. Looking through a lens of reflexivity allows us to work with the idea that our view is neither objective nor independent and to question those findings that are discriminatory or favour those conducting the research.

SECTION SUMMARY

- Reflexivity is a lens that looks inward at our own practice.
- It helps us see the relationship between research questions and research conclusions.
- There are different ways of thinking about reflexivity. Wilkinson (1988) suggested three types, one of which, disciplinary reflexivity, is particularly important for research methods in psychology.
- Disciplinary reflexivity focuses on how psychology operates and how it is supported by the institutions and structures of academia – what is included and what is excluded.

Feminist science and feminist methods

So what happens when we look at the world through a feminist lens – one that expects equity? The method is not in itself constitutive of knowledge. That is to say, while it may be true that you can use any method to make feminist or anti-feminist claims (as many feminist authors argue), it is also true that the tool can limit the outcome. Statistical analyses don't let you study meaning and discourse analysis is not generalisable to populations. The tool you use, like the question you ask and the lens you see it through, all play their part in how and what knowledge can be produced. At the beginning of this chapter, we referred to the role of epistemology in making sense of research and then proceeded to consider the different lenses that we can use to focus on and explore the elements of research. In the next chapter, we discuss the different epistemologies that psychology draws on to make sense of the world and their relationship to the feminist project.

CHAPTER SUMMARY

- Research questions tell us what a researcher believes needs explaining. We should think carefully about how we do this and consider who benefits and who loses when we conduct research/design a project.
- In this chapter, we have presented six lenses through which we might look at research questions: place; power; social justice; ethics; representation and intersectionality; and reflexivity.
- The methodological approach you take (e.g. the tool you use, the question you ask, the lens you see it through) affects how and what knowledge is produced.

3 Sense-making in psychology

Learning objectives

Study of this chapter should enable you to:

- Learn about the different epistemological approaches that psychologists take in their research.
- Practise doing 'sweaty work' (Ahmed, 2016).
- Learn about the elements of a research paradigm.
- Consider four of the main paradigms in psychology: positivist (and post-positivist); critical/transformative; interpretivist/phenomenological; and social constructionist.

We've said quite a bit already in this book about the importance of questions. This chapter explores the different questions we can ask by exploring the different approaches psychologists take based on different *epistemologies*. This is a challenging chapter which tries to present some very different ways of making sense of psychology. Some of the arguments may benefit from being read more than once. This is the kind of 'sweaty work' we talked about in Chapter 1 (Ahmed, 2016), so buckle up for the read, so to speak. We hope you will find it informative and useful. In each case, we discuss how questions shape knowledge in ways which can be used to disadvantage women or to support equity, or indeed distract us from issues of gender by arguing that gender isn't relevant to the question. You might have come across this often quoted reflection – one of Rose's favourites – on questions and answers: "If they can get you asking the wrong questions, they don't have to worry about the answers" (Pynchon, 1973, p. 251). So we also discuss the relationship between questions and answers. How do we know whether something is right? Psychology has a number of ways of thinking about this, which you will most likely be familiar with. Consider terms such as *reliability*, *validity*, *rigour*, *transparency*, *trustworthiness*, and *credibility*. These are the ways in which researchers try to make sure that findings and conclusions are meaningful – but are there other ways to judge the relevance of psychology?

How do we know what we know? Different approaches to research

We argued in Chapter 1 that knowledge and power are intimately intertwined. If this is the case, then it is really important to understand how knowledge is produced and what assumptions are being made in the process. One way of thinking about this is to see psychological knowledge as being shaped by a number of different (and often competing) research *paradigms*. A research paradigm is "the set of common beliefs and agreements shared between scientists about how problems should be understood and addressed" (Kuhn, 1962, p. 45). In other words, a research paradigm is a system of thinking. This system of thinking connects ideas about the nature of the world or reality (known as *ontology*), to how we think this world can be known by researchers (*epistemology*), to how we make sense of something (*theory*), to the specific processes and tools we can use to discover or produce this knowledge (*methodologies and methods*), and to what sources of data we draw on (see Figure 3.1).

How might this work in psychology? Say you were wanting to explore something like 'attitudes'. First, you would need to believe that they were in some way real (ontology), then you would need to consider how you might be able to know about them (epistemology). You would need a theory of what they might be, say, for instance, cognitive theory. You would need to consider how you might go about studying them (methodology). You can't measure them directly as they are not solid objects, so you might want to study their effects (method), by asking people what they like or don't like directly using a questionnaire (data).

Figure 3.1: Elements of a research paradigm.

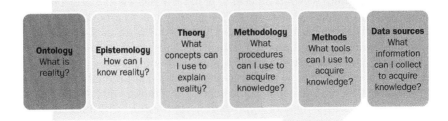

SECTION SUMMARY

- This is a challenging chapter and will involve some 'sweaty work'.
- We can think about psychological knowledge as being shaped by different research paradigms.
- Paradigms bring together ontology, epistemology, theory, methodology, methods, and data sources.

Research paradigms

Now that we've considered what makes up a research paradigm, we can look at four of the most common ones in psychology: positivist (and post-positivist), critical/transformative, interpretivist/phenomenological, and the social constructionist research paradigm. Although an over-simplification, the latter three are often presented as emerging out of a critique of positivism, while post-positivism is the way that positivist researchers have responded to this critique. Although positivism has been the dominant paradigm in psychology, the other three have become more widespread over the last few decades. These changes over time reflect social and political shifts in the wider culture as well as in academic thought. All four are evident in contemporary psychological research and all are adopted by feminist researchers.

Positivism (and post-positivism)

Positivism has dominated academic psychology for decades and, though other research paradigms are growing, it continues to be the dominant approach in psychology internationally. Part of the reason for this dominance is that psychology has long sought to position itself as a 'science' which produces robust 'hard' evidence which accurately describes reality. Positivism argues that there is an objective reality which is independent of the research (it exists 'out there' and available for psychologists to discover) and aims to produce knowledge which is trustworthy and reliable (as close to the truth as possible). This approach values unbiased research which depends on accurate observation and which controls for factors which might distort or misrepresent knowledge. This is the approach that is primarily taught on undergraduate psychology degrees and, most likely, the one you will be most familiar with. Researchers in this tradition adopt the logic of **hypothetico-deduction**, which involves posing a logically derived statement (**hypothesis**) about how two (or more) **variables** (items of psychological interest) might be related. In order to do this, variables must be measurable so that through the use of **statistical probability**, researchers can test the relationship between the variables in order to prove that no relationship exists (*falsification*). If they cannot do so, then they can claim that there is evidence to support the existence of a relationship. For instance, you could suppose that secondary school students learn more if they've had breakfast than if they haven't. The hypothesis would be that 'Secondary school students who have eaten breakfast that day will score more highly than those who had no breakfast on a test of amount learned at the end of each day'. We would then collect the data – which students ate breakfast and how they scored on the test – and use *inferential statistics* to test whether the two groups of students performed equally. If we find that there is a *statistical difference*, then we can claim that the results support our hypothesis.

As you can see from the example above, positivism relies on quantification, measurement, and experimental or quasi-experimental research designs. Positivism is often presented as conventional (including by some feminists), but as Carla Willig and Wendy Stainton Rogers (2017) point out, it has a radical history. Scientific reason was originally conceived as an alternative to religious ideology and a way to challenge prejudice and superstition. It is perhaps not surprising, then, that a key strand of feminist research, particularly in the early days of psychology, uses scientific reasoning and quantitative methods in a radical attempt to challenge assumptions, prejudices, and dogma about women. This includes contesting stereotypes, faulty thinking, and bias within the discipline of psychology itself. For instance, Helen Thompson Woolley (Thompson, 1903) argued that it was effectively 'unscientific' to assume that physical variation in *brain* size should be taken as evidence of intellectual variation because it didn't account for social influences. This is often referred to as the 'bad science' critique of sexism because it points to flaws in the application of the scientific method – more of which later.

In the 1960s, psychology's reliance on the experimental method and scientific rationality began to come under intense critical scrutiny. Psychologists started to identify different kinds of bias which threatened the integrity of the scientific bedrock of psychological methods and epistemology. In a series of experiments, Robert Rosenthal (1967) demonstrated how the expectations held by the researcher could exert a potent influence on the outcomes of the research (known as *experimenter expectancy effects*) through subtle communication cues between the researcher and human (and even animal) participants. This is commonly referred to as a *self-fulfilling prophecy*, whereby what experimenters expected to find, based on theoretical supposition and their own 'common-sense' assumptions, turned out to be what they 'discovered' in their research. At the same time, others demonstrated that the people who participate in research are curious about, and try to work out, the purpose of experiments and respond in ways which support the aims and hypotheses (known as *demand characteristics*; Orne, 1962), or feel motivated to give *socially desirable responses* (Crowne & Marlowe, 1960). Although this research threatened the integrity of experimental methods, the greatest challenge was yet to come.

Key questions about the usefulness of treating psychology as a natural science began to emerge in the 1970s, influenced by a range of emancipatory social movements which challenged 'established' knowledge, agitated for social change, and placed inequalities in power centre-stage – these include women's liberation, anti-psychiatry, lesbian and gay liberation, and civil rights movements. Collectively, these movements raised concerns about four different aspects of psychological research:

1 the generalisability of *laboratory findings* to everyday life;
2 the *unequal relationships* between investigators and research participants;
3 the potential for the broader *social and political context* to produce bias;
4 the implication of psychological knowledge in *systems of power*.

Laboratory findings

Conducting experiments in a laboratory setting is an excellent way of trying to isolate one or two specific aspects of behaviour (like eye contact) in order to study the effect that this has on human psychology (say feelings of intimacy or threat) in order to develop universal laws (for example, is prolonged eye contact always interpreted as aggressive?). However, does placing people in strange, artificial environments to complete unusual tasks, reveal anything about how people act in their ordinary lives? This is the main point that produces dissatisfaction with the scientific approach as it rests on a fundamental disagreement about whether people can or should be studied by psychologists in the same way as chemists study molecules or biologists study plant cells. As well as failing to recognise the complexity of human behaviour, this approach, it has been argued, removes the very context that makes behaviour meaningful to us and to others. Humans are reflexive, meaning-making beings who, when placed in unusual or strange environments, try to make sense of what is happening, and use clues from the environment, previous experience, and values to try to work out how to behave or what is expected of us. Knowing how we behave on one occasion in one very specific context, like an experiment, may say very little about how we respond on the next occasion when so many other factors are involved.

Unequal relationships

Within the positivist paradigm, the researcher–participant relationship is explicitly hierarchical where researchers have more power, importance, and control – it is, after all, their experiment. The researcher decides what questions to ask and how to conduct the research. This includes designing and controlling the environment, deciding who participates, and how participants can or should respond, as well as determining what counts as data, how to record it, and how to interpret it. Moreover, in order to reduce bias, positivist investigators create research relationships that are distant, non-intrusive, and 'objective' – ideally, researchers and participants might never meet in person! This means participants are completely excluded from all of these processes so nothing unexpected can happen – at least from the researcher's perspective.

Social and political context

There has been a growing discomfort that the scientific method in psychology could generate biased knowledge about often marginalised and already disempowered groups of people, who are misrepresented by research which excludes their own values, priorities, and perspectives. For instance, a researcher might conceptualise something as a 'problem' that participants themselves might understand differently. As we mentioned in the previous chapter, a popular example of this is environmental activist Greta Thunberg who considers her autism as a 'superpower' rather than a disability.

Systems of power

The 1960s and 1970s saw the rise of anti-psychiatry movements. These were user-led and aimed to destigmatise mental health difficulties and enhance civil rights. These movements looked to the psychological disciplines and professions such as psychology, psychiatry, psychoanalysis, and psychotherapy through the critical lens of power and in particular, the abuse of power. The 'psy' complex, as Nikolas Rose (1985) referred to it, was seen as a form of social control through which large groups of people were categorised as mentally unwell. As an example, the DSM (Diagnostic and Statistical Manual of the American Psychiatric Association, widely used by psychiatrists and other mental health professionals to diagnose patients) *pathologised* lesbians, gay men, and other sexual minorities by including 'homosexuality' as a sexual 'perversion'. This led to the abuse of these minority groups through the utilisation of brutal 'treatments' such as conversion therapy (Haldeman, 1994). Further psychological 'treatments' were understood by activists as brutalising or abusive (e.g. isolation within asylums, sedation with powerful drugs, surgical procedures such as lobotomies, aversion therapies), not to mention the treatment of women, who could be and were placed in asylums for failing to meet social conventions (e.g. becoming pregnant outside of wedlock, infidelity, etc.). As a result, users began to describe their experiences of the mental health system in terms of survival.

Attentive to these issues of context, inequality, and power, feminist researchers began to re-imagine the relationship between the researcher and the researched. This included considering whether 'better' knowledge – richer, useful, more embedded in everyday life – could be produced. They favoured collaborative partnerships with research participants by developing close and respectful research relationships, using qualitative methods which 'gave voice' to participants, enabling them to describe their experience in their own words. They adopted and championed ethical practices which sought to minimise power differences and maximise the benefit of research for those who kindly agreed to participate and share their lives.

Rather than reject positivism and scientific rationality, however, post-positivists were prompted to identify new ways of conducting research which avoided these methodological pitfalls. Post-positivists retain the idea of an external reality that exists separately from human attempts to understand it, and that scientists should strive to accurately map this reality. However, importantly, post-positivists acknowledge that all psychological knowledge is imperfect, shaped by bias, subject to error, and subject to faulty logic or mistaken assumptions, making it impossible to completely or accurately reflect reality. Nonetheless, they endeavour to find the *best* way to address the inherent flaws in the process through methodological checks and balances such as:

- adopting multiple methods to examine the same hypothesis (e.g. using diaries, self-report questionnaires, and experiments to examine a particular relationship, such as whether children who play computer games are more aggressive), known as *triangulation*;
- collecting data from multiple sources (teacher and parent reports), also a form of *triangulation*;
- having a different research team repeat exactly the processes and procedures used previously, known as *replication*;
- collating evidence gathered by different research teams in different contexts, for instance *meta-analysis*;
- transparency and *open science* to allow others to check the work underpinning a published research study;
- *peer review* and rigorous critique of one another's work.

By using such techniques, post-positivists believe that the limited and partial knowledge acquired from individual studies will be overcome by the accumulation of confirmed findings. Although post-positivists have responded to some of the criticisms, the more fundamental critique about how researchers' values and social contexts inevitably influence what questions researchers ask and what kinds of knowledge they produce, has not received enough attention in this research paradigm.

SECTION SUMMARY

- Positivism has dominated academic psychology for decades and it continues to be the dominant approach to psychology internationally.
- Positivism positions itself as a 'science' and argues that there is an objective reality which is independent of the researcher.
- It takes a hypothetico-deductive approach to the production of knowledge and makes use of inferential statistics to make claims about statistical differences and associations.
- Many feminist psychologists have been critical of this approach, arguing that it strips out the context and, with it, meaning.
- We have looked at these critiques in terms of the generalisability of laboratory findings to our everyday lives, the lack of equality between the researcher and the researched, the production of bias due to the social and political context, and the implication of psychological knowledge in wider systems of power.

Critical/transformative

Critical or transformative research foregrounds the activist agenda of feminist research by explicitly seeking social change through working collaboratively with groups and communities. Reason describes the two overriding objectives of this type of inquiry as being the production of "knowledge and action directly useful to a community" and empowerment through "consciousness-raising" (1994, p. 48), although change at a broader social or cultural level is often an additional implicit goal. These approaches share three key principles:

1 Work is *inquiry based* and topics of investigation are grounded in people's lived experiences and concerns.
2 It is *participatory* as researchers and communities collaborate in the research process.
3 It is *transformative* since the purpose is to actively create change.

This approach to research tries to address the power imbalance between researcher and researched by emphasising a collaborative approach in which each person involved in the research has their expertise and experience valued: the psychologist's expertise in research methods and scholarship and the community members' expertise in relation to their own lived experience. Ideally, researchers and communities work together to identify the research goals, develop the methods that will be used, and participate in collecting and analysing the data.

Working in partnership to identify the goals of the research means that inquiry is grounded in the lived experiences and concerns of community members. Together, they decide how best to communicate the research and take action based on the key findings in a way that will promote positive change in the lives of those involved. This more collaborative approach is reflected in the description of all those involved in the research – researchers and participants – as co-researchers. In this sense, doing research which is explicitly for the benefit of the community-based co-researchers represents a shift from doing research *on* people, to doing research *with* people. It also reflects a move which has been gathering momentum since the 1960s to ensure that academic research is of practical benefit to societies, communities, and organisations, and which has been embraced in particular by feminist researchers (e.g. Fine & Torre, 2019; Lykes, 2017; Moane, 2014).

SECTION SUMMARY

- Critical or transformative research is interested in activism and explicitly seeks social change.
- This approach argues that research should be directly useful and should empower the communities in which the research is conducted.
- It is a participatory and transformative approach that is based on inquiry grounded in people's everyday concerns

Interpretivism/phenomenology

Interpretivism and phenomenology are concerned with understanding the *lived experience* of individuals – what is it like to be a survivor of sexual violence, a single parent, living in poverty, to be diagnosed with chronic fatigue, to be dependent on informal care, or to be excluded from school. Interpretative phenomenological analysis (IPA), for instance, is an ***ideographic*** mode of inquiry as opposed to the ***nomothetic*** approach which dominates in psychology (Smith et al., 1995). In a nomothetic study, analysis is at the level of groups and populations and the only claims that can be made about individuals are based on probabilities. This is the case for the experimental approaches favoured by positivism. For example, that there is a 70% chance that person X will respond in this way because 70% of the participant sample meeting these characteristics in the study responded in that way. (You might want to dwell on that for a moment. Is that assumption justified?). In an ideographic study, however, because it has been derived from the examination of an individual case, it is also possible to make specific statements about those individuals. For IPA, the analysis always begins with the detailed reading of the single case. The focus is on people's perceptions of the world, and how they make sense of their everyday lived experience.

Phenomenologists argue that there is a separation between the world as it is (reality) and the world as it appears to people (individual perception), although the former is inaccessible to us. Consequently, in practical terms it does not make sense to see the world as separate from how people perceive and make sense of it – since our perceptions (that of researchers and research participants alike) are viewed through the lens of our own experiences, and that this also relies on the context in which this perception is taking place. For instance, the experience of being a single parent may feel different in conversation with a researcher, a friend or relative, your child's schoolteacher, or a welfare officer. Phenomenologists are therefore more interested in finding out about what orients an individual's personal perception or account of a phenomenon or event and less interested in attempting to produce an objective statement of the event itself.

Moreover, phenomenologists argue that both researchers and research participants have an active role in sense-making. Making sense of the participant's experience depends on the researcher's own experience as they try to comprehend the participant's subjective world through a process of interpretation. As such, this is a two-stage interpretation process: the participant is trying to make sense of their world while the researcher is trying to make sense of how the participant is trying to make sense of their world. This approach fits well with feminist concerns about respecting and acknowledging the value of people's own experiences of the world.

SECTION SUMMARY

- Interpretivism and phenomenology aim to understand people's lived experiences of the world.
- Interpretivism and phenomenology take an idiographic approach that is derived from the examination of a single case.
- Phenomenologists argue that reality is not accessible to us, so we should study the world as it appears to people.
- This approach values the sense-making of both the researchers and the research participants.

Social constructionism

Social constructionism is an umbrella term that is used to describe a range of critical, radical, and alternative approaches to studying and theorising about psychology and social life. In her foundational text, *Social Constructionism*, Vivien Burr (2003) describes this approach as being characterised by four key features:

1 a critical stance towards taken-for-granted knowledge;
2 locating ideas in cultural and historical context;
3 knowledge is produced and sustained through social processes;
4 knowledge, power, and social action are interconnected.

A critical stance towards taken-for-granted knowledge

Social constructionism questions the idea that the nature of the world can be revealed through objective and unbiased observation, and invites us to be suspicious and sceptical of our assumptions about the world. An example of this, which sits at the centre of much feminist theorising, is the assumption that there are two categories of person – male and female. Our observations of the world might lead us to confirm this assumption – after all schools, toilet facilities, changing rooms, clothing, toys, occupations, and friendship groups are very often organised or segregated into these two categories. More than this, these categories of being are often thought to be rooted in essential biological differences between 'the two sexes' and reflective of differences in genes, hormones, and reproductive organs. This is referred to as sexual dimorphism (and we will come back to this a few times in this book). However, there are a multitude of chromosomal patterns beyond XX female and XY male, considerable variability in levels of hormones such as testosterone and oestrogen, as well as diversity in the configuration of reproductive organs. Social constructionism encourages us to question these distinctions. Are they as natural as they might appear? Why do these categories exist? How have they come into being? Who benefits and who loses from this distinction? How might the world be organised differently? Social constructionists have drawn attention to the blurry biological lines around the categories of male and female arguing that this distinction is not a clear as some would have it (Jordan-Young, 2010). Moreover, social constructionism draws attention to the diversity of gender identities and expressions. These include but are not limited to drag kings and queens, the **androgynous**, those who identify as transgender, non-binary or gender queer, transvestites, or gender noncon-forming. Finally, social constructionism would note all of the social processes involved in producing and policing gender categories – from gender assignment at birth and gender confirmation surgery, to the ways in which we learn what it means to think, act, talk, and move like a 'woman' or a 'man'. This isn't just the popular distinction between 'sex' as apparent differences rooted in biology and 'gender' as social and cultural ideas about masculinity and femininity. Social constructionism questions the relevance of gender as a meaningful mechanism for organising ourselves and our world. Actually, it questions many of the **dichotomies** we've become used to in everyday life, and often don't think about, that we accept as taken-for-granted – adults/children, sane/insane, criminal/law-abiding, white/Black, disabled/able-bodied.

Locating ideas in cultural and historical context

Social constructionism has often sought to examine how **taken-for-granted** knowledge shifts across different cultures and time periods as a way of demon-strating how unusual, fleeting, narrow, and changeable our current assumptions about the world are. Indeed, it aims to show how knowledge is the product of a specific time and sociocultural place which is dependent on the particular social, economic, and political arrangements of the time. This is an important mecha-nism for challenging our views, which we often believe to be universal and time-less (i.e. the world is like this, has always been like this, and will always be like this). The distinction of different racial categories, for example between Black and white 'races', is a product of colonialism which involved the occupation and economic exploitation of one country by another. This distinction served as a mechanism for justifying slavery and the systematic and widespread oppression and abuse of those deemed 'Black' for financial (and social) gain. Although slav-ery was outlawed in the UK and many British colonies in 1833, the effects of colonialism, the social organisation of people into 'races', and the 'othering' of Black people continues and is powerfully reflected in social inequalities in hous-ing, employment, mental and physical wellbeing, schooling, political participa-tion, victimisation, and engagement with the criminal justice system.

Knowledge is produced and sustained through social processes

For social constructionism as a research paradigm, knowledge is not an objec-tive observation of the world, nor is it an imperfect reflection of an underlying reality. It is, instead, constructed through the continual production and reproduction of everyday practices and interactions. So, it's not just that the distinction between (the socially created categories of) men and women was decided one day and everyone agreed. This distinction is continually being produced and reproduced, or constructed, as meaningful through our everyday practices. The first thing that people often ask about a baby is 'What is it?', alluding to the sex of the child. Expectant parents sometimes throw gender reveal parties where blue or pink balloons or confetti are used to announce whether the baby is expected to be a boy or a girl. Young girls who are being loud or unruly are casually referred to as 'unladylike' or boys are told that 'big boys don't cry'. The use of gendered pronouns and language serves as a constant reminder of these two categories. Which one we belong to is so important that it is embedded in all of our basic communication. The use of gender segregated wards in hospitals, government surveys which ask about gender as the first question and limit responses to male or female, separation of sports teams into exclusively male or female competitions, and many more provide a host of examples about how this distinction is created, maintained, and policed. It is worth noting though that these can also be challenged. For instance, old school buildings will often have boys' and girls' entrance signs, but these are no longer used.

Box 3.1: Gender and the loo

If you have every used a public toilet in a busy environment you may well have had the experience of finding a long queue for the women's loo with no one waiting for access to the men's. Now that can be really frustrating, can't it? You would think after all these years designers of such spaces would have cottoned on to the differential need. Given that obvious inequities have not been addressed, you may not be surprised to hear that the less obvious are often completely bypassed. You're probably aware of recent discussions around the gendering of public toilets. In fact, many secondary schools, colleges, and universities in the UK now have gender-neutral toilets and there have been concerns about the safety of such spaces. Slater and Jones (2018) conducted an arts-based research project around what makes a safe and accessible toilet. It began as a project around the experiences of trans people and those with a disability of using public toilets. However, it soon became clear that the remit would need to be expanded to include many other groups such as parents, mobile workers, and those with religious beliefs that affect toilet use to name but a few. The gendering of shared resources, such as public toilets, serves not only to discriminate by gender but also, because of many of the assumptions embedded in these distinctions, ends up making life that bit more difficult for lots of different groups that don't fit with those assumptions.

Knowledge, power, and social action are interconnected

From a social constructionist perspective, knowledge is always contested. It is always local and contingent. That is to say, it depends where you are and what environment you are in, so there are often multiple versions of knowledge which vie for popularity and authority. We have seen, for example, increasing challenge to the dominance of knowledge about gender and race. But, knowledge brings with it distinct forms of social action. When homosexuality was constructed as a criminal offence in the UK, lesbians and gay men were forced to hide their sexuality or risk prosecution. When homosexuality was constructed as a psychological disorder, lesbians and gay men were subjected to *'aversion therapy'* (the repeated pairing of an unwanted behaviour such as sexual arousal to images of naked people of the same sex with discomfort such as electric shocks or drug-induced nausea).

SECTION SUMMARY

- Social constructionism includes a range of critical, radical, and alternative approaches that take a critical stance towards taken-for-granted knowledge which is produced and sustained through social processes.
- This approach highlights the value of locating ideas in cultural and historical context.
- Knowledge, power, and social action work together to produce what we experience as reality.

Conclusion

In this book, we adopt a *pluralistic* approach. We understand psychology as pluralistic in the sense that there are different ways of making sense of psychology or psychologies. We adopt the same approach to feminism, which means that we consider feminism not to be one unified set of beliefs, theories, or way of being in the world. Instead, we embrace the eclectic diversity of feminisms which share a concern with gendered (and intersectional) inequalities and a desire to redress these. If we conceive of psychologies and feminisms in the plural, then it comes as no surprise that feminist research in psychology engages with all of the different research paradigms outlined above. It is our intention, with this book, to showcase the rich variety of feminist approaches to research and demonstrate how feminist researchers use all of the methods and research tools at their disposal to generate excellent robust knowledge to challenge inequality and social injustice.

CHAPTER SUMMARY

- This chapter has looked at some of the most common approaches to research in psychology and explored some of the ways in which each makes sense of the world.
- We looked at the different elements of a research paradigm to think about how this impacts on the questions a researcher might ask.
- Positivism, and more recently post-positivism, is the dominant paradigm in psychology but has been subjected to sustained critique by feminists.
- We have looked at three other research paradigms that are growing in popularity in psychology that vary from positivism in terms of the primary aim of their research.
- These different paradigms take a more critical approach to the production of knowledge.
- This book takes a pluralist approach to both psychologies and feminisms.

4 Cognitive psychology: 'false' memories, sexual abuse, and memory experiments

Learning objectives

Study of this chapter should enable you to:

- Develop a critical understanding about classic memory experiments in cognitive psychology, including some of the methodological pitfalls, limitations, and problems with experiments.
- Recognise how experimental research within cognitive psychology has influenced, and been shaped by, the controversy surrounding false/recovered memories of sexual abuse.
- Develop an awareness of ethical issues in research.
- Understand alternative ways of conceptualising and researching memory using a feminist poststructuralist and discursive framework.

Imagine that you have just witnessed a car accident. When asked to remember and give an account of what happened, you are asked: 'How fast were the cars going when they smashed into one another'? You could replace the word *smashed* with *collided*, *bumped*, *contacted*, or *hit*. The question (***hypothesis***) is: Would a change in the question wording cause people to give different estimates of how fast the cars were moving? When Elizabeth Loftus and John Palmer conducted this notorious ***experiment***, they found that people estimated the cars to be travelling faster when the word *smashed* was used in the question. One week later, they re-tested people's memory of the event (which was a film of a car accident – not a real accident) by asking, 'Did you see any broken glass?' Importantly, there was NO broken glass depicted in the film. Yet, the people who were originally questioned using the word smashed were more likely to answer 'Yes'. The authors concluded that the "questions asked subsequent to an event can cause a reconstruction in one's memory of that event" (Loftus & Palmer, 1974, p. 585). At first glance, this study may seem fairly bland. However, this experiment (and others that followed) radically changed how psychologists understood memory and the act of remembering by:

- challenging the dominant idea in *cognitive psychology* that memory operates like a computer in which information (memories) is processed, labelled, and stored in a mental filing system which we later search to retrieve memories of specific events. Loftus and Palmer's research demonstrated that remembering is a more dynamic and malleable process in which people construct memories in response to the demands of the present situation;
- extending research beyond examining memory errors by considering whether memories could be generated for events which did not occur;
- drawing attention to the importance of language in shaping perceptions of reality (we return to this at the end of the chapter).

This research also has important implications for the criminal justice system, which often relies on the memory of events described by witnesses, victims, and the accused. It is this application of cognitive memory experiments to legal contexts which sits at the heart of controversial debates about *recovered/ false memories* of childhood sexual abuse.

So, what *is* an experiment?

We start this chapter by looking at this notorious *experiment* in cognitive psychology, which examined how we remember complex events such as a car accident. Cognitive psychology is one of the core areas of psychology. It is the study of internal mental processes (things that go on inside your brain), including how we make sense of what we see (perception), how we learn and use language, how we solve problems, how we think, how we learn, and how we remember. As noted in Chapter 2, experiments are the foundation of the scientific method that is central to the *positivist paradigm* in psychology. So, what is an experiment?

According to the American Psychological Association, an experiment is 'a series of observations conducted under controlled conditions' in order to study a relationship between two or more *variables* with the purpose of drawing conclusions about whether a change in one variable causes a change in the other (APA Dictionary Online, n.d.). A variable is a psychological thing-of-interest which is liable to change or vary; psychologists distinguish between *independent variables* and *dependent variables*. The independent variable is the thing-of-interest which the experimenter manipulates or alters to see whether it has a direct effect on the thing that is being measured (the dependent variable). In Loftus and Palmer's experiment, the independent variable is the different words used in the question (smashed, collided, bumped). The estimated speed of the vehicles is the dependent variable. Experiments sit firmly within the positivist approach to producing knowledge which we discussed earlier in the book (Chapter 3). This includes using the techniques of hypothesising, *objectivity*, controlled observation, and *deduction* to develop laws about the nature of mental processes which apply to everyone. Following the principles of the scientific model, experimental psychology promotes **reductionism** (trying to identify the most elementary causes of mental events) and **predictability** (knowledge based on laws which enable psychologists to predict how someone will think or behave). Experiments are very useful to psychologists because by controlling the research situation carefully, by manipulating only one variable at a time, and by carefully observing changes in the dependent variable, researchers can (or at least try to) draw conclusions about **causal inference**. In other words, changing the wording of a question *causes* a change in how the speed of a car involved in an accident is remembered. This is very powerful! Perhaps not surprisingly, then, some feminists have been keen to harness the power of experiments and the scientific method (see Box 4.1), whilst others have developed alternative ways of knowing and innovative methodologies.

Box 4.1: Examples of feminist experiments

That swimsuit becomes you: **Objectification** theory claims that in Western cultures girls and women measure their self-worth against sexually objectifying and unrealistic standards of beauty. In two related experiments designed to test this theory, participants tried on either a swimsuit or a sweater alone in a dressing room in front of a full-length mirror. The idea was that the more body-revealing swimsuit would evoke in participants a process of observing and evaluating their body as an object (known as self-objectification) compared with the less revealing sweater. Researchers Barbera Fredrickson, Tomi-Ann Roberts, Stephanie Noll, Diane Quinn, and Jean Twenge (1998) found that not only did women who tried on the swimsuit report more body shame (supporting objectification theory), these women also later did worse in maths tests and were more likely to restrict what they ate. This suggests that body objectification not only influences how women think and feel about themselves, it also limits their achievements and has harmful consequences for how they behave.

Benevolent sexism: British psychologist Aife Hopkins-Doyle and her colleagues have conducted a series of experiments looking at **benevolent sexism** (Hopkins-Doyle et al., 2019). In contrast to hostile sexism, in which overtly nasty ways of characterising women (e.g. as manipulative, devious, and inferior to men) are associated with support for aggressive and discriminatory behaviours, benevolent sexism characterises women in superficially positive ways (e.g. as compassionate, gentle but in need of protection), which ultimately undermine gender equality. Given that perceptions of a person's warmth influence the judgements that are made about them, these researchers investigated whether the warm tone associated with benevolent sexism masks its misogynistic ideology. Thus, they experimentally manipulated warmth in order to test whether it plays a causal role in people's misunderstandings of benevolent sexism by asking participants (211 British adults) to read vignettes about a male and female protagonist described as having either a warm (i.e. '(s)he likes women, has warm feelings, and positive attitudes toward them') or cold (i.e. '(s)he dislikes women, has cold feelings, and negative attitudes toward them') attitude toward women. They found that protagonists' warmth played a causal role in participants' misunderstanding of benevolent sexism. So, although the literature suggests that men who report higher levels of benevolent sexism are more likely to disapprove of public breastfeeding, blame rape victims, justify domestic violence, enjoy sexist humour, and believe men should initiate dating, the superficial warmth associated with benevolent sexism meant that participants perceived benevolently sexist men to be less likely to endorse these views than men who demonstrate hostile sexism.

Bogus pipeline experiment: In **bogus pipeline** experiments, participants are attached to a non-functioning lie detector and are led to believe that the machine can identify when they are giving dishonest answers to questions posed by the researcher. Their answers are usually compared to those of a **control group** who are not attached to the machine. This is one of the ingenious ways that psychologists conducting experiments try to avoid the difficulties associated with reactivity – like people lying or giving answers that they think will show them in a better light (**social desirability**)! The idea is that people will give more honest answers to avoid the embarrassment of being caught out in a lie by the machine. Using this technique, Michele Alexander and Terri Fisher (2003) looked at sex differences in sexual behaviour typically reported in surveys (e.g. that men report more sex outside of committed relationships, more frequent and explicit sexual fantasies, more sexual partners, and are more likely to masturbate than women). They wondered whether these differences reflect participants' accommodation to gender norms about sex rather than being accurate reports of their sexual attitudes and behaviours. So, to test this they asked male and female college students to complete a sexual attitudes and behaviour questionnaire under three **experimental conditions** in which they were led to believe that:

- their answers would be seen by a peer;
- their answers were completely anonymous;
- their answers could be identified as true or false by the **polygraph** machine.

Sure enough, reported differences in sexual behaviour between men and women were greatest when participants believed that their answers would be seen by a peer, and smallest in the bogus pipeline condition.

Feminists have explored alternative forms of knowledge production, which means that they have often been at the forefront of methodological innovation. Despite methodological diversity, experimentation remains the foundational method in psychology – as reflected in textbooks and curricula.

SECTION SUMMARY

- Experiments are a core method in psychology and have frequently been used in cognitive psychology to study memory. Psychologists have begun to explore some of the difficulties inherent in experiments, and are using inventive ways to overcome these problems.

- Loftus and Palmer showed that how questions are asked influences the way that people answer them. They argued that this tells us something about how memory operates, but also tells us something important about research – how we ask questions (including research questions) influences the answers we get.

- Feminist researchers also use experiments to expose gender bias and inequality.

'False' memories and child sexual abuse

To understand how Loftus and Palmer's experiment about how people remember car accidents became swept up in debates about false/recovered memories, we need to understand the socio-political climate of the early 1990s. Specifically, we need to understand the *invention* of 'false memory syndrome'. In her analysis of British newspaper coverage, feminist media scholar Jenny Kitzinger (2003) argued that the concept of 'false memory syndrome' originated in the USA in the 1990s when Jennifer Freyd (herself a cognitive psychology professor) spoke about beginning to recall (recover) experiences of being abused by her father. Claiming that these memories were untrue, her parents set up the False Memory Syndrome Foundation, which attracted international attention (the British False Memory Society, established in 1993 by an accused father, is the closest UK equivalent). Note that the language being used here – describing memories as being either 'false' or 'recovered' – does important work. Proponents of *recovered* memory (mostly therapists and survivors of sexual abuse) argue that memories of traumatic experiences – such as childhood sexual abuse – can be unconsciously blocked so that the individual does not remember the abuse. Such memories may be recovered during adulthood, sometimes during therapy, as the individual begins to process the trauma associated with the abuse. Proponents of *false* memory (memory researchers and those accused) argue that is it impossible to repress memories of repeated child abuse and then later to recall them accurately in adulthood. They argue that these memories are fabricated during therapeutic encounters between susceptible and vulnerable clients, and the clumsy lines of questioning adopted by inept therapists.

The debate about false/recovered memory is, then, partly a debate about how memory works and how accurate memory is. This is why experiments like those conducted by Loftus and Palmer are so important. But the debate is about much more than the science of experimental cognitive psychology. It is also:

- wrapped up in debates about the practice and regulation of therapy;
- has implications for the media framing of child sexual abuse (see Box 4.2);
- is entrenched in the legal system;
- is deeply entwined in gender politics;
- is used to discredit those who report abuse.

It is precisely because of this melting pot of life-changing consequences, vested interests, and political implications that some feminists argue that objective scientific experiments are necessary to cut to the 'truth' about how memory works. Other feminists argue that *all* science is political and can never be truly objective. For the purposes of this chapter, though, we return to cognitive psychology, memory science, and the use of experiments.

Box 4.2: Recovered/false memories, the media, and the court room

Feminist researcher Jenny Kitzinger (2003) argued that the mass media played a vital role in creating 'false memory syndrome' as a social issue at the forefront of public awareness. Analysing media coverage, interviews with journalists and editors, and interviews with key professional organisations (e.g. psychological societies) and pressure groups (the British False Memory Society), Kitzinger noted four key aspects related to the extent of media reporting and how the 'false memory' story evolved in Britain:

- the *rapid speed* of the media response which occurred alongside substantive pressure group activity contrasted sharply with attempts to interest the media in reporting male violence;
- the *consensus* view that false memory syndrome was a real and common problem which dominated coverage despite a lack of official endorsement;
- the priority given to *lay opinion* (especially accused parents) rather than professional experts in contrast to typical journalistic practice;
- the *privileging of those denying abuse*, such as accused parents, who were seven times more likely to be quoted in newspapers than the person recalling the abuse.

Explaining why the media ran with the 'false memory' framing of child abuse so quicky and extensively, Kitzinger argued that alongside a need for a 'new angle' on child abuse reporting amongst news outlets, the story was used to illustrate underlying conservative messages about the threat of political correctness, inappropriate state intervention into family life, and the destructive power of feminist ideology. It also played into a familiar sexist rhetoric about science vs. emotion by dismissing girls/women as unstable, suggestible, and over-emotional, whilst depicting proponents of false memory syndrome as giving objective and unbiased scientific facts to support their views (we come back to the power of scientific rhetoric below).

The false/recovered memory debate inevitably entered legal circles. From the mid-1980s, the US courts saw a dramatic increase in criminal and personal injury cases alleging child sexual abuse, with similar trends in the UK. This coincided with a period of intense feminist advocacy on behalf of victims of sexual violence, including childhood sexual abuse, and some including British feminist Erica Burman (2010) interpreted the false memory counter accusations as (in part) a backlash against these efforts. As Milchman (2012) observes, the lawsuits were a primary cause of the 'recovered memory wars', and meant that the legal system had to grapple with this controversy in the absence of clear and convincing scientific evidence.

SECTION SUMMARY

- Ideas about how memory works are not just important to psychologists, they have real world impact. Some psychologists believe that experiments can produce objective knowledge which can challenge bias by finding out the truth about how memory works.
- Others think that psychology and politics cannot be separated, and that psychological research can always be used for political ends.

Memory experiments and psychological research

In contemporary cognitive psychology research investigating the accuracy of memories, two different types of experiment have come to dominate – those which examine errors in remembering details (e.g. in list-learning paradigms) and those which focus on confabulations of whole events (e.g. research in which memories for entire events are examined). We briefly examine these types of experiment and draw attention to the methodological difficulties these illustrate (such as *generalisability*, *ecological validity*, and *ethics*) before considering how these are implicated in the false/recovered memory debate.

The *list-learning approach* has a long history and is used to study errors in remembering details. Typically, participants are asked to study a list of related words – for example, *sandal, foot, toe, slipper*, all of which are related to feet and footwear. In an early study using this method, Deese (1959) demonstrated that some memory errors happen in predictable ways – people often 'recall' words which were *not* included in the original list, but which are related to the topic (e.g. *shoe*). Deese (1959) referred to this as an 'intrusion' error. According to Anne DePrince and her colleagues (DePrince et al., 2004), Deese's research received little attention at the time of its publication. This changed with the publication of Roediger and McDermott's (1995) study using a similar list-learning experiment in which they also found that people sometimes remembered a related-but-not-presented word. However, rather than describing this as a memory 'intrusion', Roediger and McDermott explicitly referred to this as "dramatic evidence of false memories" (1995, p. 812) – we return to this point about language later.

The *misinformation approach* refers to experiments which examine to what extent, and under what conditions, people might remember events which are suggested to them, but which did not actually happen. Using this method, people are asked to elaborate on specific events, several of which *did* actually happen to them, but one that *did not*. In an early study by Elizabeth Loftus and Jacqueline Pickrell (1995), close relatives of 24 participants (college students) were asked to supply information about three real-life events that had happened to the participants as children. An additional event (e.g. being lost at a shopping mall), which had not actually occurred, was added by the research team to those provided by the relative. Each event was described in a short paragraph with participants being asked to write additional information about each of these events. They were also later interviewed about these events on two separate occasions. The 'lost at the shopping mall' event was created by the research team based on information provided by relatives about the types of stores visited when the participants were aged around 5, and which would have attracted their attention. In addition, the event description always included information that the participant was (a) lost for an extended time, (b) was crying, (c) was around age 5, (d) was helped by an elderly woman, and (e) was reunited with their family. Participants were told that if they did not remember an event, they should write 'I do not remember this'. Seven out of 24 people (29%) 'remembered' the misinformation about being lost in the shopping mall by writing a description of being lost. The authors concluded that "people can be led to believe that entire events have happened to them after suggestions to that effect" (Loftus & Pickrell, 1995, p. 723). Using this procedure, researchers have presented misinformation about other events, including being bitten by a dog or abducted by aliens (for an overview, see Otgaar et al., 2021). In sum, these studies have shown that it is *possible* for suggestions and misinformation to lead to the creation of autobiographical memories of events that did not actually happen. Studies such as these have been taken as strong evidence in support of false memory syndrome – something which is exacerbated by the use of terms like 'suggestibility' and the description of this research as 'false memory implantation' studies. However, although this research demonstrates that it is possible to create memories for events that did not happen, this does not mean that this is likely or easy. One review which analysed the findings across many misinformation studies found full-blown false memories in only 15% of participants (Brewin & Andrews, 2017).

Ethics in memory research

A range of scientific methodological flaws in the 'lost at the mall study' have been identified, including the lack of a **control group** and poor detail about the methods which limit **replicability**. This led us on to some of the broader issues surrounding experimental methods and their use in the false/recovered memory debate.

What are the ethical responsibilities of psychologists when studying such sensitive and complex issues as memory in the context of child sexual abuse?

The British Psychological Society's Code of Human Research Ethics (2021a) is underpinned by four key principles:

- **Respect:** for the autonomy, privacy, and dignity of individuals, groups, and communities.
- **Scientific integrity:** research should be designed, reviewed, and conducted in a way that ensures its quality, integrity, and contribution to the development of knowledge and understanding.
- **Social responsibility:** psychology has a shared collective duty for the welfare of human and non-human beings, both within the societies in which psychology researchers live and work and beyond them.
- **Maximising benefit, minimising harm:** psychologists strive for the avoidance of harm and the prevention of misuse or abuse of their contribution to society.

Memory experiments of the kind conducted by Loftus and Pickrell often brush up against two ethical issues: deception and participant wellbeing. Let's take the issue of deception first. The BPS Code states that: "Deception or covert collection of data should only take place where it is essential to achieve the research results required, where there are no alternatives, where the research objective has strong scientific merit and where there is an appropriate risk management and harm alleviation strategy" (1995, p. 23). The Code notes many psychological processes are altered by individuals if they are aware that they are being studied. This means that telling people the exact purpose of a study would make researching the psychological processes accurately impossible! This speaks to some of the earliest debates about whether it is possible for psychology to be a science, and to use the scientific method. As feminist psychologists Jill Morawski and Gail Agronick put it, "psychology is inherently a reflexive science" (1991, p. 569) not only because scientists produce knowledge about a class of objects (humans) of which they are a part, but also because the people involved in research as participants reflexively try to make sense of what is going on in experimental situations. People taking part in research may try to guess what the experiment is designed to test, or what researchers expect to find, and try to please the researchers (known as ***demand characteristics***). Likewise, people may behave differently because they know that they are being observed or studied (known as the ***Hawthorne effect***). These very human responses to being placed in odd or unusual situations are seen as a problem for researchers using the scientific approach, since they introduce bias and inaccuracies.

Researchers adopt a range of creative strategies to address these issues. Deception is one of these strategies. So, in Loftus and Pickrell's lost-at-the-mall study, participants were told that the study was about "the kinds of things you remember from your childhood" (1995, p. 721) rather than about trying to create a false memory. In the debriefing at the end of the study, the researchers "apologized for the deception and explained why it was necessary" (p. 722). They also asked whether participants had guessed the purpose of the study or which of the four memories was the false one (another way of checking for bias/inaccuracies). Nineteen participants (out of 24) correctly identified the 'lost at the mall' memory as the false one. One could argue, then, that the deception was relatively mild but also pretty ineffective!

The second ethical issue concerns participant wellbeing. At first glance, you may think that studying memories of childhood sexual abuse is not easy or even impossible. How do you research traumatic events whilst making sure that this is not harmful to participants? But of course, psychologists study a whole range of complex, sensitive, and troubling issues (including death and dying), and they study them directly, by asking people about their experiences. The issue for cognitive memory researchers is the attempt to marry the scientific method with sensitive issues. It is not ethical to experimentally manipulate traumatic events – for example, by randomly assigning participants to be involved in a car accident! It is difficult to study memories of traumatic events with the precision and control that experiments require, whilst also ensuring that people are not harmed by taking part in psychological research. Attending to ethical guidelines inevitably means weighing up different elements of the research – perhaps compromising on ecological validity to manage concerns about wellbeing. Talking about the early experiments with Pickrell (who was, by the way, an undergraduate student supervised by Loftus), Loftus said: "I want to plant a whole memory ... traumatic, but not so traumatic that the experiment would be rejected as unethical" (Loftus & Ketcham, 1994, p. 94).

Can this research really be generalised to memories of childhood sexual abuse?

When people participate in experiments, they are often asked to complete tasks which may bear little resemblance to everyday life. How often in our day-to-day lives do we have to remember a list of related words (as described above)? So, can information gained from research on abstract tasks (such as learning a list of words) be extrapolated to explain the ordinary, everyday ways that memory works – especially autobiographical memories? Perhaps it is also not too difficult to see how the *generalisability* of these kind of memory errors is problematic! Can errors about words which were or were not included in a list that people have learnt in a psychology laboratory tell us anything meaningful about real life memories of child abuse? This problem is known as *ecological validity*. Participants in word list experiments do not, for example, remember whole word lists to which they were never exposed. However, we noted earlier that Roediger and McDermott used the term 'false memory' to describe their list-learning research, and indeed, this is reflected in their study title, 'Creating false memories: Remembering words not presented in lists' (1995). Since the publication of this work in the 1990s, there has been a dramatic increase in cognitive psychology experiments which use this list-learning approach (and others) describing their work as evidence of false memory (DePrince et al., 2004). Although Roediger and McDermott (1995) may not have explicitly stated, or intended, that their research could be generalised to false memories of child abuse, by using this term at the height of the false/recovered memory controversy it is easy to see how it might be taken up in this way. This is problematic given that science and scientific rhetoric can be, and is, mobilised for ideological, political, and economic gain.

Studies using the misinformation approach may be considered a better approximation to memories of child sexual abuse since they focus on autobiographical memories. Yet, the ecological validity of these studies has also been called into question as they typically focus on memories for one-off events, rather than repeated events (which might better approximate child sexual abuse). Although recent studies have attempted to address this, albeit using the example of a repeatedly lost cuddle toy (Calado et al., 2020), and have tried to incorporate negative events (such as being lost or bitten by a dog), these are still a far cry from the traumatic memories associated with abuse.

How can feminist ethical frames expand psychologists' engagement with ethical practice?

Ethical guidelines are sometimes treated like an insurance exercise to protect the researcher/organisation from litigation or liability, or as a box-ticking exercise to gain institutional approval to conduct the research – see Loftus' comment about trying to avoid the project not being approved on ethical grounds. Feminist psychologists have consistently challenged this administrative approach and have argued instead for a more expansive understanding of ethics – an approach which raises questions about the values, interpretations, and intended uses of science, about the relationships between researchers and researched, and about institutional power.

Power dynamics between researchers and participants

Research adopting the scientific method (like experiments) encompasses an explicitly hierarchical relationship between the 'experimenter' and the dehumanised 'subject' of research. Researchers design and conduct the experiment, control the setting and the information shared with participants, manipulate variables, and interpret the outcomes. These processes imbue the researcher with authority, which is strengthened and reinforced by the institutional power afforded to them by the university, science, and psychology as a discipline – as well as other contextual features, such as wearing a white lab coat, as demonstrated in Milgram's (1974) infamous experiments about obedience to authority. This unequal power relationship is unsettling to some feminists because it reflects power inequities in everyday life (especially when the researchers are white, male, and middle class while the objects of research are women, ethnic minorities, or working class). This is even more unpalatable when marginalised or traumatised people are represented in stigmatising ways – i.e. by presenting women who have been abused in childhood as making false accusations. Rather than purporting to produce 'expert' knowledge about people, feminists have proposed that research should be conducted *with* (rather than *on*) people in as compassionate and democratic way as possible. Inherent in this stance of feminist ethical science is a process of attending to power differentials in the research process, in the knowledge that is generated, and in the way that this knowledge is taken up and used. This might mean asking questions like:

- What is the impact of this research on minoritised and marginalised peoples?
- What is the role of power and authority in what is being said and what is being believed?
- Who stands to benefit from this research and who stands to lose out?
- How have people who are the subjects of this research contributed to the design and implementation of the research?
- What is our own power as researchers, and as individuals who have our own gender, sexuality, race, class, and other social and economic locations as well as our own unique lived experience?
- How is science and research put to ideological work?

SECTION SUMMARY

- We have introduced the four principles which are embedded in the BPS guidance about ethical practice in research: respect, scientific integrity, social responsibility, and maximising gain while minimising harm.
- We have explored how feminist researchers have attempted to expand our understanding of ethics by paying particular attention to issues of power and how research can be taken up and used outside of academia.

Language, memory, and discourse

We noted at the beginning of this chapter that one of the important contributions of Loftus and Palmer's (1974) research was that it showed the importance of the language used in asking questions about memory – that asking whether cars collided or smashed into each other changed how people remembered the event. Language is not simply descriptive, rather it has the power to evoke different versions of reality – in the case of Loftus and Palmer's research, participants perceived the reality of the speed of the cars differently. But this notion of language as constructive and powerful (rather than descriptive) has much wider consequences than this.

We have opted throughout this chapter to talk about false/recovered memories to reflect the controversy surrounding different understandings of memory.

These are not neutral terms; each has embedded within it the power to evoke a different set of understandings about memory and about perpetrators and victims/survivors of sexual abuse. In more recent research, the term 'recovered memories' has been replaced by 'traumatic memories' by researchers seeking to understand the impact of traumatic events on processes of remembering and forgetting. We have considered, then, how language does *ideological* work. Publishing their foundational article in 1974, Loftus and Palmer did not use the term 'false memory' anywhere in their paper, but this phrase was later taken up within cognitive psychology and has increasingly been used to describe cognitive experiments conducted since the 1990s. DePrince and colleagues (2004) make a compelling argument that using the term 'false memory' to describe these experiments aligns this research with heated debates about child sexual abuse in misleading ways, and lends scientific legitimacy to claims that accusations of child abuse are false. They argue that it is "imperative that research on human memory occurs in an intellectual environment that acknowledges and considers the political, ethical, and theoretical implications of the language used" (2004, p. 214). A key feminist critique of objective science (including experimental research within the positivist perspective) is that science does ideological work – often, feminists would argue, ideological work that impacts negatively on women and girls. Feminist researchers who adopt experimental methods to expose gender inequality are often explicit and transparent about their value position *as* feminists, acknowledging that this has shaped the research.

See and hear for yourself

Have a look at the cognitive psychology textbook you are using on your course. Is the false/recovered memory controversy mentioned in this textbook? If so, have a look at how this is reported, and ask yourself:

- What language is used to describe different elements of this controversy?
- Is discussion of recovered memories limited to the concept of repression?

In the final part of this chapter, we draw on the work of British feminist psychologist Paula Reavey who, with a variety of colleagues, has presented an alternative understanding of memories about child abuse drawing on *poststructuralism* and *discourse analysis*. The cognitive psychology tradition is concerned with identifying both the mental building blocks of memory, and with establishing the accuracy or reliability of memory. In contrast, the discursive approach is particularly interested in *autobiographical memory* and treats memory as a social activity which is implicated in people's ongoing concern with creating and maintaining self and identity. Poststructuralist theory rejects the possibility of absolute truth and objectivity. This idea has been popular with some feminists because, as we have noted, observations about reality and statements of truth in psychological science have tended to perpetuate patriarchal power interests. Moreover, feminist research which produces different truths and highlights alternative realities has increased scepticism towards the idea of one reality and one truth. The term 'false memory' is problematic from this perspective, because it suggests that there is a simply binary between memories which are *true* and memories which are *false*. This oversimplifies the very complex relationship we have (individually and collectively) to memories of the past as we seek to re-examine and make sense of such experiences in the present. Two key books, *New Feminist Stories of Child Sexual Abuse: Sexual Scripts and Dangerous Dialogues* (Reavey & Warner, 2003) and *Memory Matters: Contexts for Understanding Sexual Abuse Recollections* (Haaken & Reavey, 2010) bring together poststructuralist feminist work on child sexual abuse and memory.

A central idea within poststructuralism is that we never encounter or experience the social world unmediated by the meanings that are given to it. In other words, our memories of experiences are inevitably shaped by the meanings we give to these memories. These meanings are constructed through language or other forms of representation and are highly contingent on context. This means that the meanings which are given to memories, and through which experiences become known, are always in flux and are being actively produced and negotiated each time we talk about, write about, or otherwise represent them. In their introduction to the book *New Feminist Stories of Child Sexual Abuse*, Reavey and Warner reflect this approach arguing that child sexual abuse "is never transparent in terms of what it means: either as an event itself or in the memory of it"; rather, it is

> something that, as survivors, theoreticians or practitioners, we *make sense of* in the re-telling, and how we make sense of it shifts according to the contexts in which we speak, with whom we speak with, and who we speak about.
>
> (2003, p. 1)

In *Memory Matters* (2010), Haaken and Reavey explore the question of why some memories matter more than others, depending on the social and emotional investments we have in these memories. They acknowledge the vital role of the feminist movement of the 1970s in opening up spaces for women to publicly recount and share their experiences of sexual assault (such as consciousness-raising spaces, workshops, and self-help groups), and moving towards a collective understanding of sexual abuse as a social, rather than individual, problem. To this, we would also add that feminist academic work also bore witness and gave voice to these experiences using qualitative research methods. Nonetheless, Haaken and Reavey attempt to move beyond the true/false binary in relation to memory, and provide an alternative to the way that feminist concerns about validating women's experiences became fused with literalist understandings of memory. Their volume is not concerned with the veracity of memories of child sexual abuse, but instead with the ideological work that these memories are put to, by whom, and under what circumstances. The contributors consider how memories of abuse are scrutinised, responded to, and reworked in professional and interpersonal settings. The sources of data they draw on are primarily qualitative, including interviews, case histories, focus groups, video-recordings, published media, and legal materials. This approach asks a different kind of question – rather than asking whether memories are true or false, it asks: 'How are notions of truth and falsity produced in specific contexts, and what are the implications of this?'

We can see these elements in action in one of the chapters in *New Feminist Stories of Child Sexual Abuse* written by Marcia Worrell (2003). Drawing on stories shared by women in a self-help group for adult survivors of child sexual abuse, Worrell demonstrates how the group actively worked to reframe women as *survivors* rather than *victims* of sexual abuse by focusing not on how women survived abuse but on the fact that they did survive, or by focusing on post-abuse strengths or resiliencies. Worrell observed how women monitored themselves, and each other, to challenge 'victim-blaming' by foregrounding the agency and resilience of the survivor as a form of mutual support. Overall, then, we can characterise this alternative, post-structuralist, and discursive approach to understanding memory as encapsulating three elements:

1 Rather than conceptualising memory as a capacity of the mind to store information as discrete records of past events, memory is understood as a social and cultural activity.
2 Memories of past events are open to many interpretations and power dynamics play a role in determining which interpretations stick.
3 Processes of remembering and forgetting are inherently ethical and political.

SECTION SUMMARY

- Researchers drawing on a social constructionist paradigm for research place a lot of emphasis on language. This is because language is not just descriptive but can shape our understanding of the world in powerful ways.
- We have looked at contrasting ways of using language – like false/recovered memories or victim/survivor of sexual abuse – to demonstrate how powerful language can be.

CHAPTER SUMMARY

- Using the example of memory experiments in cognitive psychology, we have explored how experiments are often considered to be the 'gold standard' for research because they offer a high level of control, allowing cause-and-effect conclusions to be reached. They are infused with a high level of scientific authority.

- We have also explored the ways in which this control can also be methodologically problematic: it lacks connection to everyday experience and real life (ecological validity), people are difficult to study in the same way as the objects of the natural sciences because they react and respond to experimental environments (*reactivity*), and because ethical concerns mean that sensitive topics often have to be studied in abstract ways (and therefore lack generalisability).

- Feminists have also drawn attention to more profound concerns with the experimental method, including the impossibility of maintaining an objective stance, the ways in which experimental research is shaped by the (patriarchal and other) socio-cultural context, and the problematic unequal power relationship between researcher and researched.

- We have also looked at the social constructionist approach to understanding memory, which sees memories and the meanings given to these memories as inseparable and draws attention to the ideological function of language.

5 | Personality and individual differences: tests and scales

Learning objectives

Study of this chapter should enable you to:

- Understand how psychometric tests are developed and some of the issues associated with psychometric testing, including objectivity, reliability, and validity.
- Demonstrate awareness that how psychological constructs are conceptualised, defined, or imagined is inherently political (linked to power, status, and inequality).
- Become familiar with feminist critiques of psychometric testing, including essentialism and context stripping.
- Develop a critical understanding of sex differences research and how psychometric testing can be used to oppress and support discrimination against women and other marginalised groups.

In 1974, American feminist psychologist Sandra Bem developed a psychometric test, the Bem Sex Role Inventory (BSRI), which challenged the relationship between biological sex (male and female) and gender (masculinity and femininity). Traditional assessments of masculinity and femininity widely used at the time assumed that masculinity and femininity were binary opposites, and that people could be categorised as masculine *or* feminine largely in line with their biological sex. In other words, that men would (largely) display 'masculine characteristics' such as assertiveness, problem-solving ability, and leadership, whilst women would (largely) display 'feminine characteristics' such as being understanding, nurturing, and soothing hurt feelings. Radically, the BSRI treats masculinity and femininity as two *independent* dimensions. Bem argued that the dimensions of masculinity and femininity are empirically as well as logically independent, rather than being polar opposites, and that they were not inherently linked to biological sex. Any one individual might, she claimed, have *both* masculine *and* feminine traits, and that whether or not these characteristics came to the fore might be more dependent on context than biological make-up. So, although some individuals were identified as exclusively feminine or masculine using this inventory, Bem also found that some people have strongly masculine *and* strongly feminine traits. She described these people as *androgynous*. More than this, Bem was keen to challenge an important assumption often made by psychologists at the time – that gender appropriate characteristics and behaviour indicated good mental health, whilst gender atypical behaviour (i.e. boys displaying 'feminine' traits and playing with dolls, or girls being aggressive or fighting) was indicative of mental disturbance. Bem hoped that her research would

> encourage investigators in the areas of sex differences and sex roles to question the traditional assumption that it is the sex-typed individual who typifies mental health and to begin focusing on the behavioral and societal consequences of more flexible sex role self-concepts.
>
> (1974, pp. 161–162)

It was Bem's hope that the androgynous person would be held up as the standard of psychological health. Although this did not prove to be the case – actually so-called masculine traits were found to be most associated with good mental health (Whitley, 1984, 1988) – Bem's work did highlight how assumptions about mental health, personality, and gender stereotypes are connected. The BSRI is one of the most widely used tools in research on *gender roles*, and Bem's work significantly shaped feminist psychology and gender studies (see the special issue discussing her work over 40 years later in the journal *Sex Roles*: Keener & Mehta, 2017). Although the BSRI is not without criticism, it does illustrate many important points about one of the cornerstones of research methods in psychology – psychometric tests.

See and hear for yourself

Find out more about Sandra Bem and her work at Feminist Voices: https://feministvoices.com/profiles/sandra-bem

So, what are psychometric tests and why are they used?

Tests, scales, and questionnaires form one of the most popular and widely used research methods in psychology. Psychometric tests are *applied* in different contexts. In educational contexts, tests of ability (like intelligence tests and aptitude tests) may be used to monitor individuals' progress over time, to predict individuals' achievements and educational outcomes, or to select children for entry into (private) schools (see Table 5.1). In employment or occupational contexts, personality tests are used in recruitment to select the candidate who has the right traits for the role (e.g. to recruit an extrovert into a sales job), or perhaps to find out what motivates different employees to work hard. Someone

Table 5.1: A summary of the uses for different types of psychometric tests

Type of test	Purpose	Examples
Personality	To measure a set of psychological attributes, traits, or characteristics of an individual and allow comparison between individuals or groups	Bem Sex Role Inventory (Bem, 1974) – measures masculinity, femininity, and androgyny Minnesota Multiphasic Personality Inventory (Hathaway & McKinley, 1940) Five Factor Inventory (FFI; Costa & McCrae, 1992) – measures openness, conscientiousness, extraversion, agreeableness, and neuroticism
Ability	To measure a specific ability (like comprehension, reasoning, spatial ability, creativity) or aptitude	Wechsler Adult Intelligence Scale (Wechsler, 1955) – measures intelligence Mental Rotation Test (MRT; Peters et al., 1995) – measures spatial ability by asking someone to identify a rotated version of a shape from a range of possible options
Motivation/ attitude	To measure beliefs or opinions	Rape Myth Acceptance Scale (Burt, 1980) Attitudes Towards Women Scale (Spence & Helmreich, 1972)
Psychological wellbeing	To measure specific aspects of mental health (such as self-esteem, body image, coping style) or to identify mental distress/ill health	Rosenberg Self Esteem Scale (Rosenberg, 1965) Beck Depression Inventory (Beck et al., 1961)

who is motivated by money, for example, might work hard to achieve a bonus, whereas someone who values work/life balance might be more attracted by flexible hours. Psychometric tests in clinical settings are used as a way of diagnosing psychological disorders. In this sense, tests are used to gain insight into an individual, but are also valued because they allow comparison between individuals or groups.

In this chapter, we look at the issues surrounding psychometric testing by exploring how it is used to examine one of the core areas of psychology – personality and individual differences. The study of *individual differences* is about how people are both similar and different to each other in how they behave, how they think, and how they feel. As this book is concerned with the research methods used by psychologists, our focus is largely on how such differences are defined, measured, and tracked in order to reach conclusions about what differences exist (and the magnitude of any differences) as well as the consequences of these differences for life outcomes. As will become clear, this area of research is highly controversial, and is particularly of interest to feminist psychologists because of the almost obsessive focus within psychology on the study of *sex differences*. Bem's research focused on one particular aspect of sex differences – masculinity/femininity – but research into sex differences covers a vast range of different areas. To demonstrate, here are some examples of commonly reported sex differences:

- Boys are more intelligent than girls.
- Boys are better at visuospatial tasks than girls.
- Women are more agreeable (nurturing, tender-minded, and *altruistic*) than men.
- Men are more dominant, assertive, risk-prone, thrill-seeking, tough-minded, emotionally stable, utilitarian, and open to abstract ideas.

These reported sex differences are concerning since this research has real world effects – by reinforcing stereotypes and shaping popular opinion, by supporting prejudice and discrimination, and by shaping policies and practice. For example, sex differences research is often reported in the popular press. British newspaper *The Daily Mail* consistently runs stories reporting psychological and neuroscience research about sex differences with headlines like: 'Women ARE the fairer sex and have stronger morals than men when it comes to being caring and fair, study finds'; 'Surprise! Men and women really ARE different: Sexes share just 10 per cent of their personality traits'; 'Female brains really ARE different to male minds'; and 'Proof that girls and boys are born to be different: Controversial study finds that brain differences between the sexes begin in the womb'. Of course, they also run stories which refute the idea of fixed sex differences: 'Largest study to date debunks myth that male and female brains are different'. Importantly, feminist researchers have demonstrated that newspaper reports which are politically conservative and express traditional gender roles also use a biological explanation for these differences. More than this, when people read newspaper reports like this, exposure to a biological explanation of sex differences (rather than a socio-cultural explanation) was found to increase their endorsement of gender stereotypes (Brescoll & Lafrance, 2004). Psychological research is not neutral; it is always political. The study of group-based differences is problematic and controversial, then, because it is inherently political – no matter how much psychologists argue that it is 'objective' science. If we want to understand if, where, and when sex differences in thoughts, feelings, and behaviours exist, we need to examine the research methods and procedures used to identify such differences. The questions we can ask about sex differences, and the answers we get, depend on the methods we use to define, measure, and assess such differences.

One key area of focus within the psychology of individual differences is *personality*. When we talk about personality, we are interested in the type of person someone is or what they are like as an individual, often drawing on a list of qualities or attributes to describe them – she is selfish/kind/intelligent/ thoughtful/caring/warm/difficult/sensitive, and so on. Personality researchers often seek to explain why people behave in the ways that they do, and to consider whether these personality traits (characteristics or attributes) motivate and explain such behaviour. The idea of personality traits implies something which is relatively consistent, fixed, and enduring. In other words, personality is a psychological construct – we cannot observe personality directly, as psychologists we infer personality from behaviour or, more typically, from the ways in which individuals respond to personality questionnaires. Personality is a hypothetical construct invented by psychologists to try to explain individual differences in behaviours, thoughts, and feelings. A key message in this chapter is that how psychological constructs are conceptualised, defined, or imagined is inherently political (linked to power, status, and inequality). As noted earlier, when Sandra Bem developed her sex role inventory, she was looking for an alternative to traditional assessments which defined masculinity and femininity as binary opposites and assumed that this aligned with biological sex. The assumption that women are, by their very nature, nurturing, gentle, affectionate, or sympathetic, for example, is one which has historically been used to justify the unequal treatment of women (such as their exclusion from the armed forces or certain sports) and to oppress women by limiting their employment opportunities (see Box 5.1) or exploit their labour (when state policy exploits women's unpaid caring work). Conceptualising personality traits and individual differences as natural, biological, or inherent to the individual (known as *essentialism*) has formed a central axis of the feminist critique of individual differences research, and feminists have offered alternative explanations for why such differences may exist – based on gender stereotypes, differences in power, the effects of trauma and inequality, and so on. Importantly, how constructs are measured, the tools we use to assess these constructs, and the knowledge about individuals and groups which is generated using the tools and methods is inevitably political. Feminism, with its careful attention to power – especially unequal power based on gender and its intersection with other dimensions of inequality – exposes the ways in which power operates in and through the development and use of psychometric tests.

Box 5.1: Women, leadership, and the glass ceiling

Psychometric tests are often used to identify whether potential job candidates possess certain traits. This is one of their key applications. Yet, as we know, women remain underrepresented in top leadership positions in work organisations (Ryan et al., 2016). The metaphor of the *glass ceiling* is commonly used to describe the invisible barriers women face in securing promotion to these top positions. British psychologist Michelle Ryan has extended this by introducing the notion of the *glass cliff* to describe how poor company performance can trigger women's appointment to more precarious leadership positions.

Scholars of personality and individual differences tend to focus on individual-level factors. One body of work focuses on women's apparent lack of assertiveness, drive, and/or competitive spirit as an explanation for their failure to secure top leadership positions in higher numbers. A classic example is Babcock and Laschever's *Women Don't Ask* (2003), which suggests that women are much less likely than their male peers to ask for promotions. The implication of such individual-level explanations is that if women were only more assertive, many more would be appointed to leadership positions. Such explanations largely fail to consider the range of institutional factors that shape appointment decisions. This highlights three problems that feminists often raise about psychological research of this kind – that it is individualised, pathologising, and victim-blaming.

According to role congruity theory (Eagly & Karau, 2002), women who are assertive and meet the agentic requirements of the leader role are evaluated less favourably than their male counterparts. This form of prejudice places female leaders in a bind, as the agentic behaviour required of leaders (e.g. assertive, dominant) is incompatible with the non-agentic behaviour required of women (e.g. tentative, submissive), while being tentative in leadership reduces the likeability and influence of women, but not of men. Although approval of agentic behaviour from women in leadership reflects progress, evidence that women are quickly singled out for disapproval if they fail to show agency is important for understanding how they continue to be at a distinct disadvantage to men in leadership roles (Bongiorno et al., 2014). Moreover, this fails to account for the ways in which personality traits themselves are not neutral – some are more socially valued than others. Agentic traits – like assertiveness, strength, dominance, and decisiveness – are positively valued (so in a patriarchal society it is no accident that such traits are associated with masculinity), whilst other traits are seen as negative (for example, the 'dark triad' of narcissism, psychopathy, and Machiavellianism). It is this association between particular (positive) traits and masculinity that Bem was keen to disrupt.

SECTION SUMMARY

- We have used Sandra Bem's work in developing the Bem Sex Role Inventory as an example of a 'classic' study examining how gender, masculinity, and femininity are associated with personality.
- We have noted that research on sex differences is a 'hot topic' in psychological research and the media, as it often reinforces stereotypes about men and women – often in ways which disadvantage women.
- Tests and scales to measure personality (and other attributes) are often used (applied) in a range of different settings, such as the workplace. This means it is especially important to interrogate *what* these instruments purport to measure, and the implicit assumptions which underpin them.

How are psychometric tests developed?

Psychometric tests are designed to be *objective* measures – this means that they are designed to be free from *subjective* factors such as the researcher's personal beliefs, feelings, and experiences. Typically, when completing a test or scale, people are presented with a set of statements, questions, or adjectives (see, for example, adjectives about masculinity and femininity from the BSRI in Table 5.2) and are asked to indicate how accurately they describe their personality using a limited set of predetermined response options (true/false, yes/no, agree/disagree, etc.). What is objective about this, is that the psychologist administering the test does not need to rely on judgement to classify the individual as feminine, masculine, or androgynous. Instead, this judgement is based on the scoring of the test according to a pre-existing set of criteria.

Step 1: Identify and define your psychological construct

The development of a psychometric test begins by identifying a psychological construct that you want to measure, such as sex roles, cognitive ability, aggression, or intelligence). We noted earlier that personality is a hypothetical construct – an idea invented by psychologists to explain why people think, feel, or behave in the ways that they do. Behind any psychometric test is a construct which is being measured. It is important to remember this because when a construct becomes widely used and enters into everyday vocabulary, it is easy to forget that it is an invented idea – some good examples include the concepts of personality, body image, and the unconscious, all of which are now such taken-for-granted words that we sometimes forget that they were invented. When concepts are treated as if they are real, it is known as *reification*. A first step in producing a questionnaire or test is to define the

Table 5.2: Examples of masculine, feminine, and neutral traits from the Bem Sex Role Inventory

Stereotypically masculine	Stereotypically feminine	Stereotypically gender neutral
Ambitious	Shy	Tactful
Competitive	Affectionate	Conventional
Forceful	Childlike	Happy
Self-sufficient	Gullible	Reliable

construct so that it can be measured objectively (i.e. without bias). Feminist psychologists have pointed to the ways in which assumptions about gender often enter into the definition and measurement of constructs. As noted earlier, prior to the development of the BSRI, masculinity and femininity were treated as polar opposites (people were identified as *either* masculine *or* feminine). Bem radically altered the perception of gender by developing a measure which assessed the extent to which one identified with *both* masculine *and* feminine traits. In other words, the way that gender is conceptualised influences the way it is measured through self-report questionnaires, which in turn shapes the kind of knowledge and understanding of gender that is produced (as knowledge is power). We pick up this point again in Box 5.3: Challenging the Gender Binary.

Thinking critically about psychological constructs and their measurement has been an important aspect of feminist work – this includes both reimagining existing constructs (like gender) but also introducing new constructs. As we noted in Chapter 1, one of the problems with research identified by feminists is that the experiences that are studied often inevitably reflect the interests and lives of the researchers themselves. This is not, in itself, problematic. Some of the best (most interesting, most productive, or most influential) lines of inquiry have resulted from psychologists drawing on their own experience. Historically, however, feminists have shown how the predominance of white, middle-class men within the profession (coupled with a focus on WEIRD samples) has skewed research and theory in ways which marginalise women and women's interests. Feminist researchers have been consistently working to move women 'from the margins' by placing women at the heart of their research by foregrounding women's experiences and concerns. This means developing constructs to describe and explain women's experience and developing sound psychometric measures to objectively and rigorously assess the extent of these experiences within individuals and across groups of individuals. As we saw in Chapter 2, asking (the right) questions and thinking like a feminist are important. Here are some examples where feminist research using tests and scales has transformed psychological knowledge by centring women's experiences.

Box 5.2: Examples of feminist conceptual analysis

Feminist psychology is full of examples of researchers who question and deconstruct how particular ways of defining concepts have influenced their measurement in problematic ways and skewed the knowledge produced.

Mary Koss on 'hidden rape' and redefining rape. Koss (1985) argued that because of the ways in which sexual assault was measured, there was a serious underreporting of this crime. In addition to conviction rates as an indication of the extent of sexual assault, which are acknowledged to be unreliable due to issues of underreporting and low prosecution rates (which persist long after Koss began writing about this in the 1980s), National Crime Surveys are the key mechanism for estimating crime rates. Here individuals are interviewed in their own homes or by phone and are asked about whether they (or members of their household) have been a victim of crimes during the last six months (known as victimisation studies). Based on a combination of these two sources of information, rape was generally considered to be a rare or unusual crime which was infrequently experienced by women. Koss noted a number of problems with the way that questions about sexual assault were posed in such surveys, in particular the assumption that the term 'rape' was a recognisable and meaningful way for women to conceptualise their experiences of sexual assault. Widely held rape myths, such as the belief that rapists are mentally deranged strangers, you cannot rape an unwilling woman, or you cannot rape someone you know, argued Koss, meant that many women did not recognise sexual assault as rape or use this term to describe their experiences. For example, among a sample of women who described assaults primarily by acquaintances that met legal definitions of rape, only 53% believed their experience qualified as rape (Koss, 1985). Asking women about whether they had 'Had sexual intercourse with a man (woman) when you (she) didn't want to because he (you) threatened to use physical force (twisting your [her] arm, holding you [her] down, etc.) if you (she) didn't cooperate?' (i.e. the legal definition of rape), Koss found that many more women had experienced rape than indicated in crime statistics and victimisation studies. Using this survey, Koss, Gidycz, and Wisniewski (1987) conducted a nationally representative survey of US higher education students and found that from the age of 14, 27.5% of college women reported having experienced an act that met legal definitions of rape, which includes attempted rape. Importantly, Koss also argued that rather than seeing sexual assault as categorical (i.e. categorising women as a victim of rape/not a victim of rape), sexual assault should be conceptualised as dimensional with rape representing the extreme end of experiences. The Sexual Experiences Survey was revised in the mid-2000s – you can find it here: https://ncvc.dspacedirect.org/handle/20.500.11990/1482. This work revolutionised the way in which instances of rape are counted, and was pivotal in shifting recognition that rape and sexual assault are highly prevalent in many societies.

Martha Burt on measuring rape myths. Research into rape myths emerged in the 1970s when radical feminists such as Susan Brownmiller and Martha Burt argued that rape was a way for men to exert control over women (i.e. rape is about power, not sex) and that rape myths served to justify this sexual dominance. Rape myths are "prejudicial, stereotyped, or false beliefs about rape, rape victims and rapists" (Burt, 1980, p. 217); they are myths that blame the victim, exonerate the perpetrator, imply that only certain types of women are raped, or suggest the claims of rape are not to be believed. The most widely used measure is Burt's (1980) Rape Myth Acceptance Scale. Research has consistently found that men are more supportive of rape myths than women (for a review, see Lonsway & Fitzgerald, 1994). Rape myth acceptance has been found to be associated with male-on-female sexual violence (Yapp & Quayle, 2018), and the acceptance or rejection of rape myths shapes police officers' judgements about the credibility of rape victims' accounts (Parratt & Pina, 2017). In her article on the truth about false accusations of sexual violence (they are not very common), Lazard (2017) argued that studying these type of rape myths can help us understand, and contest, how specific conditions scaffold and support sexual assault.

As well as producing measures which speak to the reality of women's lives, feminists have also been keen to produce measures which foreground context (and consequently avoid biological essentialism). One example is the Objectified Body Consciousness (OBC) Scale developed by Nita McKinley and Janet Hyde (1996) and now widely used in research on body image and eating disorders. This scale is embedded in feminist theory about body image. Noting that "negative feelings toward their bodies take a heavy toll on women's economic, personal, and political lives" (p. 181), McKinley and Hyde observe that body image measures typically ask people to rate how positively/negatively they feel about a list of discrete body parts (stomach, waist, legs, breasts, etc.), which "emphasizes the *intrapersonal* factors that are related to body experience, rather than the context in which body experience takes place" (p. 182). In contrast, the concept of objectified body consciousness places social context centre-stage. Feminist theory argues that the female body is socially constructed as an object to be looked at and judged in relation to a set of cultural standards of attractiveness and sexual desirability – think about all the sexualised images of (predominantly white, slim, young, able-bodied) women's bodies which we see plastered on advertising and magazine covers, pornographic pop-ups when we are online, or which encourage us to 'eat well' and exercise. Through these social messages, women learn to also view their body as an object, becoming detached from sensory experience and instead imaging themselves from the position of an outside observer judging and assessing their own appearance. Instead of looking at individual differences in body dissatisfaction, the OBC scale examines the differences in the extent to which women have resisted or internalised these cultural beauty standards so that they appear to originate from their own beliefs or desires (e.g. 'I want a breast enlargement so that I can feel more confident', or 'I am cutting down on my carbs so that I can fit into my new dress'). The authors foreground the pernicious and toxic cultural context in which women are sexualised, valued for their appearance/body, and held to impossible standards. Without attention to this context, high levels of body dissatisfaction among women might be seen as a deficiency within the individual (i.e. women are too vain, appearance-obsessed, narcissistic, easily influenced by the media, etc.), effectively holding women responsible for their own *oppression* in a form of *victim-blaming*.

Step 2: Write good questions

The key to writing a good test is to write good questions! The questions must provide a way of measuring the psychological construct (which has been defined by the researcher – see above). The researcher also decides what questions are important to ask, and how to ask them. Psychometric tests typically use closed questions – questions in which participants can respond in only a fixed number of ways – which are convenient for the researcher as they allow the data to be easily *quantified* (or counted), enabling it to be analysed using statistical techniques. Therefore, a lot of control and power rests with the researcher. To temper this power, and to ensure objectivity, researchers can use a number of techniques to develop questionnaire items:

- review the theoretical literature;
- recruit experts;
- ask colleagues;
- consult people who are targeted by the research – this is the one which many feminists would recommend and democratises the research process.

To develop her sex role inventory, Sandra Bem compiled a list of 200 personality traits that were positively valued and stereotypically masculine or feminine, and 200 gender-neutral traits. Bem asked undergraduate students at Stanford University to rate whether the items were socially desirable either for a man or for a woman (rated from 'Not at all desirable' to 'Extremely desirable'). Twenty personality traits that were deemed socially desirable for a man, and 20 deemed socially desirable for a woman were selected for inclusion in the inventory alongside 10 positive and 10 negative neutral traits (i.e. those associated equally with men and women). In contrast to the essentialism of traditional personality tests, the BSRI acknowledges that personality characteristics are not socio-culturally neutral, but rather that some are more socially valued than others. Consequently, it is perhaps not surprising that in patriarchal societies the attributes associated with (certain versions of) leadership (such as being assertive, competitive, risk-taking, or decisive) are also those that are stereotypically associated with masculinity. Personality tests typically seek to strip away this important context, assuming that an attribute like femininity (or assertiveness, competitiveness) is an essential essence of the individual and can therefore be accurately and objectively measured irrespective of its social status (valued or devalued) and stereotypical association with groups. ***Context stripping*** is a problem that feminist researchers try to avoid in their own work, and we return to look at other examples of this later.

There's lots of advice available on writing good questions: ones that are clear, not leading, and that are easy for people to answer. This advice has become increasingly sophisticated as psychologists try to find ways of avoiding the problems which inevitably arise when human beings complete these questionnaires. This includes problems like social desirability where people might give answers which they hope will present them in a good light (e.g. by exaggerating how likely they are to help others in need or by not being completely honest about how likely they are to discriminate against others). These human processes are treated as sources of bias (as preventing psychologists from obtaining a true or accurate measure of people's attitudes) which psychologists attempt to address by introducing 'lie scales' in an attempt to identify when participants are not being entirely truthful by asking about the same issue in different ways. The idea is that if everyone receives exactly the same questionnaire in the same format, with the same questions, any differences observed in responses are due to the individual. The measure is ***standardised***.

Step 3: Test the reliability and validity of your questionnaire

Tests are (ideally, but not always) rigorously tested to establish their quality. Typically, different types of test are conducted: tests of ***reliability*** and tests of ***validity***. Reliability assesses the extent to which the test consistently performs the same. There are two types of reliability. ***Internal reliability*** (or internal consistency) assesses whether all the elements of a test or all the individual items are measuring the same underlying construct. This is tested by looking at whether there is a relationship (known as a ***correlation***) between the items on a scale. Items which are not strongly related to the others are often excluded from the final version of the scale. ***Test-retest reliability*** assesses the consistency of the questionnaire when used over different points in time. You might also look at the average score for each item (the mean score). A high mean score means that most people would agree with this item. Therefore, you might exclude this item from your scale as it does not differentiate well between people. Tests of *validity* examine whether the questionnaire really measures what the researchers intended to measure: *convergent validity* (does this questionnaire show similarities with other established questions which we would expect it to show a relationship to?), *concurrent validity* (does this questionnaire show a relationship to questionnaires measuring the same construct?), and *discriminant validity* (does the questionnaire NOT show a relationship to questionnaires measuring other constructs?).

SECTION SUMMARY

- We have looked at some of the key stages involved in developing psycho-metric tests and scales as well as some of the ways in which psychologists test the reliability and validity of scales.
- A test is only as good as the construct it is designed to measure and we have explored how using a feminist lens can work to define constructs in ways which avoid victim-blaming.

But how do people make sense of questionnaires?

Researchers who use self-report measures such as tests, scales, and questionnaires, whether feminist or not, often assume that the psychological construct which is being measured is universally shared and easily understood. Researchers who want to use surveys across different groups (for example, cross-cultural research) recognise that this may not be the case. To account for this, and with the aim of developing *an* item or scale that can accurately measure between group differences or variance, a range of methodological techniques have been developed to increase the validity of questionnaires. These involve exploring how diverse groups of individuals interpret and make sense of survey items and the constructs underpinning these items. The aim is to move towards conceptual coherence where all individuals share the same understanding of the concept and where questionnaire items are equally meaningful and understandable to all.

To illustrate the value of examining how people make sense of questionnaires, we draw on Sara McClelland's (2011) work examining the measurement of sexual satisfaction – although the critical points she raises could be applied to questionnaires designed to measure any other area of psychological experience. McClelland observes that studies of 'sexual satisfaction' often assume that this concept is universally understood, or that by leaving it undefined participants can apply their own unique understanding when responding to items such as 'I am satisfied with my sex life' (Neto, 2012). What this misses, argues McClelland, is that individuals and groups who have developed within social and political contexts that routinely limit their rights, voices, behaviours, and expectations (such as women and LGBTQ+ folk) might have very different interpretations of sexual satisfaction. In addition, self-report questionnaires typically assume that when people respond they are engaged in a process of looking inwards and reflexively evaluating and appraising their own experiences or beliefs. In the case of questionnaires regarding sexual satisfaction, in order to respond to the question 'I am satisfied with my sex life', a person is assumed to be either reporting a pre-existing appraisal (or belief or attitude) which they already hold, or to be reviewing their sex life to reach a position. Questioning this assumption, McClelland (2011) adopted a multi-method approach in which men and women were asked to both evaluate their sexual satisfaction using a series of survey items *and* talk about their sexual satisfaction appraisals during a semi-structured interview. Using multiple methods allows researchers to *triangulate* the information collected – i.e. to compare and contrast the information gleaned from using different methods to study the same phenomenon (in this case, sexual satisfaction). In particular, McClelland looked at the *benchmarks* that people used to evaluate their experiences of sexual satisfaction. Analysis of the quantitative responses to the three questionnaire items suggest that the four groups (heterosexual men, heterosexual women, sexual minority men, sexual minority women) reported approximately the same frequency of orgasm, enjoyment of sex with their partner, and roughly the same level of sexual satisfaction. Importantly though, while some people reported on their own sexual satisfaction, others prioritised whether their partners were satisfied. McClelland (2011) found that reliance on a partner's experience was not limited to women in this study. LGBT and queer-identified men also described fulfilling a partner's expectations as the primary benchmark used to evaluate their own level of sexual satisfaction.

SECTION SUMMARY

- Questionnaires, tests, and scales are often treated as if they are standardised and objective tools which are the same for everyone.
- We have looked at how these measures are interacted with and made sense of by the people who are asked to complete them, and show how responses to questionnaires can reflect social inequalities.

Meta-analysis and the future of sex differences

In 1979, American feminist psychologist Rhoda Unger asked fellow feminists: 'Should we study sex differences?' Fifteen years later, in 1994, Celia Kitzinger again posed this question. So, one use of psychometric tests, scales, and questionnaires is to measure a set of psychological attributes, traits, or characteristics of an individual and make comparisons between individuals or groups. The latter allows psychologists to make generalisations about different groups. Of particular interest to feminists is the ways in which psychological research explores gender or sex differences. The goal of understanding the extent to which social groups are different from – or similar to – one another is perhaps one of the most controversial and politically charged areas of psychology. The mid-1990s saw a flurry of debate in feminist academic circles about the value or otherwise of studying sex differences. Similar controversies were (and still are) being discussed in relation to differences between racialised groups. Here is a list of some of the common problems that feminists identified in relation to sex differences research:

1   Preoccupation with sex differences overlooks and diminishes similarities between the sexes. "The fact that the sexes are similar in far more ways than they are different is not considered startling psychological news" (Unger, 1979, p. 1090).

2   Sex differences research often rests on the assumption that different does not mean equal and that psychological research often measures attributes and abilities in ways which position women as deficient compared with men.

3   Differences are often attributed to biological or inherent differences between men and women – despite this not being explicitly tested.

4   Statistical vs. social significance – statistical tests often allow researchers to calculate an *effect size*, which is a measure of the magnitude of difference between two groups (in this case men and women), but it does not give any indication of whether this difference is socially meaningful.

5   Publication bias – studies which report statistically significant sex differences are more likely to be published than studies which report no differences.

6   The interpretation of differences – research which documents differences between men and women, but which offers no way of explaining why these differences exist, may reinforce stereotypes and perceptions.

7   False universalism – the assumption that 'all women' or 'all men' are the same.

8   Assumption that gender is binary – that people are either male or female and that only these two – opposite – sexes exist.

Box 5.3: Challenging the gender binary

Sex differences research is predicated on the assumption of a gender binary – that there are two (and only two) types of people, men and women. This assumption has been seriously challenged by both academic research and social activism. In a review of the academic literature, Hyde et al. (2019) identified five key challenges to the gender binary arising out of empirical research: evidence from neuroscience refuting the idea that the human brain is systematically different between men and women; findings from behavioural neuroendocrinology challenging the notion of genetically fixed, non-overlapping hormonal systems; psychological research highlighting the similarities between men and women; psychological research on transgender and non-binary individuals' identities and experiences; and developmental research suggesting that the tendency to view gender/sex as a meaningful, binary category is culturally determined and malleable. Responding to these challenges the authors argue that a distinction needs to be drawn between whether sex should be analysed as a variable and who should be included in research. Samples of people recruited for psychological research should be as diverse as possible to ensure that the research speaks to the rich variety of human experience, and to avoid silencing and marginalising groups. At a basic level, this might include shifting towards asking participants open questions, such as 'What is your gender?', rather than offering a choice between 'male' and 'female'. It might also include measures which acknowledge fluidity in gender identity, such as asking about birth-assigned and self-assigned sex/gender, or asking how people currently identify. Finally, it might include conceptualising sex/gender as continuous (i.e. identifying as more or less female/male rather than as one or the other) and multidimensional (i.e. consisting of many different elements). In this sense, Sandra Bem's sex role inventory was ahead of the curve! A final consideration is whether asking about people's gender identity, especially at the beginning of the research (which is when this kind of information is often collected), reinforces the idea that sex/gender is important – a simple change might be to ask these questions at the end of the research.

Some feminists argued that the study of sex differences should be abandoned, while others argued that 'better science' – research which attended to and corrected methodological errors – was needed to debunk myths and misconceptions prevalent in sex differences research and to develop a more accurate picture of what (if any) sex differences exist. These debates were both political *and* methodological; focusing both on the scientific rigour of sex differences research, and on the real world uses and abuses of sex differences research. We use the term *sex differences* here to reflect the problematic grouping of people into female and male binary categories; the term *gender* reflects the social and cultural meanings given to the categories of male and female.

Although methodological innovations, such as the development of **meta-analysis** as a technique for synthesising quantitative research findings from multiple studies, have radically altered research on sex differences, they have not brought about the widespread social change that some feminists had hoped for. A meta-analysis consists of several stages:

1 Researchers systematically search for, and identify, empirical research which reports on the area of interest (e.g. sex differences in mathematical ability). The idea is to identify all of the relevant data that is available in order to get the most accurate picture possible. Given the publication bias mentioned above, this might also include unpublished studies or 'grey literature'.

2 Researchers compute an **effect size** based on the data reported in each study. The effect size is calculated by looking at how far apart the mean scores for men are from the mean scores for women (i.e. between-group differences), but also takes into consideration variability within the groups (i.e. the differences between individual women included in the study). In other words, it acknowledges that the groups are not homogeneous (not all women or men are the same).

3 Researchers calculate the mean or average effect size obtained from each of the studies, which allows them to draw conclusions about the size of any sex differences across all of the studies included in the meta-analysis. Rather than concluding that, say, some studies find evidence of sex differences while other studies find none, meta-analysis enables researchers to draw more specific conclusions.

Feminist psychologists, most notably US psychologists Janet Shibley Hyde and Alice Eagly, enthusiastically applied this new meta-analytic technique to studies of sex differences in cognitive ability and intelligence.

Although some feminists hoped that meta-analysis would put an end to the controversy about sex differences research by being able to definitively show what differences (if any) exist, this has not (yet) proven to be the case. Controversy exists over how to interpret the results of these meta-analytic syntheses – some (like Hyde) argue that sex differences in cognitive ability are negligible, whilst others contend that there are important sex differences (for an overview, see Eagly, 1995).

Other developments include:

- Asking more sophisticated, contextual questions, such as: under what circumstances are sex differences smaller or larger?, under what conditions are the sexes more similar than different?
- Moving beyond nature or nurture to consider the dynamic interplay of biology and social context, e.g. the environmental influence on gene expression.
- Exploration of intersectionality and nuanced consideration of power.

SECTION SUMMARY

The study of sex differences is controversial, not only because it remains difficult to pin down with scientific certainty which (if any) differences exist, but also this research is political in that it often reproduces and perpetuates harmful stereotypes.

CHAPTER SUMMARY

- In this chapter, we have used the Bem Sex Role Inventory to explore how feminists have used scales to explore the relationship between gender and personality.
- We have identified some of the problems and pitfalls of research which uses these kinds of instruments to examine sex differences in traits and abilities.
- We have addressed how people make sense of these scales as they complete them.

6 Biological psychology: biological sex differences and fMRI

Learning objectives

Study of this chapter should enable you to:

- Describe the roles of genes, hormones, and brains in relation to gender dimorphism.
- Consider the use of fMRI technology in neuroscience.
- Think critically about the claims made about sex/gender based on biological data.

In 2006, when my (Rose's) eldest daughter was small, we went shopping to buy a present for her best friend who would be turning five. Her friend was really excited about a princess-themed board game she had seen somewhere that had a twinkling musical slipper in the centre of the board. The game was pink and sparkly and very much what many people would think of as 'girlie'. So, into the catalogue shop we went, filled in a form to order the game, received our order number, and waited for the coveted game to come down the conveyor belt. After a few minutes we could see the box headed towards us in all its pink and glittery magnificence. We could also see it had a big label on it which, at first, we couldn't read. As it approached and the label became clearer, we were able to see what was written on the label. 'BOY'S TOY' it proclaimed in big upper-case letters! My daughter and I looked at each other a bit confused. Oh well, off we went home, removed the sticker, and wrapped it up ready for the party. Although we agreed it was a game that could be played by both girls and boys, we weren't sure why it should be labelled just for boys. This experience nagged at me, so I emailed the customer services office of the catalogue shop to ask about it. The response I received was very straightforward. All their competitive toys were designated 'boy's toys' and all their creative toys were designated 'girl's toys' – it was just a way of organising their inventory and, it was implied, I shouldn't be reading any more into it. After that I started paying closer attention to where games were placed in toy shops and department stores. While the princess game was an extreme example, the tendency to separate toys into creative/girls and competitive/boys seemed to be standard across most shops. This, we would suggest, is the outcome of the process Gina Rippon and her colleagues are referring to when they say that, in our culture we treat as self-evident, or even intuitive, that sex/gender differences emerge "from a causal pathway that runs from genes to hormone to brain to behavior to social structure" (Rippon et al., 2014, p. 2).

In the previous chapter, we looked at personality and individual differences and how the research methods in psychology that investigate these, such as psychometric tests, can and have been used to support practices that discriminate against women and other marginalised groups. In this chapter, we will focus on the research psychologists carry out on the body, to look at ways in which biological psychology has contributed to our understanding of ourselves. Of course, as we have all along, while we discuss the methods used (this is a book about methods after all) we will consider how some questions and some designs might produce results that consistently fit with existing practice rather than challenging it. From genes to hormones to brains, this chapter considers the complex relationships between biology and sex/gender and the ways in which feminist scholars are informing and shaping the discipline.

Measuring the body and measuring up – biological psychology and sex differences

According to Stephanie Shields (1975), back in the late 1800s when psychology was just getting its act together and establishing itself as a discipline, the emergence of the functionalist movement brought attention to the study of **sex differences**. In particular, the interest in Darwin and evolutionary theory underpinned research into the presumed different but complementary functions of males and females. At the time, Shields argued, the main theme of *evolutionary theory* in the social sciences "was the evolutionary supremacy of the Caucasian male" (1975, p. 739). Ideas around **phrenology** and **neuroanatomy** were popular and sex differences were mostly thought about in terms of the size and structure of the brain. So, when women's brains were found to be smaller than those of men, the assumption was made that this was the biological explanation for men's (presumed) intellectual superiority. When this claim was not substantiated by the data, the explanation shifted to argue that different parts of the brain were of different sizes in men and women. When it was not possible to establish a clear link between brain size (in whole or in part) and intelligence, the next move was to develop another evolutionary theory, known as the **variability hypothesis**. You may recall that the variability hypothesis came up in Chapter 2 when we mentioned the idea that men's brains were more variable than those of women, and that this was used to provide a rationale for the superiority of men. Variability had been established early on in Darwinian theory as a key mechanism for evolution. The argument goes something like this: more variability provides a greater likelihood of survival and thus a superior system.

However, as you've no doubt guessed, these claims did not go unchallenged. Mary Whiton Calkins (who was, coincidentally, the fourteenth – and first female – President of the American Psychological Association in 1905) was an early critic of this approach. You may recall that in Chapter 2, we pointed out that the studies in support of the variability hypothesis for sex differences didn't even consider or engage with the possibility that there might be any social or environmental factors at play. Whiton Calkins (1896) argued that it was impossible to make a distinction between the male and female intellect, as it was not possible to eliminate the effect of environment. Leta Stretter Hollingworth (1914) took this critique and applied a rigorously methodological approach to it. She challenged the assumption that all mental traits were normally distributed, which, she argued, was critical to the validity of the variability hypothesis. At the same time, there were far simpler explanations for some of the phenomena observed, other than sex differences were biologically based. For instance, the lack of comparable access to formal, and particularly university, education seems like it could be a reasonably important consideration. Hollingworth's methodological critique also pointed out that, importantly, social factors impacted not only the behaviour of participants but also the ways in which the data was interpreted. Eventually, the variability hypothesis lost favour, Shields (1975) argues, because it became more and more evident that the variation within each sex was far greater than that between the sexes and so the effect was trivial. We will return to the question of variability and the role of the normal distribution later in this chapter, as they are rather important to the arguments around sex/gender. For now, though, we'd just like to spend a little time on the issue of qualities and quantities in measurement because, in well over a hundred years, while the ways in which we 'measure' the body have changed, it is still widely assumed that performing measurements is indeed what we ought to be doing.

You may have noticed in your reading of psychology so far that biological psychology relies heavily on *quantitative measures* and the description of those measures. Biological psychology, maybe more than any other subdiscipline of psychology, sees itself as a natural science and, as such, adopts the methods of the natural sciences – a *hypothetico-deductive* approach – to knowledge production. As we discussed in Chapter 3, this approach requires that all relevant variables be measurable so they can be quantified, thereby allowing for statistical probability testing. As we also discussed in Chapter 3, this approach has a number of limitations, which means it is not appropriate for many issues of psychological concern. One issue that is particularly relevant to biological psychology relies on the translation of scientific interest into quantifiable variables, which are operationalised and subjected to experimental manipulation to produce outcomes which are statistically tested to provide findings, which are most often numbers, which must then be translated back into everyday language by the scientists conducting the research.

In their classic text *Laboratory Life* (1979), sociologists of science Bruno Latour and Steve Woolgar argue that this notion of the scientific method, the experiment, as the basis on which theories are confirmed or discarded is more narrative than fact and is inconsistent with observable laboratory practice. Latour and Woolgar describe scientific laboratories as messy places where data is rarely clean and scientists make decisions on what to include, what to discard, and what to develop. Importantly, these decisions are often shaped by environmental factors such as the researchers' access to equipment and funding, their relationships with other research teams, and so on. What Latour and Woolgar do in their exploration, is to step back from the quantitative aspects of the practice of science to look at the everyday qualitative context in which it takes place and by doing so find a very different 'science' than the one you might expect.

SECTION SUMMARY

- The functionalist movement in psychology in the late 1800s kicked off interest in the study of sex differences. At the time, ideas around phrenology and neuroanatomy which involved measuring the brain were popular.
- The functionalist movement received thorough and sustained critique from women psychologists who challenged it as 'unscientific'.
- Biological psychology is considered the most scientific of the subdisciplines in psychology.
- Based on their close observation of laboratory practices, Latour and Woolgar (1979) argued that the practice of science was much messier than we would expect, which impacts on what facts become established.

Genes

So, what does biological psychology focus on when studying the body? Well, many things, but in terms of the discussion of sex differences, the main areas are **genes**, **hormones**, and **brains**. We won't go into too much detail here, as there are many textbooks and websites available which cover this. In simple terms, what are referred to as the 'sex' **chromosomes** in our genes are labelled X and Y, with the vast majority of the population being either XX (female) or XY (male). While a small number of people do not fit this pattern (less than one in a thousand), chromosomes are generally understood to be **dimorphic** – that is, things that exist in two distinct forms. Things like gonads and genitals are similarly dimorphic in over 99% of the population. According to Daphna Joel (2012), who refers to the trio of genes-gonads-genitals as 3G-sex, these three Gs, as well as being almost completely dimorphic, are highly consistent with each other. That is to say, if someone has female genes, it is highly likely that they will also have female genitalia. Joel reckons, as a conservative estimate, that about 1% of the population do not follow this pattern. So, here are three things – Joel's 3G-sex – that support the notion that (most) humans are one of two kinds: male or female. If this is what biological science tells us, then what is the fuss about? Let's continue and see where it takes us.

Hormones

This gender dimorphism is the basis of what is often referred to as the **sex/ gender binary** – the idea that there are two types of humans: women and men. As we mentioned above, this distinction has shaped psychological science since its inception. However, hormones are much more complex and cannot be fitted easily into this dichotomy in spite of many efforts to do so. In fact, Hyde et al. argue that there is evidence from "behavioral neuroendocrinology findings that challenge the notion of genetically fixed, nonoverlapping, sexually dimorphic hormonal systems" (2019, p. 171). So what does that mean in practice? Fixed, non-overlapping, sexually dimorphic …

The assumption is often made that hormones are dimorphic – that is, **oestrogen** and **progesterone** are 'female' hormones while **testosterone** is a 'male' hormone. This assumption is based on the idea that the levels of these hormones in one's body are genetically determined and fixed. It's not difficult to follow this logic. It's the one we mentioned in the first paragraph of this chapter – that causal pathway that goes from genes to hormones (then to brain, behaviour, and social structure, but we'll get to that in a bit). So the argument is, if genes are dimorphic – and we have established that they mostly are – and they are responsible for hormone production, then it is reasonable to assume that hormones are also dimorphic and, importantly, that they are fixed. However, this is not actually the case. All of the so-called 'sex' hormones are produced by and are present in all our bodies. So they are not dimorphic in the sense that the 3Gs are. However, it is the case that different bodies have different levels of these hormones – at which point we can ask, are these fixed?

The first thing to note here is that levels of hormones in your body vary according to a number of factors, such as what you are doing and at what point in your life you find yourself. Hormones are not 'fixed' in the sense that the 3Gs are. They can vary quite a bit within individuals in response to social context and behaviours. For instance, when we are involved in a contest for dominance – say, playing a competitive game like the princess slipper game – our progesterone levels will increase. However, it is also the case that progesterone levels increase when we experience social closeness.

Before puberty, the difference in hormone levels between girls and boys is negligible. Although testosterone levels rise during puberty, the difference seen between males and females is small and the overlap is considerable (remember this was an issue with the variability hypothesis as well). In addition, women who are not pregnant have levels of oestradiol and progesterone much closer to those of men that to those of pregnant women. As Hyde et al. (2019) suggest, if we divide people into two groups according to their levels of what have been referred to as 'female' hormones, the obvious divide would be between pregnant women and the rest of the world.

Furthermore, Sari van Anders (2013), a **neuroendocrinologist**, has argued that testosterone has mostly been studied as a cause rather than a product of behaviour, an approach which lacks scientific rigour as we know that behaviour impacts on hormone levels. She suggests that rather than conceptualising testosterone in terms of male/female, it is more helpful to think of it as a trade-off between competition and nurturance. Van Anders further argues that our assumption that there are 'female' and 'male' hormones has made for bad science because instead of studying the impact of hormones on bodies more generally, much of the research has focused exclusively on 'male' hormones in men and 'female' hormones in women, and this limited perspective on hormone functioning has produced incomplete and biased knowledge.

The brain

As was the case for the study of hormones, feminists have argued that the study of the brain as 'female' or 'male' is methodologically flawed. The ***brain organisation theory*** that underpins some of the dominant theories around gender differences (Jordan-Young, 2010) suggests that our brain's development is shaped through the organising influence of prenatal and perinatal sex hormones, which produce sex differentiation of the brain. So we're back to that causal pathway that goes from genes to hormones and now to the brain (on its way to behaviour and social structure), and we know that feminist psychologists have challenged this assumption at every point. In Chapter 5, we summarised Hyde and colleagues' (2019) five challenges to the gender binary. In this chapter, we will examine one of these challenges – the evidence from neuroscience that refutes the idea that the human brain is systematically different between men and women.

The first thing to note is that the link between structure and function in the brain is not well defined. That is to say, the bits of the brain you can measure directly (e.g. its size, shape, and configuration) are not clearly and directly linked to what the brain actually does, and the behaviour measures we have for studying this. Although neuroscience is getting better at this (in the next section we'll introduce *fMRI technology*), there is quite a lot of **black boxing** required. In science and engineering, a black box is any complex device for which we can observe the inputs and outputs, but the inner workings are unknown. That means you can push a button or turn a dial and you know what will happen, the lights will turn on or the volume will increase, but you have no idea how it happens. While research has found differences in both brain structure and function between women and men, many scholars have pointed out that even the largest sex differences show considerable overlap. Hyde et al. (2019) have further argued that these average differences need to be considered in the context of other relevant data. For instance, the assumption is often made that these differences are innate or pre-programmed when this is not the case. Like the examples we looked at with hormones, these brain differences are often context dependent and vary across the lifespan. Joel points to those studies indicating that there are interactions between sex and environment, for instance between stress and ***cannabinoid receptors***, which provide clear evidence that sex is not the only determinate of brain structure and function. The final point, and you may have seen this one coming, is that these differences, it turns out, are not ***additive*** – they don't produce a typical male or a typical female brain. That is to say, when specific differences can be found, these differences are not "highly dimorphic in the population" (Hyde et al., 2019, p. 172), which means they don't divide the population clearly into two groups. Also, they are not "internally consistent in the individual" (p. 172), which means that all elements of the brain would need to be typical of females or typical of males. Instead, most people have some of both.

Daphna Joel and her colleagues (2015) conducted a study looking at brain structure using MRI data from over 1,400 human brains and found that the internal consistency was remarkably low. Based on these and other findings, Joel and Vikhanski (2019) have argued that the brain is *multimorphic*. As a result, they propose that each brain is a unique 'mosaic' comprised of numerous features – some that are more common in women, some that are more common in men, and some that are common to both. On this basis, they state that "human brains cannot be categorized into two distinct classes: male brain/female brain" (Joel et al., 2015, p. 15468)

Box 6.1: The allure of the average differences

As you will know, many of the studies carried out in psychological research look to identify differences between groups, often a control group versus an experimental group, but also men versus women. If you were to test thousands of men and women on lots of different variables, you would at the very least find slight differences between them. The larger the number of participants in the study (n), the more likely that you would find a significant difference as the power of the study would increase. However, this does not mean that if you picked a man and a woman at random, they would be different on this dimension.

This way of testing statistically for differences is based on the 'average difference' between groups. The idea of 'average difference' is very alluring. We think that it tells us something important about ourselves and other people – some might argue, why 'men are from Mars and women are from Venus'. Both Maccoby and Jacklin (1974) and Hyde (2005) published papers that relied on extensive evidence to argue very specifically that claims to the existence of sex differences are over-reported and that in fact they are limited to a very small number of variables. In spite of this, both papers are often cited as evidence for the very differences they were intended to dispel.

We hope by this point you can see the issues with claims of this kind and the way they reinforce our existing biases and prejudices. In this and the previous chapters, although we have discussed how weak the evidence is for most gender differences, we've also argued that asking about difference might not be the best way to proceed or lead to the best research. So, it is worth thinking about why we are so interested in these average differences. What does being able to say groups of people are different allow us to do? It allows us to treat certain groups differently from others, for instance providing more resources for disadvantaged groups. However, it can also be used to justify excluding some groups from societal resources. So it is always important to ask: why do we care about this particular difference?

SECTION SUMMARY

- In the discussion of sex differences, biological psychology has generally focused on genes, hormones, and brains.
- *Neurofeminist* Daphna Joel refers to 3G-sex (genes, gonads, genitals), which she identifies as being almost completely dimorphic and internally consistent. This appears to support the idea that humans come in two kinds: male and female. This has shaped psychology in unhelpful ways.
- Hormones are not dimorphic. They can be found in all our bodies, albeit at different levels. However, they vary not just between 'men' and 'women' but are also heavily influenced by age, stress, and countless environmental factors. The variation within gender categories is much greater than the differences between them. It has been argued that it is bad science to attribute gendered characteristics to hormones without considering the context.
- Feminists have argued that the study of brains as either 'female' or 'male' is methodologically flawed because differences in the brains of females and males are not additive or internally consistent. Most people have some elements more typically found in males and some more typically found in females, as well as areas that are not distinguishable based on sex.

What is fMRI testing and how has it revolutionised psychology?

Having referred to the work of Joel and her colleagues based on existing MRI data, this might be a good time to have a closer look at magnetic resonance imaging and its role in the collection of data in psychological research. Theories relating to differences in the brains of men and women date back to before it was possible to study the brain directly. Fortunately, the advent of fMRI technology opened up a world of possibilities. You may be familiar with fMRI scans – you may even have had one. Basically, *functional magnetic resonance imaging* (fMRI) is a technique developed in the 1990s to measure brain activity, albeit indirectly. Critics have referred to it as a form of modern-day phrenology. Phrenology is the (completely discredited) practice of measuring the shape and size of the skull to make claims about the mental abilities and character traits of the individual. It's an interesting artefact from the early days of psychology. You might well have come across a phrenology head (Figure 6.1) at some point sitting on a desk or a shelf in a psychologist's office, though the psychologist in question is very unlikely to be a phrenologist. I (Rose) have one that was given to me with humorous intent when I completed my PhD.

Figure 6.1: Phrenology head.

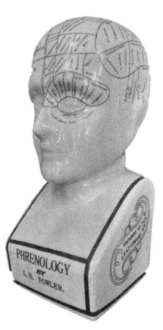

So, neuroscientists use this technique as a way to measure the brain. Unlike the phrenologists, however, neuroscientists have reason to believe there may be a relationship between these measurements of brain structure and brain function and that they may, ideally, be able to link these to behaviour. The MRI machine works by detecting the magnetic signal from hydrogen in water which allows it to detect changes associated with blood flow. When an area of the brain is 'in use', blood flow to that region increases. This process produces a 'picture' of the brain. Other neuroimaging technologies are available, including *electroencephalography (EEG)* and *positron emission tomography (PET)*, but in recent years fMRI has emerged as the favourite. fMRI is a promising yet limited technique. Unlike X-rays, it is non-invasive, has excellent spatial and good temporal resolution, and is easy to use – well once you know how. According to the Wellcome Centre for Integrative Neuroimaging (WIN, 2021): "Most fMRI investigators seek not to localize brain function but to map the parts of the system that act in different combinations for different tasks". So they are trying to examine the relationships of various activities within the brain. According to Hannah Devlin at WIN, fMRI is a more 'objective measure' of an individual's mental state than a tick-box questionnaire. This is not an uncontentious statement, which we will return to later. What there is general agreement on is that the technology is full of promise. It may also be the case that, as we currently stand, it is more promise than fact.

There are a number of limitations to fMRI scanning. Many fMRI studies rely on correlational data which, as you will know, does not allow you to make claims about causality. So, although we can say a certain brain activity is linked to a specific behaviour, how they interact remains unclear. At the same time, all fMRI data is representational, so you aren't actually seeing the brain activity itself, just an image captured of the movement of water molecules. This means that any data is mediated by the technology, which limits what information you can collect. Moreover, you might think that representation of the brain would be approached in the same way, but this is not the case. According to Bijsterbosch et al. (2020), different research teams take different approaches to reduce the fMRI data produced in order to analyse and interpret it; on top of that, these representations are sufficiently different that they have become an impediment to communication within the scientific community which hinders future development in the field. This may sound like they are being a bit silly, but actually it is a critical point. When we spoke earlier of Latour and Woolgar's work around the functioning of laboratories, we pointed out that many decisions are made that escape the strict limits of the scientific method. These decisions rely on many things, including (and here comes the broken record you've been hearing about throughout this book) what kinds of questions they are asking and all the assumptions that come with them.

It is also interesting how these representations of the brain are portrayed in both the media and academia.

Bijsterbosch and her colleagues also argue there is a broader 'sloppy science' issue going on akin to the 'bad science' argument we discussed earlier. Although, given the points we have already discussed in this book, you may be thinking that this might not be any truer of neuroscience than it is of any other approach. It suffers from many of the same issues we saw in Chapters 4 and 5. For instance, you may not be surprised to hear that the participants in neuroscience research are not representative of the population as a whole. According to Mamlouk, Dorris, Barrett, and Meitzen (2020), there is a notable imbalance in the use of males versus females as participants in neuroscience research. In their review of findings published across six key journals, they found that 26% of studies used male-only samples whereas a mere 5% used female-only samples. We won't even go into the representation of other diversity with respect to other markers of difference such as ethnicity, class, and age which are virtually non-existent (Duchesne & Kaiser Trujillo, 2021). Mamlouk et al. (2020) also found that sex/gender bias and omission are related to the research model used. Let us pause here to reflect back on Chapter 3, where we discussed different paradigms for knowledge production, and consider why some approaches may result in more unbalanced samples than others. Questions anyone?

Another issue that arises in these studies is the impact of **effect sizes**, which we also touched on in Chapter 5. Hines (2020) argues that, based on existing research, including the classic studies by Maccoby and Jacklin (1974) and Hyde (2005), there is little evidence of sex differences. She compares sex differences with differences in height, a more familiar measure, using **Cohen's d**. Let's examine this methodological point more closely here. Cohen's d, or **standardised mean difference**, is a measure of the **significance** of the difference found between two groups, usually once a **test of difference**, such as a **t-test** or an **analysis of variance (AnoVa)**, has already been conducted. The convention is that $d = 0.80$ and above represents a large effect, scores between $d = 0.80$ and $d = 0.50$ are considered to represent a medium effect, and those between $d = 0.20$ and $d = 0.50$ a small effect. This is one way of conceptualising it. Another is to consider the overlap of two groups at each of these points.

Looking at Figure 6.2, you can see that even at $d = 0.80$ the overlap in the data is considerable: 68.7% in fact. At $d = 0.50$ it is over 80% and at $d = 0.20$, which is conventionally understood to be a small effect, the overlap is 92%. This means that even for large effects there will be large numbers of individuals that go against the population-level pattern. Going back to Hines' use of height as a comparison for sex/gender difference claims, she states that height has a d of 2 – much higher than the numbers we've been discussing and substantially higher than the vast majority of sex/gender differences that have been reported. Now, we know that men tend to be taller than women, but we also know there is a lot of overlap, so we don't refer to it as 'female' height and 'male' height. So when you read that a small effect has been found indicating a difference between males and females on a specific variable, this is what it means. It can often be

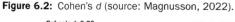

Figure 6.2: Cohen's *d* (source: Magnusson, 2022).

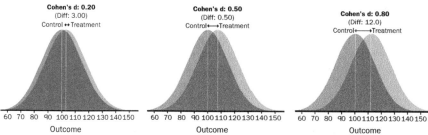

helpful to keep the visual image of these effect sizes in mind when you are reading about newly discovered sex/gender differences.

To summarise, there are a number of limitations to fMRI research that we need to be aware of: such studies rely on correlational data so causality cannot be established; the data are always representational rather than a direct measure; there are issues around how it is visually represented and the consistency of representation, which hinders communication between research teams; there are concerns around 'sloppy science'; biased representations of the population and, finally, a tendency to overclaim by reporting small effect sizes as meaningful. In fact, Logothetis, while maintaining that "despite its shortcomings, fMRI is currently the best tool we have for gaining insights into brain function" (2008, p. 877), warns that the conclusions that are drawn "often ignore the actual limitations of the methodology" (p. 869). There may be many reasons for why this is the case. Gina Rippon (2019) has argued that the approach taken with fMRI testing was problematic from its inception. According to Rippon, from the first studies in the early 1990s, the focus has been on finding biological evidence for 'robust' differences (again the issue around asking the right questions comes up) rather than exploring a phenomenon and, on top of that, the data tends to be interpreted in terms of existing stereotypical gendered characteristics.

This takes us back to the narrative and translational aspects of research that we discussed earlier. Quantitative research requires us to translate our questions into numbers and then back into our everyday language so we can say something intelligible about our area of study. With fMRI technology we use the findings to narrate 'who we are' based on our brains. In many ways, psychology is all about making sense of 'who we are'. What are we doing, then, when we tell a narrative about difference? How does this affect how we make sense of the data we collect and the findings from our analyses? In the next section, we look at research which claims to have found female and male brains and consider what we are being told about ourselves through this narrative. We will not be arguing that you cannot find differences in the brain but instead we'll be considering how these differences are used, what assumptions are made about them, and what they are understood to mean.

SECTION SUMMARY

- Functional magnetic resonance imaging (fMRI) technology is a fairly new, promising, and popular way of 'measuring' the brain. Neuroscientists use fMRI to explore the relationships between brain activity and behaviour. There are different approaches to analysing the data produced by this technology and they are not always comparable.
- fMRI studies have been critiqued for their lack of representativeness – most participants are white males from WEIRD countries.
- Sex/gender differences that have been found have small effect sizes and meta-analyses appear to indicate that there is very little evidence of sex differences.
- There are a number of methodological limitations around fMRI research. For example, because the effect sizes are so small, it makes little sense to define these two, mostly overlapping groups, as male and female. Also, there are translational aspects to this research, so it is important to avoid overinterpreting or overclaiming from limited scanning data.
- Neurofeminists have argued that neuroscience is asking the wrong questions and so getting the wrong answers (we bet you saw that one coming!).

How do people make sense of fMRI technology?

One of the most prominent theories around the idea of male/female brain theory has been proposed by Simon Baron-Cohen. In his book *The Essential Difference* he states, quite categorically, that "The female brain is predominantly hard-wired for empathy. The male brain is predominantly hard-wired for understanding and building systems" (2003, p. 1). On this basis Baron-Cohen has developed the 'empathising-systematising (E-S) theory'. According to this theory, 95% of the population has one of three brain types: the type E brain that prioritises empathising; the type S brain that that is better at systematising; and the type B which is the balanced brain. Baron-Cohen argues that more females show the E brain profile than males and more males show the S brain profile than females, so he refers to them as the female brain and male brain respectively. The type B, however, is dominant in neither males nor females. It is worth noting here that about two-thirds of the population, that is most of us, have neither a female nor a male brain.

Now, let's think about the logic here. Just because one group displays a behaviour more than another group (rather than exclusively), does it make sense to 'label' it as such? As we mentioned earlier, we don't refer to tall people as having a male height and shorter people as having a female height in spite of the fact that Cohen's *d* for height is considerably larger than that for the different brain types identified by Baron-Cohen. We might want to ask *why* we need to attribute sex/gender dimorphism to these different types of brain. What purpose does it serve if we know, from Baron-Cohen's own evidence, that they are not dimorphic at all? Besides, the E-S theory focuses on just two aspects of brain function, when we know that the brain does much more than just empathise and systematise. This brings us back to Joel and Vikhanski's (2019) claim that sex/gender differences in the brain, regardless of their origins, rather than adding up are mixed up in a complex mosaic so that each individual will have a distinct pattern. Some brain areas, at some points in time, in some environments, will show signs of fitting in with a pattern that is more common in females and at others one that might be more common in males.

See and hear for yourself

You won't be surprised to find that there has been 'lively' debate about the topic of male and female brains. If you are keen to read some more, take a look at this exchange between Cordelia Fine and Simon Baron-Cohen in *The Psychologist*. The debate starts here: https://thepsychologist.bps.org.uk/volume-23/edition-11/battle-sex-differences – and you can follow the links from this page to the responses and counters by each of them.

This debate around the notion of male and female brains took place between Simon Baron-Cohen and Cordelia Fine, author of *Delusions of Gender* (2005) and *Testosterone Rex* (2017), in the pages of the British Psychological Society's publication *The Psychologist* in 2010 and 2011. The debate picks up some of the points we've been discussing here as well as others you might find interesting.

See and hear for yourself – follow the discussion on sex, gender, brains, and behaviour

Del Giudice, M., Puts, D. A., Geary, D. C., & Schmitt, D. P. (2019). Sex differences in brain and behavior: Eight counterpoints. *Psychology Today*, 8 April. https://www.psychologytoday.com/gb/blog/sexual-personalities/201904/sex-differences-in-brain-and-behavior-eight-counterpoints

Fine, C., Joel, D., & Rippon, G. (2019a). Eight things you need to know about sex, gender, brains, and behavior: A guide for academics, journalists, parents, gender diversity advocates, social justice warriors, tweeters, facebookers, and everyone else. *Scholar & Feminist Online*, 15. https://sfonline.barnard.edu/neurogenderings/eight-things-you-need-to-know-about-sex-gender-brains-and-behavior-a-guide-for-academics-journalists-parents-gender-diversity-advocates-social-justice-warriors-tweeters-facebookers-and-ever/

Fine, C., Joel, D., & Rippon, G. (2019b). Responding to ideas on sex differences in brain and behavior: Agreements, ghost disagreements, and points for continued debate. *Psychology Today*, 17 July. https://www.psychologytoday.com/gb/blog/sexual-personalities/201907/responding-ideas-sex-differences-in-brain-and-behavior

Why might it be that the authors of the papers tend to be gendered – either all male or all female?

In a more recent attempt to potentially mediate the debate around gendered brains, Yi Zhang, together with an international team of 30 scientists (2021), used neuroimaging data from 9,620 participants to explore the relationship between biological, psychological, and environmental factors and how they impact on the development of brain function and connectivity. Whilst acknowledging that our understanding in this area is still limited, their findings, they claim, indicate that androgynous brains – those that do not show gender-typical structure or functioning – are associated with better mental health. Their advice based on these findings is that we need to avoid extreme stereotyping in our education of children and adolescents. This may remind you of the discussions of Bem's work around androgyny in Chapter 5. In fact, Zhang et al. draw explicitly on Bem's work in their research. So you can see how the arguments around gender differences research, because they are conceptual, can often be applied to the notion of difference in a variety of domains and subdisciplines. And to loop back, it is worth noting that Baron-Cohen has also suggested that a balanced brain is potentially preferable, having himself proposed an 'extreme male' brain theory of autism (Baron-Cohen et al., 2005) whereby the systematising brain is held to be linked to autism spectrum disorder.

Box 6.2: Check out *The Conversation*

'Male' vs. 'female' brains: having a mix of both is common and offers big advantages – new research

https://theconversation.com/male-vs-female-brains-having-a-mix-of-both-is-common-and-offers-big-advantages-new-research-153242

SECTION SUMMARY

- Simon Baron-Cohen has argued that there are male and female brains but neurofeminists have argued that the research does not support this designation, as the vast majority of male and female brains fall into the same category. There are identifiable differences between the brains of males and females, but these are highly context dependent, and as we saw earlier in chapter, the differences are neither additive nor internally consistent.
- A large population study conducted by a group of 30 neuroscientists from across Europe suggested that androgynous brains are associated with better mental health. These arguments resonate strongly with those proposed by Sandra Bem in the 1970s and are subject to similar critiques.

Neurofeminism and the future of sex and gender

In this chapter, we've looked at some of the research around the biological basis of sex/gender differences and we've drawn on the work of various feminist scholars to explore some of the claims that have been made in this area, particularly the work often referred to as **neurofeminism**. Neurofeminism is "a field of critical neuroscience that challenges neuroscientific assumptions, methods and interpretations of data that reinforce sexism" (Duchesne & Kaiser Trujillo, 2021, p. 1). Part of this, you will not be surprised to hear, is about asking the right questions. For instance, Rippon has argued that a question such as 'Are there male and female brains?' is not the one to ask. This question structures, as all questions do, the possible answers and limits what you can learn about a phenomenon. Is that what we want to know about the brain? Even if sex is embodied, neuroimaging and other measurements of the body will not tell us how it got there, as Fausto-Sterling (2019) reminds us.

As Fine (2010) points out, neurological explanations for the difference in roles and achievements of men and women have been evolving along with the technology. According to Rippon (2019), women's 'difference', often understood as inferiority, has over the years been attributed to brain weight, the ratio of mass to brain, the variability hypothesis, the relative size of specific areas of the brain, and most recently connections to whatever 'lights up' in an fMRI. She humorously refers to these as the Whack-a-mole myths of sex/gender differences – as soon as you whack one down the next one pops up. The most pressing acknowledgement is probably that the complexity of the brain makes it particularly susceptible to "overinterpretation and precipitous conclusions" (Fine, 2010, p. xxvii)

For this reason, Rippon et al. (2014) have proposed four key principles that should inform all neuroimaging research design, analysis, and interpretation.

- *Overlap.* The awareness that characterising sex/gender differences as dimorphic (the idea that there are two clearly distinct groups) is not accurate because the overlap makes it difficult to identify reliable difference.
- *Mosaicism.* An acknowledgment that gender is multi-factorial rather than one- or two-dimensional, and 'masculine' and 'feminine' characteristics tend to be weakly inter-correlated or not at all.
- *Contingency.* Gender stereotypical behaviour can be affected by framing, training, and general life experience, all of which are variable across time and place. In the nineteenth century, women were seen as unfit for university education; in many countries today, women outnumber men in these institutions.
- *Entanglement.* Fausto-Sterling (2000) has argued that as a social phenomenon, biological sex and gender are 'entangled', one affecting the other. As we learn more about the brain through technologies such as fMRI, it is becoming clearer that the brain-behaviour relationship is not one-way. In spite of the importance of the study of neuroplasticity in neuroscience, it has received very little attention in the work on sex/gender.

See and hear for yourself
Here is an excellent TEDx talk by Daphne Joel titled 'Are brains male or female?': https://www.youtube.com/watch?v=rYpDUO4Oyzc

Beyond these more specific issues, in recent years there have been wider discussions across academia around the growing Open Science movement. Open Science refers to a set of practices that increase the transparency and accessibility of scientific research (van der Zee & Reich, 2018), such as: the preregistration of research to avoid publication bias; moving away from the reporting of significance and towards effect sizes; the use of meta-analysis and others. In their discussion of Open Science, Persson and Pownall offer a feminist reading of the movement, suggesting that it "may be the novel and disruptive tools needed to dismantle claims about hardwired brain sex differences" (2021, p. 493).

Box 6.3: The Open Science/ Open Research movement

You may be familiar with recent efforts to move towards a more open research culture. This has been referred to as the Open Science – or, more inclusively, the Open Research – movement, and aims to open up access to the research process. According to its supporters, this movement is disruptive and inherently critical – it doesn't take decontextualised science for granted – and these fundamentals for openness promote equity and inclusion. In September 2021, the journal *Psychology of Women Quarterly* published a special issue on Feminist Psychology and Open Science (https://journals.sagepub.com/toc/pwqa/45/4) that discussed many of the possibilities afforded by the movement. We recommend you take a look if you would like to find out more. We would also, however, like to add a note of caution. There have been some concerns that without careful vigilance open research might simply reproduce structural privilege – sometimes referred to as #bropenscience (Whitaker & Guest, 2020).

SECTION SUMMARY

- Neurofeminism challenges assumptions in neuroscience that reinforce sexism.
- Four specific considerations have been proposed to inform the future of neuroimaging. Researchers should attend to overlap, mosaicism, contingency, and entanglement.

Concluding thoughts

In 1914, Helen Thompson Woolley suggested that: "The general discussions of the psychology of sex, whether by psychologists or by sociologists show such a wide diversity of points of view that one feels that the truest thing to be said at present is that scientific evidence plays very little part in producing convictions" (p. 372). Resonantly, over a century after Woolley's claim, Rippon, Eliot, Genon, and Joel (2021) have critiqued the role of hype and hyperbole in research reporting and how it distorts neuroscience. Partly because it is inherently interesting to the public and thus the media, and partly because its association with 'science' makes it sound more convincing, it is often the case that such studies are picked up unproblematically and used to validate sexism in society. Rippon et al. recommend that for this reason, it is particularly important, both ethically and methodologically, that when neuroscience communicates findings around the question of sex/gender differences in the brain, this research should be held to the highest standard. "Given the real costs of entrenched sex/gender disparities across society, neuroscientists have a duty to prevent the spread of misinformation about the neural basis of such differences" (Rippon et al., 2021).

As we've said before, this is not to argue that biological differences don't exist but rather to take a more critical look at them. Few feminist psychologists would argue for a 'gender blind' approach, for instance. We know that when science ignores sex/gender we risk making women invisible. As Criado Perez (2019) has cogently argued, a lack of acknowledgement of gender leads to a world built for men. This argument extends to people of colour, those with disabilities, and any other group that is marginalised. This latter point is critical for neuroscience and neurofeminism, both of which, according to Duchesne and Kaiser Trujillo (2021), fail to meaningfully consider intersectionality in the research process. Similarly, our critical engagement does not argue that biological measurements are not meaningful. As Elizabeth Wilson (2015) has argued, we need to take science seriously, but we need to be careful about taking it literally when we have extensive evidence that it is embedded in social narratives and practices.

CHAPTER SUMMARY

- Our culture often assumes that, with respect to sex/gender, there is a direct causal pathway from genes to hormones to brain to behaviour to social structure.
- This chapter has explored the evidence and claims made around sex/gender and different elements of this pathway. While there is strong evidence for the dimorphism of the 3Gs (genes, gonads, and genitals), the relationship starts to dissolve at the hormone level. By the time we reach the brain, the relationship with sex/gender become very complex – like a mosaic – and heavily mediated by the environment.
- Scientific practice is far more nuanced and contextual than the scientific method would lead us to believe.
- Neurofeminism has added richness to theorisations of gender within biological psychology through expertise in and critique of the dominant research methods.

7 Developmental psychology: observing human development

Learning objectives

Study of this chapter should enable you to:

- Consider the relationship between developmental psychology and feminist approaches to knowledge production.
- Review the theory and research around attachment in developmental psychology.
- Consider various critiques and feminist engagements with 'attachment' and the 'Strange Situation'.
- Become familiar with some of the different uses of observation in psychological research methods.
- Explore the role of feminist ethnography in developmental psychology.
- Reflect on the role of language in the production of knowledge in developmental psychology.

You may be familiar with the saying 'Give me the child until he is seven and I'll give you the man', generally attributed to St Ignatius de Loyola (founder of the Jesuits, an order of the Roman Catholic Church dedicated to education, research, and culture). Let's set aside for a moment the sexist language to consider the intention of the quote. What it is alluding to is the importance of education but also the belief that the first few years of life are decisive for the future of the person. Sigmund Freud (we don't think we need to introduce him) similarly argued that there was something 'special' about the early years and that childhood lays the foundations for the rest of one's life. It makes sense from this perspective that any issues that arise during this period might re-surface later on, in the form of deviant behaviour or 'maladjustment'. This position has been taken up more generally by psychoanalytic – as well as a number of other psychological – approaches to development and continues to be widely held in the psychological literature. It should not be surprising to find, then, that developmental psychology has historically tended to focus on the child. Indeed, in spite of admirable efforts to extend the focus of the subdiscipline to adulthood, this project is still a growing one. It often takes place through other subdisciplines such as health or organisational psychology. By and large, developmental psychology continues to focus primarily on, and be seen as, the study of childhood. For this reason, while acknowledging that excellent feminist and critical research is being conducted in development across the lifespan, in this chapter we will focus on childhood. The reasons for this are both psychology's historical foregrounding of children and, as this is a methods book, that it allows us to consider the challenge of collecting data from participants who may not be very participative such as babies and toddlers. It has been argued that some methods suit some subdisciplines better than others and that, for this reason, observational research is particularly common in developmental psychology. So we'll talk a bit about that as well.

In Chapter 6, in our discussion of neuroscience and sex/gender, we finished on the notion that science is embedded in social narrative and practices. Here we turn to how these social narratives and practices play out in developmental psychology to examine the challenges of studying children. This chapter examines the use of observational research for exploring children's social and emotional development. Drawing on early studies on attachment and maternal sensitivity, we investigate how parenting – and specifically mothering – was conceptualised in them and how it has impacted current research. We explore the potential for 'mother-blaming' embedded in this early research and make connections to contemporary research in the context of 'intensive parenting'.

Attachment theory (theory) and the Strange Situation (method)

The focus on the child in developmental psychology in particular, and in psychology more broadly, is often about trying to understand how we first make sense of the world. For John Bowlby (1958), the most important thing we do as early as possible is attach to our mother/caregiver. According to Bowlby, we have an innate need to form emotional bonds with a caregiver in the first six months of life. Drawing on Freudian and evolutionary theory, he developed an *attachment theory* which moved away from psychoanalysis but continued to prioritise the early years as critical to healthy development. He argued that attachment performed two functions. The first was to keep the baby safe, and the second to regulate their emotions after negative experiences. The idea behind Bowlby's work was that our relationship with our mother serves as the template for all future relationships. He saw attachment as a dyadic relationship between the mother and child with any disruption of this bond resulting in negative outcomes for the child. It's probably not lost on most people that this image resonates quite strongly with traditional understandings of mothering, including those portrayed in art and religious iconography. The Madonna (Mary with Jesus), for instance, is a dominant and powerful image within Christian cultures that serves as a reminder of the importance of this relationship. Burman (1995) argued that the relationship between mothers and children is so preeminent that you cannot define them independently of each other. However, what then happens within these approaches is that the mother somehow becomes peripheral to the child, who becomes the priority. Sharon Hays (1996) talks about this as the 'sacred child' being prioritised over all else – the mother's role now limited to ensuring her child's success.

It is worth stepping back for a moment to consider what was going on in the wider society at this time. Bowlby was developing his theory in the aftermath of the Second World War. During the war, with so many men off fighting, many women joined the the labour force which provided them with financial independence. However, with the end of war it became necessary to free up these jobs for the returning soldiers, so Bowlby's warning of the effects on the developing infant of maternal depravation was the perfect motivation for women to retire to their homes to mother their children. The psychological theory fitted perfectly with the needs of society at the time. It provided jobs for the men and care for the children, but what of the women?

None the less, attachment theory became a dominant theory in developmental psychology and in broader psychological understandings of relationships throughout the lifespan, including loss and bereavement. There have been many critiques of this approach over the decades and we will get to those later in the chapter but before we do so, let's return to our discussion of research methods. Whilst based on Bowlby's experiences, both personal and professional, the research evidence for this theory was sparse until Mary Ainsworth entered the field.

Box 7.1: Relationship between theory and method

The theory that underpins a researcher's approach to their study and the method that they use to conduct the study are closely interwoven. However, it isn't a one-to-one mapping. Just because two projects use the same method, you can't assume they also take the same theoretical approach. For instance, observational methods are used by researchers from very different paradigms and epistemologies. The methods psychologists use in observational studies can range from tightly structured observation in an experimental context, as is the case in Bowlby and Ainsworth's work discussed in this chapter, to the observation of already occurring behaviour when conducting participant observation as we described in Chapter 3 and we will discuss later in this chapter. What the researcher is doing may look similar, but it is based on asking very different questions which, as we know, can produce very different findings. Keep this in mind as you read through the rest of this book.

Ainsworth became interested in the concept of attachment. However, while Bowlby's initial proposal was that it was an all-or-nothing process – there either was or wasn't a bond – Ainsworth believed that there were different kinds of attachments and individual differences in the quality of these. In order to test this, Ainsworth developed a method to investigate how attachments might vary between different children and called this the 'Strange Situation' (Ainsworth et al., 1978/2015). This involved bringing the mother and child into a room, separating the two of them, and then bringing them back together in different situations to observe their behaviour (see Box 7.2 for a detailed explanation of what this involved).

Box 7.2: The Strange Situation (Ainsworth et al., 1978/2015)

The 'Strange Situation' is a structured observational procedure developed to assess the attachment behaviour of infants and toddlers with their caregiver. It involves eight stages, during which the child is observed through a one-way mirror.

1 The mother and baby enter the playroom.
2 The child is encouraged to explore.
3 A stranger joins the mother and baby.
4 The mother leaves baby and stranger alone.
5 The mother returns and the stranger leaves.
6 The mother leaves the infant completely alone.
7 The stranger returns.
8 The mother returns and interacts with the child.

The researcher observes and measures four interaction behaviours:

- Proximity and contact seeking
- Contact maintaining
- Avoidance of proximity and contact
- Resistance to contact and comforting.

Between 1964 and 1967, Ainsworth carried out what is referred to as the Baltimore Longitudinal Study of Attachment. The sample consisted of 26 white, middle-class, US mother-infant pairs from families in which the parents were married and living together. The procedure was conducted both in the lab and in the family homes. The emphasis in the study was on observing the behaviour of the participants rather than rating a psychological construct. The researchers assigned scores based on a set of behaviours rather than on single acts. According to Ainsworth and her colleagues (1978/2015), the Baltimore studies were able to validate Bowlby's attachment theory.

Ainsworth proposed three types of attachment with a fourth being added later (Main & Solomon, 1990):

- Insecure-Avoidant (Type A). The infant will ignore the mother when she leaves or returns and will not explore.

- Secure (Type B). The infant will explore while mother is present, be upset when she leaves and happy when she returns.
- Insecure-Resistant (Type C). The infant shows distress and is clingy and difficult to comfort.
- Disorganised (Type D). The infant is confused, indecisive, and disoriented.

Ainsworth's early empirical work in the US (before Type D was introduced) indicated that 70% of infants were classified as 'secure'. The remaining 30% were split evenly between insecure-avoidant and insecure-resistant.

In the Preface to the 2015 classic edition of *Patterns of Attachment*, Waters, Bretherton, and Vaughn argue that "Conceptualizing the four caregiving and interaction constructs, translating them into measures, and relating them to attachment outcomes in a truly modern and theoretically grounded way was one of the singular accomplishments of the Baltimore study" (1978/2015, p. xx)

Based on the findings of the Strange Situation, Ainsworth and colleagues further developed the Maternal Sensitivity Scale. According to Waters et al. (2015), these remain the key instruments in infant-mother interaction and have been used for studies across the lifespan. The Maternal Sensitivity Scale includes measures for:

- sensitivity to signals;
- cooperation with ongoing behaviour;
- acceptance of age-related requirements;
- physical-psychological accessibility.

In a ***meta-analysis*** of 66 studies, De Wolff and van IJzendoorn (1997) found only a moderately strong relationship between ***maternal sensitivity*** and attachment. However, Waters et al. (2015) describe the scales as some of the most elegant descriptions of behaviour used in psychology.

See and hear for yourself

BBC Mind Changers radio programme on Mary Ainsworth hosted by Claudia Hammond: https://www.bbc.co.uk/programmes/p00f8n6q

Mary Ainsworth's work has been hugely influential and so has been widely reported. Here are some examples you might find interesting:

Psychology's Feminist Voices website has an entry on Mary Ainsworth which talks about her experience of being a woman in psychology: https://feminist-voices.com/profiles/mary-ainsworth

The Simply Psychology website also has an entry on Mary Ainsworth which includes a short video of the Strange Situation procedure in action: https://www.simplypsychology.org/mary-ainsworth.html

Ainsworth and Bowlby shared their work and interest in attachment theory and research for many years. In 1991, they wrote a paper together providing a historical account of their common project. An interesting point made there is that for both of them, their initial interest, even before graduate training, was not in infant attachment *per se* but rather in personality development. Would it be unreasonable to suggest that this admission might provide some insight into the kind of questions they were asking, and so what methodological approaches they used?

SECTION SUMMARY

- John Bowlby's attachment theory is based on psychodynamics and evolutionary theory. He believed that the child forms an attachment in the first six months of life (most often with the mother) that serves as the template for all of the child's future relationships.
- Attachment theory is a dominant theory in developmental psychology.
- Mary Ainsworth came up with the Strange Situation – a research method that allowed her to explore the attachment relationship between a child and their mother.

Critiques of attachment theory and methods

As we mentioned above, there have been many critiques of both attachment theory and the Strange Situation over the decades. Here we focus primarily on the method and divide these critiques into methodological, feminist, and intersectional.

A clear methodological critique that you've come across before in this book was raised early on in the history of the Strange Situation. That is, in controlling the environment, the procedure is stripped of context producing a highly artificial environment that lacks ecological validity. For instance, it only identifies the type of attachment to the mother. More recent research has shown that the child might have different types of attachment to different people such as their father, a grandparent, an elder sibling or, as was the case for Bowlby, their nanny. Similarly, the same child might show different attachment behaviours on different occasions. As the values of both the mother and the child are replaced with those of the researcher's values, we're not sure why certain behaviours are taking place from the participants' viewpoint. Why assume that a child that does not get distressed when their mother leaves the room is unhappy? As Hays points out (1998), this ignores the fact that separation from mother is a normal part of growing up. It might be the case that the child is repressing their distress – but is that the only possible, or indeed most likely, explanation? Similarly, the infant might be clingy because they feel unwell. We'll come back to this critique in the next section but, just to return to the point that by limiting the responses to the questions being asked, what can be observed also becomes limited as well. You could argue that this is unavoidable, and we would agree; however, if that is the case, then it needs to be acknowledged.

Another of the earliest queries that was raised about the Strange Situation procedure, as you might expect, was around the cultural specificity of the findings. Remember the Baltimore study included only a small number of participants and not a very diverse sample at that. A ***meta-analysis*** of Strange Situation research by Van IJzendoorn and Kroonenberg (1988) found that there were high levels of both intercultural and intracultural variation. That is to say, not only were there differences between different places but also between different groups of people in the same place. The issue wasn't so much that the behaviours identified by Ainsworth et al. weren't observable – they were. However, the distribution of infants across the different attachment styles was highly variable in ways that reflected the values of the community in which the research was taking place. For instance, in countries like Germany, where individual independence is highly valued, more children were classified as Type A Insecure-Avoidant. Analogously, Japanese infants, who are rarely separated from their mothers, were more likely to be classified as Type C Insecure-Resistant. There was even more variability, according to Van IJzendoorn and Kroonenberg, between different groups within the US where the original Baltimore studies were conducted. Gaskins argues that for each culture, healthy attachments "cluster around the culture's ideal balance point" (2013, p. 40) between, for instance, dependence/independence or the need for intimacy/autonomy. What comes into sharp relief here as well is how what constitutes a 'normal' childhood is predefined by the researchers along with the unquestioned assumption that a 'normal' childhood is superior to an exceptional one. Both of these are widespread in the developmental psychology literature as well as the broader discipline.

Box 7.3: What is 'normal'

The use of the term 'normal' in psychological research methods is worth paying attention to. Like many words we use in psychology, 'normal' can be used in an everyday sense or it can be used to mean something very specific. For instance, in statistics normal is defined as those scores within two standard deviations from the mean. This may seem quite innocuous but when it is used to refer to people, and particularly children, it can have some very unpleasant consequences. We've already discussed how what is normal can often be defined in relation to a white, middle-aged, middle-class man from the global North, and thus exclude the experiences of many of us who don't belong to or fit into that category. This can be particularly worrying when it is applied to children. What is a 'normal'? A society based around graphic representation of communication, that is writing, makes dyslexia a problem. A society based around multi-levelled buildings and transportation makes certain physical conditions difficult to manage. These contexts might make it seem like these impediments are naturally determined, but it doesn't take

much consideration to see that they are the result of how we choose to organise ourselves. Crafter (2015) has argued that assumptions about 'normal'
development have been taken up unproblematically by many teachers, parents, and young people themselves and we need to question these. In her
book *Deconstructing Developmental Psychology* (2017), Burman draws on
intersectional feminist theory and research to question the assumptions surrounding child development, critiquing the role that developmental psychology has played in how we make sense of children and 'normal' childhood that
has all the hallmarks of WEIRD cultures. According to Crafter, Burman's book
has "provided the space to tell a different story about developmental psychology" (2015, p. 398). If you have an interest in developmental psychology that
makes use of an intersectional feminist lens, we highly recommend this book.

SECTION SUMMARY

- In spite of its enormous success, there have been critiques of attachment
  theory and the Strange Situation almost from their first introduction.
- The methodological critique focused on many of the same issues that
  we've already read about in previous chapters: lack of ecological validity,
  the prioritisation of the researcher perspective, and the cultural specificity
  of the findings.

Feminist critiques of the Strange Situation

Many feminist researchers concurred with these methodological critiques of
attachment theory and the Strange Situation. According to Sharon Hays, the
basic theory of attachment was developed from "small unrepresentative samples of and poorly designed experiments on monkeys and on children raised in
wartime orphanages" and "is arguably simple-minded and shallow because it
fails to recognize the deep complexity of child development" (1998, p. 789). For
Susan Franzblau, "The notion that there is some inherent glue that unites
mother and child, simplifies, depoliticizes and removes from historical review
the exploitative and oppressive conditions under which most women reproduce
and mother" (1999, p. 29). In the following paragraphs, we'll explore the reasoning for these claims in more detail but for now we'd like to call your attention
to the repeated claims that the theory is 'simple'. While we all appreciate simple
explanations, these often replicate the status quo and exclude voices from the
margins such as those of feminist critique.

Maternal deprivation, maternal sensitivity, and other carers

Kirsty Budds (2021) has argued that it is difficult for women to resist parenting
advice that is presented as being in the best developmental interests of their

child. And this remains the case even when it compromises the mother's own interests. We couldn't agree more. Motherhood is a powerful discourse. It is closely tied to notions of femininity and worth. In particular, the notion of the 'good mother' is a difficult one to resist for a woman. At the same time, the role of mother is open to scrutiny at any time by virtually anybody. Attachment theory positions the mother at the very centre of the narrative, yet she is there *only* to serve the interests of the child. The Strange Situation is, in effect, a judgement of the quality of a woman's mothering. As such, this approach pits the interests of the child and the mother against each other, adjudicating in favour of the child – of course! But why pit them against each other in the first place? Franzblau has argued that "the ideology of overdetermination and control as applied to women's reproductive abilities and the needs of children is implicitly structured in the language of attachment, by virtue of its specification of the tasks of woman as mother" (1999, p. 23). Basically, attachment theory requires the woman as mother and in doing so functions to control how women are and can be.

You may have noticed that throughout this chapter we have stuck with the traditional language of 'mother' and 'maternal' rather than 'caregiver' and 'parental'. We've intentionally avoided this more generic terminology. This is partly because the original studies included only mothers, no matter how often they are referred to as parents. Also, even when the language used is gender neutral, the descriptions of and the assumptions about the participants are highly gendered. The conflation of caregiving, mothering, and parenting in many developmental psychology texts can be highly misleading (see Box 7.4 for a discussion of this point).

Box 7.4: What's in a word?

In this book we've tried to bring your attention to the importance of language. The psychological literature around children, families, and parenting is a prime example of this, including much of the work we discuss in this chapter. When reporting research findings in this area, authors are careful to use terms such as 'parent' and 'caregiver'. However, the data and examples that are provided refer almost exclusively to mothers and mothering. The writing, while using gender-neutral terms, often assumes the mother and often uses the language of 'mothering'. Examples such as maternal deprivation theory and maternal sensitivity are some of the most obvious examples. Next time you are reading a text about parenting, be it in a book or a newspaper, pay attention to how the parent is described and what assumptions are made about the role. Is the use of non-gendered terms alone sufficient to make the language less sexist?

The intensive mothering agenda

In her classic text on the cultural contradictions of motherhood, Sharon Hays (1996) argued that attachment theory underpins the prevalent parenting ideology in the US and other high-income counties such as the UK – that of ***intensive*** *parenting*. It is a direct response to the requirement for exclusive mothering embedded in attachment theory and methodologically established through the Strange Situation. According to Hays, intensive parenting is "child-centred, expert-guided, emotionally absorbing, labor intensive and financially expensive" (1996, p. 8). And who is doing this parenting? Well you might not be surprised to hear it is primarily mothers. By defining women exclusively in relation to their children, argues Budds (2021), it serves to isolate and overburden women. It is worth mentioning that this positioning is so successful because it offers women a positive and agentic role – who doesn't want to be a good mother? As a result, this process reinforces the gendered division of labour that already exists in our society. Hays further argues that intensive parenting causes guilt and exhaustion, which "diminish women's chances for advancement in the political and economic realms and contribute to the reproduction of larger gender inequalities" (1998, p. 789). And so intensive parenting is both bad for gender equality and unrealistic. Moreover, it fails to consider how this type of mothering impacts on the gendering of children. What do young girls learn about their role in society when this is the way in which childcare becomes understood? It is worth considering again here the point we raised in Chapter 2 about the importance of accessible childcare in facilitating possibilities for women both personally and professionally.

Intersectional critiques of the Strange Situation

The ways in which attachment theory positions women, like most things, vary along with other markers of difference. Like others before her, Budds (2021) has pointed out how most of the research on intensive parenting continues to be carried out on white, middle-class women and that the small number of studies of other groups indicates the way 'good mothering' is constituted varies. Quinn and Mageo (2013) refer to attachment theory as profoundly ethnocentric, based as it is around culturally biased assumptions around methodology such as the 'decontextualised' lab experiment we've already discussed. Accordingly, anthropologists have come to conceptualise the approach as a 'folk theory' which relies on the experiences of the hegemonic class as universally representative and normative. For Quinn and Mageo, the confounding of the theory and the method has meant that the importance of the meaning of the child-caregiver relationship requires a broader critique and they recommend other, more appropriate methods (we will get to these in a bit) that allow for the consideration of non-maternal caregivers such as fathers, grandparents, extended family, neighbours, and elder siblings, as we suggested above. One example of how interpretation is crucial to the understanding of the Strange Situation can be found in Weisner's (2005, p. 89) description of the mother of a child identified as 'insecure-avoidant':

> But the mother proudly commented that: 'This is what I have been working for by having him be with other kids and families while I am working. Look how independent he is! See how he can play be himself?' The mother was a single parent by choice. She had told us about her goals for independence for herself and her child, the importance of living a pro-feminist kind of family life, as she defined it, and her efforts to establish an ongoing convoy of

friends and caretakers for her child to provide relational support and secu-
rity. The meaning of the behaviors revealed in the SSP (Strange situation
procedure) were positive to her, and her construction of the situation reflected
a valorizing of her child's life path as well as the mother's. For her, the behaviors she saw meant that they both were on a positive, adaptive, virtuous
path. Her child was not in fact 'at risk' for 'attachment disorder' nor relational insecurity in her frame of meaning, whatever the scoring of her child's
behaviors might have been (and in fact, longitudinal follow-up through adoles-
cence did not show any signs of risk either).

This example highlights how a move away from the normative 'nuclear' family
where the mother stays at home to intensively parent the child, changes the
way in which the relationship between the two is made sense of.

Franzblau (1999, p. 22) suggests that feminists should be asking questions about
the language of attachment theory. Does it carry implicit social class divisions with
it? How might these class divisions play out in how the theory is used? Importantly,
Franzblau asks us to consider if the theory serves to marginalise some groups of
women or importantly to play women off against each other. You'll be familiar with
the idea that there is an unbreachable divide between working mums and those
that stay at home. Having considered these, she asks us if, regardless of its history
of misogyny, attachment theory might be useful in helping us understand the
issues and problems of motherhood and childcare. She concludes that, unfortunately this is not the case: "Only if what women do is disentangled from essentialist
arguments that she is naturally given to doing it, which requires that we look at
issues of class exploitation, racism, political and economic expediency, can we
move to a helpful understanding of the issues of motherhood and childcare" (1999,
p. 30). We can think back here to the discussions in Chapter 6 around arguments
that position gender as dimorphic and extrapolate very specific biological characteristics into the social world without evidence or justification.

SECTION SUMMARY

- Feminist scholars have been particularly critical of this approach, accusing
  it of being overly simplistic.
- The feminist critique focuses on the way this approach positions women
  as having to be always at the disposal of their children.
- Although recent texts tend to use 'caregiver', 'parent', or something that
  is more gender neutral, this is illusory. It always falls back into gendered
  language with the expectation of traditionally gendered behaviour.
- Attachment theory has fed into the intensive mothering agenda, which is
  an emotionally absorbing, labour-intensive, and financially expensive
  approach to parenting that impacts negatively on the mother in particular.
- There have also been intersectional critiques that point out the ethnocen-
  trism inherent in the design. Other feminist critics have pointed to the classed
  nature of the studies and their failure to represent non-normative lives.

Observational methods

It has been proposed that observation is the basis of all empirical attempts to understand the world (Angrosino, 2005). The critiques we've presented of the Strange Situation, however, move us in quite a different direction from what might otherwise be seen as a straightforward observation of behaviour. We have argued throughout this book that our findings are limited by the questions we ask. Accordingly, the questions we ask in an observational study limit what is observed. Although observation is something we all do every day as we go about our lives, as a methodological tool it requires us to take a systematic approach to the process. One of the ways in which this is done is through the use of *coding schemes* and this is precisely what Ainsworth and her colleagues did. Informed by attachment theory, they focused on some behaviours and not others and attributed meaning to these behaviours in particular ways. This is what is known as *structured observation*. It is a *deductive method* which allows us to measure behaviour and conduct analyses using *inferential statistics*. So it is a quantitative method, with all the limitations that we've already discussed at length. (You might want to think back to Figure 3.1 about the elements of a research paradigm.)

There are other ways of conducting observational research which are *inductive*. These are more often qualitative. Rather than using a coding scheme and working out which pre-existing categories certain behaviours fit into, the researcher makes detailed notes of the behaviour and then looks for patterns. This is generally referred to as *naturalistic observation*. Many researchers take this one step further and conduct what is known as *participant observation*. Participant observation is a method of data collection that requires the researcher to immerse themselves in the day-to-day activities of the participants in an attempt to gain an understanding of the participants' experience. It is often used as part of methods such as *ethnography* or *participatory action research*. Both of these have been embraced by feminist researchers as being more closely aligned with values such as equity and appreciation of subjective experience. We'll talk more about the latter in the next chapter. For now, we'll focus on ethnography and why many critical and feminist developmental psychologists believe it is a better way of doing research.

Ethnography in feminist psychology

Ethnography is a 'you had to be there' approach to research. The researcher immerses themselves within a particular group or culture for a period of time to capture the perspectives and experiences of the participants. If became popular in the early twentieth century amongst anthropologists, in particular, who used it to study remote communities. At that time it was intended to measure and quantify observations and, while this was fieldwork, it was expected that the researcher would maintain some kind of conceptual distance from the 'objects/subjects' of study. More recently, qualitative ethnography has become a popular research approach in a number of disciplines including psychology. Along with participant observation, the approach also often includes dense observations of life, interviews with group members, and analyses of documents and artifacts. Such qualitative ethnographic analysis brings all this information together and analyses it inductively to be able to say something about the participants in context.

Ethnography produces rich and complex data and lets the researcher observe children first hand. It allows the observation of more subtle and nuanced behaviours because it focuses on the 'insider' perspective. For this reason, in recent years, many developmental psychologists have taken up ethnography. Corsaro (2020), for instance, has argued that ethnography is the best approach for conducting research on children's friendships. He was interested in how children talk about friends rather than imposing his own definition and measuring them against it. He spent time with children, playing with them, listening to them, and becoming a member of their 'group', video recording their interactions and making detailed notes. Corsaro was able to capture nuanced and complicated influences that had been lost using more traditional methods. He was able to evidence that children as young as three could talk about friendship in complicated and abstract terms – much younger than previous research had suggested.

Alison Happel (2012) conducted a study with fifteen 11–14-year-old girls in an afterschool club to learn how they made sense of 'girlness'. Happel collected data for a year through participant observation and interviews along with club documents. In this way, she was able to investigate how these girls made sense of gender binaries, as well as exploring their relationship to race, class, and sexuality. Happel was able to evidence the social contextual nature of these identity categories and the hard work that goes into them. Once again, the depth and detail of the study was very different than if she had simply measured their responses in a controlled manner.

While the use of feminist ethnography in developmental psychology provides many benefits, there are some important issues that we need to consider. For instance, feminist scholars have highlighted the importance of the relational nature of the research. There are issues about how authentic the researcher can be in these situations if they are both conducting research and a group member – is this ethical practice? Also, because ethnographic relationships can be quite close, there is a risk of exploitation – intentional or otherwise. According to Leavy and Harris (2019), feminists have argued that attention needs to be paid to *reciprocity*. Researchers should make sure there is some benefit to the participants in a study. Feminist ethnography should improve the lives of those in the community being researched. It is not uncommon for ethnographers to see themselves as 'allies' of their participants by helping to make their voices heard.

In the context of developmental psychology, listening to children and allowing them to be heard is a key part of an ethnographic study. However, it is worth asking if it is ever possible for an adult to be a 'member' of a children's group. There will always be power differentials between adults and children so ethnography – and in particular feminist ethnography – with children needs to be permanently reflexive and respectful to participants. One way to address this is to engage with children in their full context, including those that care for and work with them such as their families and teachers as well as their social groupings. The controlled and limited context of attachment theory and the Strange Situation writes these important relationships out of their story and thus their experience of their world.

Conclusion

Erica Burman has suggested that "developmental psychology occupies a key role in the maintenance and regulation of prevailing power relations and gendered social arrangements" (1991, p. 141). In this chapter, we've looked at one of the dominant theories in developmental psychology, attachment theory, and its method, the Strange Situation, through a feminist and intersectional lens to see how this might play out. As a result, Burman argues, that there are two main issues in the relationship between feminist research and developmental psychology. Developmental psychology regulates and evaluates women as mothers, stigmatising women who don't necessarily have a choice around some of the practices around mothering (e.g. whether they work or not). At the same time, it sets up milestones in normal development creating anxiety and competition between women. We have seen how approaches such as those embedded in attachment theory underpin these issues.

CHAPTER SUMMARY

- This chapter looked at the relationship between developmental psychology and feminist approaches, in particular attachment theory and its empirical method, the Strange Situation.
- It summarises the basic tenets of the approach and then discusses the critiques: methodological, feminist, and intersectional.
- It looks at the usefulness of observation as a method in developmental psychology using the Strange Situation as an example. It addresses different types of observation: structured observation, naturalistic observation, and participant observation.
- The chapter then considers the possibilities of using ethnography as a developmental method.

8 Social psychology: helping others, field experiments, and community-based research

---

Learning objectives

Study of this chapter should enable you to:

- Become familiar with classic laboratory experiments in social psychology designed to examine bystander intervention as a form of helping behaviour, and experiments 'in the field' by exploring applied feminist research on bystander intervention into sexual violence.
- Understand how helping can be conceptualised in different ways – as heroic actions taken in emergency situations, often with strangers, or as everyday acts of care – and that these different ways of seeing helping make visible or obscure some people's experiences.
- Become aware of qualitative methods, including interviews and participatory action research, as alternative approaches to producing knowledge with and alongside marginalised communities in order to effect social change.

In 1964, a young woman, Kitty Genovese, was stabbed and murdered outside an apartment block in New York City. Weeks later, the *New York Times* reported that 38 witnesses had observed the attack, yet none had attempted to intervene. As well as prompting much media speculation about why these witnesses failed to intervene, this incident is widely credited as motivating social psychologists John Darley and Bibb Latané to explore under what circumstances people do, or do not, help each other in emergency situations. Indeed, their original paper published in 1968 opened with a description of the Kitty Genovese murder. This became known as ***bystander intervention***. This fast became a classic study in the field of ***social psychology***. Social psychology examines how individual or group behaviour is influenced by the presence and behaviour of others. This chapter explores different methods of studying helping behaviour (also known as ***prosocial*** or ***altruistic*** behaviour) which is a key field within social psychology.

Using Kitty Genovese's murder as a springboard for their research, Darley and Latané conducted a series of **experiments** to test their ideas about bystander intervention. Speculating that witnesses to the Kitty Genovese murder knew that other people were watching (perhaps "by seeing lights and figures in other apartment house windows"; 1968, p. 377), Darley and Latané wanted to investigate whether the presence of other people would lessen the extent to which any one individual felt a personal sense of duty to offer help (known as **diffusion of responsibility**). In their experiment, students were individually shown to a room in which they were to discuss personal problems associated with college life with other students through an intercom (to avoid embarrassment). The intercom system was rigged so that only one person could speak at a time. During the conversation, one of the students "underwent what appeared to be a very serious nervous seizure similar to epilepsy" (p. 378). During the apparent emergency, only the (recorded) voice of the student having the seizure could be heard in which the student explicitly asks for help five times. Participants knew that others were also aware of the event, but they did not know how anyone else was responding or whether they were offering assistance. To determine whether the number of other bystanders influenced whether any one individual offered help, participants were led to believe that they were part of a two-person, three-person, or six-person group. In fact, in each case, there was just one 'real' participant plus other individuals who posed as students, including the one who apparently had a seizure. The researchers measured the time it took for participants to respond to the emergency – from the start of the fit to the time the participant left the room to seek help (or until 6 minutes had elapsed, at which point the experiment was stopped). Eighty-five per cent of the participants who thought they alone knew of the emergency reported the seizure before the victim was cut off, and all reported it before 6 minutes had elapsed. In contrast, only 31% of those who thought four other bystanders were present reported it quickly, and 38% never reported the emergency before 6 minutes had passed. Arguing against the common assumption that bystanders failed to intervene because they are apathetic or indifferent, Darley and Latané suggested that situational factors (like the absence or presence of other witnesses) could influence people's willingness to offer help. They optimistically concluded that, "If people understand the situational forces that can make them hesitate to intervene, they may better overcome them" (p. 383). Using this type of experimental method, these two researchers went on to develop a model outlining the situational factors which influence a bystander's decision to help, including noticing and labelling an event as an emergency or as problematic, feeling personal responsibility for helping, and judging that one has the necessary skills to act (Latané & Darley, 1970).

Darley and Latané had little to say about the gender-based violence underpinning the 'emergency situation' which prompted their research (a man was later arrested for Kitty Genovese's murder). However, recently researchers and activists working to promote sexual violence (SV) prevention have adopted bystander intervention training as an alternative to information-based or attitude-change initiatives. Bystander training programmes train individuals to intervene in risky sexual situations or when witnessing sexual harassment. Key to this approach is a focus on directly changing behaviour (rather than attempting to change attitudes in the hope that this will impact behaviour).

SECTION SUMMARY

- The 'classic' experiments by social psychologists Bibb Latané and John Darley on bystander intervention aimed to investigate why people did, or did not, offer help to strangers in emergency situations.
- As social psychologists they were interested in how the social context (the presence of other bystanders) influenced behaviour rather than focusing on the individual characteristics of those offering help.

Bystander intervention in action

In 2010, the National Union of Students (NUS) published *Hidden Marks: A study of women students' experiences of harassment, stalking, violence and sexual assault* in which they reported the widespread sexual violence experienced by women students at UK universities. Some of the key findings were that:

- One in seven survey respondents has experienced a serious physical or sexual assault during their time as a student.
- Over two thirds of respondents (68 per cent) have experienced some kind of verbal or non-verbal harassment in and around their institution. This kind of behaviour – which includes groping, flashing and unwanted sexual comments – has become almost 'everyday' for some women students.
- More than one third of respondents reported that they sometimes felt unsafe when visiting their university or college buildings in the evening.
- More than four in ten victims of serious sexual assault had told nobody about what had happened to them. (NUS, 2010, pp. 3–4)

Following this, in 2014 Public Health England commissioned the development of *The Intervention Initiative* – a facilitated bystander intervention educational programme – for use by all English universities to prevent violence, abuse, and coercion. *Field experiments* have been conducted in UK universities to evaluate the effectiveness of this intervention. Field experiments are experiment which occur in natural settings (like UK universities) rather than a psychology laboratory (like Darley and Latané's experiment described above). The advantage of field experiments is that they are conducted in the actual settings in which the behaviours typically occur. In other words, if sex violence and harassment is common in universities, it makes sense to conduct research in them. Field experiments are valuable because they have greater *ecological validity* – they are closer to 'real life.' We are going to look in more detail at an example of a field experiment of the effectiveness of a bystander intervention education programme rolled out in UK universities, but if you want to know more about bystander intervention training and its application in different settings, see the *See and hear for yourself* box below.

See and hear for yourself

Put 'bystander intervention training' into your favourite search engine and have a look at the many different examples generated.

- Notice the many different areas that bystander intervention training has been applied to (workplace bullying, bullying in schools, etc.)
- Find out what is included in this training and how people are being encouraged to intervene to prevent sexual violence

Here are some examples which you might find interesting:

Hollaback.org – a global organisation which aims to end harassment in all its forms: https://www.ihollaback.org/bystander-resources/

The University of the West of England's intervention initiative website: www.uwe.ac.uk/interventioninitiative

The UK government's website on interventions to end intimate partner and sexual violence: https://www.gov.uk/government/publications/interventions-to-prevent-intimate-partner-and-sexual-violence/bystander-interventions-to-prevent-intimate-partner-and-sexual-violence-summary

---

To test whether the bystander training in The Intervention Initiative was effective, Rachel Fenton and Helen Mott (2018) conducted a field experiment. This is an example of ***applied research*** – research that attempts to provide practical solutions to everyday problems. The intervention that they tested was a ***community-level intervention*** because it targeted a specific community of individuals (university students) and was delivered collectively (to a group of students at the same time – or to a whole university at a time). To assess whether the intervention is effective at changing bystander behaviour, the researchers adopted a pre- and post-test design. This means that participants complete questions *before* taking part in the bystander training, and then again *after* they have completed the training. By comparing each individual's score before and after training, researchers can assess whether the training has had an impact. This is known as a ***repeated measures design*** because participants *repeat* completion of the questionnaires before and after the training.

The researchers had originally intended to compare a group of participants who completed the intervention with a ***control group*** of participants who did not complete the bystander training. One of the difficulties with field experiments is that the researchers do not have as much control over the research situation. In this case, not enough participants in the control group completed the questionnaires, which meant that the researchers were unable to make this comparison. When conducting experiments 'in the field', the complexities of real life mean that the research often does not go quite to plan! There are other considerations in field studies – for example, researchers might want to test the *feasibility* of an intervention. This includes assessing how *sustainable* the intervention will be in the community (i.e. will it be easy to implement and maintain once the research is completed), and the *acceptability* of the intervention (i.e. will students engage with the intervention). To aid this, the intervention was scheduled formally into the curriculum for a cohort of Law students at a large university in the southwest of England. This meant that *all* of the students in the cohort would receive the intervention rather than being delivered only to those students who expressed an interest in participating. As you can perhaps imagine, students who would be most keen to engage in bystander intervention training to lessen sexual abuse on campus might also be the students who would already be most likely to intervene if they witnessed harassment. In this way, conducting a community-level intervention avoids this kind of self-selection bias.

So, what did the bystander training intervention involve? The intervention is designed to take participants through the different stages of bystander intervention identified by Latané and Darley, moving from inaction to action. Sessions 1–5 aim to help students to recognise sexual and domestic violence as a problem. These sessions aim to raise people's awareness that violence exists along a continuum of problematic behaviours and to improve their knowledge of risk factors. In addition, these first sessions aim to encourage students to feel responsible for reducing sexual and domestic violence by developing critical awareness of their own attitudes about sexual/domestic violence as well as developing empathy for victims. Sessions 5–8 address the important action stage. These session help students to develop the capacity and skills to be able to intervene safely and effectively through planning and skills practice.

To measure whether the intervention was effective, the researchers used a range of questionnaires which focused on participants' thoughts and feelings about sexual violence and about helping. These included measures assessing:

- attitudes and beliefs about sexual violence;
- readiness to take responsibility for offering help;
- participants' confidence in their ability to offer help;
- participants' intention to offer help.

Although the researchers managed to recruit over 350 first-year Law students to initially participate in the research, only 131 of these completed questionnaires both before and after the intervention. This 'drop out' (or *attrition*) is a common problem with research that is conducted 'in the field', especially when participants are to be tested on more than one occasion. Of course, research which takes place over an extended period of time (*longitudinal* research) is very useful for assessing whether any change resulting from an intervention is sustainable. In other words, an intervention might result in a change of behaviour immediately following its implementation, but will these changes still persist 6 months, 1 year, or 5 years after the intervention?

So, was this intervention successful in changing students' attitudes and behaviours – were they more likely to intervene if they witness sexual or domestic abuse after completing the bystander intervention training? Students who participated in the programme were significantly less likely to accept rape or domestic abuse myths (e.g. women lie about rape because they regret having sex with someone, or because they want attention) after completing the bystander training than they were before the training. They were also significantly more likely to feel confident about taking action as a bystander, more likely to feel ready to help and take greater responsibility for helping, and to show a greater intention to help. But statistical significance is not as important as **effect size**. Although it is important to know that the bystander training had an effect, we also want to know whether it had a small, medium, or large effect on students' likelihood of intervening as a bystander. This is the effect size. Although these findings were statistically significant, there was a larger change in students' attitudes than there was in students' intentions to intervene when witnessing sexual or domestic abuse. More disappointingly, engaging in the bystander training programme had no significant effect on students' actual engagement in bystander behaviour. Although this shows how difficult it can be to change people's behaviour, it is a great example of feminist social psychology in action.

SECTION SUMMARY

- We have explored how field experiments are less easy to control than laboratory experiments but are often used to study the effectiveness of interventions designed to change people's attitudes or behaviours.
- Looking at the example of interventions designed to encourage people to intervene in risky situations which might result in sexual violence, we have explored how social psychological research is put into action.

Heroic helping or constant caring?

So far, we have focused on social psychological research on bystander intervention as a specific type of helping behaviour. The recent application of this research to sexual and domestic violence shows that it can be applied in the real world. When Latané and Darley started their research on bystander intervention, they were specifically interested in helping in 'emergency' situations. Social psychological studies of helping have typically been confined to short-term encounters with strangers. Alice Eagly and Maureen Crowley (1986, p. 283) referred to this type of helping as 'heroic helping' – risking one's own life while saving others from harm – and noted that heroic helping is embedded within societal values about masculinity and men's social role. According to *social role theory*, the unexpected, risky, non-routine rescuing of others in emergency situations is the kind of helping behaviour that is expected of men, and fits neatly with other aspects of masculinity such as being adventurous, strong, daring, courageous, and brave. To a large extent, then, social psychologists have focused on the kind of helping behaviour expected of men. Remaining somewhat invisible is the type of helping behaviour feminists argue is typically expected of women. The female gender role is associated with nurturing and caring for others, where women are expected to put the needs of others above their own. Feminist quantitative research has helpfully documented how the burden of caring for others falls disproportionately on women, and the detrimental effects this has on their mental health and wellbeing – see Box 8.1 for some illustrative examples.

Box 8.1: The gendered burden of care

Unpaid care work is care which is provided by family members or friends within a household for its members. This includes personal care like bathing, showering, getting dressed, or applying creams, as well as housework like doing the washing up or laundry, vacuuming, cooking, and cleaning. Because of the gendered nature of domestic and reproductive roles, women and girls are often expected to assume unpaid domestic work and care:

- Women are responsible for the majority (76.2%) of unpaid care work globally. Women spend an average of 201 days on unpaid work during a year, compared to 63 days spent on unpaid work by men (ILO, 2018a, p. xxix).

Care work, and especially unpaid or informal care work, is often perceived as low value. Since the 1970s, feminists have advocated for women's caring roles to be recognised as 'work' and launched the Wages for Housework campaign, which argued for recognition and payment for all caring work inside and outside the home. You can watch an early Wages for Housework campaign video here: https://the-lcva.co.uk/videos/5d8b5449178db841024acebd.

This work continues to the present day in the context of the Global Women's Strike – an international multiracial network campaigning for recognition and payment for all caring work for people and the planet. You can find out more about their work, and how to join in the action here: https://globalwomenstrike.net/.

Nevertheless, unpaid care work remains largely invisible and undervalued in mainstream economics despite estimates from the Office for National Statistics that unpaid household work in 2016 contributed over th1 trillion a year to the UK economy, which was equivalent to 63.1% of gross domestic product (GDP) (ONS, 2018).

Women and girls are also overrepresented in paid care work, which is typically poorly valued and increasingly precarious with zero-hours contracts, agency work, temporary employment, and so on.

- Of the 136 million workers in the health and social care sectors worldwide, 70% are women (ILO, 2020).
- Around 80% of the world's domestic workers are women (ILO, 2018b).

As if this were not shocking enough, Arlie Hochschild (2012) drew attention to the 'second shift', whereby women complete caregiving and household chores *in addition to* paid employment. This was particularly pertinent during COVID-19. Looking specifically at the UK, and based on a large, nationally representative study of UK adults:

- women spent about 15 hours per week on average doing housework in April and May 2020, while men spent less than 10 hours per week doing so during the same period;
- women spent on average 20.5 hours per week on childcare/home schooling in April, increasing to 22.5 hours per week in May, while men spent about 12 hours per week on childcare/home schooling in April and May.

Within couples, women undertook 64% of housework and 63% of childcare, and were more likely to reduce their paid working hours (21% mother only vs. 11% father only) or change employment schedules (32% mother only vs. 18% father only) (Xue & McMunn, 2021).

As this research demonstrates, when we think like a feminist, and ask questions rooted in the everyday experiences of women and girls, a very different approach to helping behaviour emerges. An approach which focuses not only on 'heroic helping', but highlights the routine, everyday drudgery of helping and caring for others. Quantitative research enables feminist researchers to draw attention to patterns in social behaviour, to name inequalities, and to provide a basis for activism for social justice. One of the limitations of this approach is that it is often only able to provide limited information about the contexts in which this behaviour takes place (***context stripping***), and about people's ***subjective experience*** and how they make sense of caring/helping behaviour. Given these limitations, feminists and other critical researchers have sought alternative ways to research people's lives and experiences – including experiences of helping.

SECTION SUMMARY

- We have explored the importance of understanding the concept of helping in multiple ways, including ways which best reflect the reality of many women's lives. Moving from thinking about helping in emergencies to thinking about everyday acts of care foregrounded the substantial burden of caring work routinely undertaken by women.
- Quantitative research is an excellent tool for identifying patterns in helping behaviour – like who is/isn't involved in childcare and housework.

Qualitative work on helping

A different way of exploring helping behaviour is qualitative research. Qualitative research involves collecting and analysing non-numerical data (e.g. text, video, audio) to understand people's opinions, experiences, or concepts through which they make sense of their experiences and the world they live in. To illustrate this, we draw on a study by Jacqueline Mattis, Nyasha Grayman, Sheri-Ann Cowie, Cynthia Winston, Carolyn Watson, and Daisy Jackson (2008) about everyday acts of helping in a low-income, urban community in New York City, USA. Looking through the lens of place (Chapter 2), these researchers thought that to understand everyday acts of helping, and how these connect to the identities and social positions of the people involved, research needs to be embedded in the communities in which people live. In this sense, qualitative research aims to be context-rich.

Specifically, their research was designed to address three shortcomings in the existing (largely quantitative) research exploring how helping is related to gender, race, ethnicity, class, age, and urbanicity:

1 A focus on individual-level – particularly intrapsychic – factors, to instead examine the ways that helping is linked to social identities and broader social forces.

2 Quantitative empirical work treats race, class, gender, and urbanicity as discrete independent variables (for example, studies looking at whether members of a specific racial group are more or less likely to help than members of another racial group). This fails to account for the reality that individuals are neither singularly, racialised, gendered, nor classed beings. It fails to account for *intersectionality*. As the authors note, socially produced behaviour such as helping "cannot reasonably be viewed as a product of either one's gender, one's race, or one's class. Further, the lived meanings and ramifications of our various identities cannot be 'controlled'" (2008, p. 419), as quantitative studies often aim to do.

3 Existing work has failed to consider how identities (such as identifying as a woman, African American, working class) are "steeped in complicated histories and systems of meaning that become all the more complicated when they are woven together" (2008, p. 419). Efforts to understand how helping is shaped by such identities needs to take this into account.

To try to address these shortcomings, the researchers adopted a qualitative approach to exploring how identities and social locations shape people's willingness to help others. To better understand the community with which they were working, the researchers spent time (several months) getting to know the residents and community stakeholders (e.g. ministers, community activists), and working with them to identify the questions or community needs that the research might address. The research team also spent time volunteering within the community – for example, acting as a chaperone to young people on trips as part of a local summer camp, developing a library in a local community centre, and leading workshops. Volunteering enabled the team to build relationships with community members, and for community members to assess the credibility and trustworthiness of the team.

Let's pause for a moment to consider these actions through the lens of ethics. Qualitative researchers often work with a different set of assumptions about how (good-quality) knowledge is produced. Quantitative researchers working within a positivist approach think it is important to be objective, neutral, and value-free when conducting research. From this perspective, it is important to remain distant from participants in order to have this impartial viewpoint from which to understand what participants say and do. Getting close to participants – by spending time with them or joining in activities – risks muddying the waters and introducing bias. How can researchers study people objectively if they are building relationships with them? For feminists (and other scholar-activists) this distance between the researcher and the researched (those whom the research is about) can be problematic. Lots of research/knowledge has been produced which has failed to accurately account for the perspective of marginalised groups. This led to calls for marginalised groups to be included in deciding what research questions should be asked, how research should be conducted, and what information should be produced. This is summed up in the slogan 'Nothing about us, without us'. Researchers also reflected on how 'keeping their distance' from participants who were sharing time and intimate life experiences with them was problematic, and that responding to descriptions of difficult life events with neutral or non-committal answers felt unsympathetic, inappropriate, or downright abusive. Feminists began to advocate for a different ethical approach to research – one which rests on the idea of reciprocity between researchers/researched, which acknowledges the power differential between the researcher and researched and tries to minimise it.

Okay, so let's circle back to the research methods that Mattias and the team used to generate knowledge about how people's willingness to help others is shaped by identity and social location. The researchers decided to use the archetypical qualitative method of ***interviews***. In simple terms, an interview is a conversation with someone – this conversation is often structured by a series of questions or topics which relate to the research question. Follow-up questions, comments, and probes are used to explore more deeply with participants their responses to the initial questions (known as a semi-structured interview). The research team interviewed 40 adults (18 women, 22 men) who were living or working in a low-income housing community in New York City. The interviews centred on two key questions: (1) 'Please tell me about a specific situation in which you saw (or heard about) someone in this community going out of their way to do something to help someone else', and (2) 'Please tell me about a time in the past year when you went out of your way to help someone who is not related to you'. To explore these questions further, the research team used follow-up questions which focused on participants' motivations for behaving altruistically: 'What do you think made them do __?', 'What made you do __?' The interviews lasted 90–120 minutes and were audio-taped. So, as you can see, qualitative research often involves a greater investment of time and energy on the part of research participants as well as researchers.

The interviews were analysed by identifying repeated themes in what different participants said about their experiences of helping. The researchers identified four overarching themes:

- narratives revealed that social identities work together to create different patterns of vulnerability and, consequently, different needs among particular groups of individuals;
- individuals' movement across particular lines of identity (e.g. class) helped to shape their subjective sense of responsibility to care for others;
- intersecting social identities shaped individuals' commitment to care for particular identity groups;
- intersecting identities worked together to shape people's perceptions of altruists.

We can see in this research a feminist-inspired attention to power. What this qualitative research reveals is the messy, complex, multi-layered ways in which social expectations of helping come together to create vulnerabilities regarding whether or not to help each other. Consider the following two extracts from interviews with participants in this research, both of which could be considered examples of bystander intervention. In the first, Paul, a man in his early thirties, describes intervening when he witnesses the police "beating up" some Black boys by "picking the kids (boys) up and slamming them down on the concrete". Concerned about the boys, Paul explains his decision to call the police and to lie about the presence of a gun:

> I thought someone was gonna get killed … I lied to make them come around. …You see, things like that is worrisome and bother you. You know, that could be me. I might be walking down the street coming from the store and got mixed up in that.
>
> (Mattis et al., 2008: 421).

Witnessing or personally experiencing assault, harassment, or public humiliation by the police, and intervening to protect other members of the community from police maltreatment, was explicitly reported by the men (especially those in their twenties, thirties, and forties) who participated in this study. Here, age, race, gender, and urbanicity work together to mark young, urban-residing Black men as particularly vulnerable to institutional police violence. That Paul intervenes by calling the police highlights the ambiguous and contentious position of state power as simultaneously a form of social control and (potentially) care. Moreover, Paul reports having to lie to the police in order to secure assistance for these young men, indicating that he is unsure whether state help will be forthcoming without this sense of heightened risk. For Paul, his own sense of vulnerability ('that could be me') is evoked by shared community location ('walking down the street coming from the store') and racialised identity, which mark him as vulnerable to police violence.

Similar ideas about vulnerability to state interventions are apparent in the second example, where Nicole describes providing informal care to 'a little girl' in her community whose mother had 'gone away and left her at home'. Nicole explains that they 'could have, you know, did the legal thing and called the police and have them take her and do everything', but instead they temporarily look after the girl until 'her mother was okay and back on her feet'. In response to a question from her son about why she offers this informal care, Nicole responds:

> I said, 'Well, she can end up some place where she might be molested, she might be raped, the people won't take care of her or things like that ... we didn't want her life to be turned up any more than what it was'.
>
> (Mattis et al., 2008: 422).

As Nicole's story demonstrates, adults in this study often engaged in altruistic behaviours that were intended to protect children and mothers from the actions of the child welfare system, recognising that such systems may fail to protect a young, poor, Black girl. Qualitative research invites us to enter into the life worlds of research participants, to understand how the world appears to them and the ways in which they make sense of being-in-the-world. Inevitably, our own social identities and locations as readers and researchers (in relation to race, class, gender, and urbanicity amongst other things) will shape our responses to Paul and Nicole's stories.

SECTION SUMMARY

- In this section we have explored the rich, contextual detail that it is possible to gain by using qualitative research methods like interviews.
- We have seen how we can pay attention to intersectionality, power, and gender in research on helping behaviour by understanding this behaviour in the context in which it occurs.

Participatory action research

In August 2005, Hurricane Katrina hit the US city of New Orleans causing widespread flooding, displacing many people from their homes and disrupting their everyday lives. With the purpose of promoting self- and other caring in this post-disaster context, university researchers M. Brinton Lykes and Holly Scheib (2016) partnered with community-based African American and Latino health promoters using antiracist feminist participatory action research. We will use their account of this process to explore participatory action research (PAR) as a research method in psychology.

Figure 8.1: Stages of conducting participatory action research.

Simply put, PAR is an approach to enquiry which involves researchers working together with people to understand a problem or difficult situation and change it for the better. PAR is not a method of conducting research as such, since it can involve quantitative or qualitative data and a range of data collection tools. For example, Lykes and Scheib used photographs and visual methods in their research (which they call photoPAR). PAR can be thought of as an approach or orientation towards research, as there is no one set way of going about it. Figure 8.1 gives an overview of the typical stages involved in doing PAR.

So, let's look at how Lykes and Scheib put this cycle into action in their research in post-hurricane New Orleans.

Understanding the research context

Bringing an antiracist and feminist lens to understanding the difficulties faced by communities following Hurricane Katrina, the authors spend time in their paper explaining to readers the socio-political and economic context of New Orleans. This mirrors the time they spent as researchers getting to know this context (although they were also both long-term residents in the city) in order to understand the differential impact of the hurricane on different communities within New Orleans. They note the increase in racial and economic inequalities in the city in the years prior to the storm, with high crime rates, low-wage jobs, and a high poverty rate. In addition, they note that following the storm, many areas of the city, but especially those areas populated by non-white and low-income residents, lacked basic services such as hospitals, schools, housing, public transport, and power. In order to be effective, then, Lykes and Scheib argued that disaster relief efforts need to recognise structural inequalities and tailor responses to the diverse cultural, linguistic, racial, and gendered needs of survivors.

Working in partnership

A key feature of PAR involves working in partnership. This takes the goals of democratising the research process a little further than in Mattis and colleagues' (2008) research. In PAR, university researchers and community-based collaborators become *co-researchers* working together to identify the important research questions, design the research, collect and analyse the data, put the data into action to create change, and communicate the research to others. In Lykes and Scheib's (2016) study, collaborators included the two white, university-based researchers who authored the paper, two health promotion programme coordinators (one a Caribbean migrant and one from Latin America), four African American and three Latina community health promoters.

It takes a lot of time and energy on the part of all the co-researchers to ensure that the team works well, to develop a shared vision for the research, and share and develop research skills. In this project, the researchers organised a number of team-building workshops in which they could get to know each other, understand the ethics and practice of PAR, and create safe spaces for sharing and hearing each other's stories. The co-researchers were invited to bring in a personally meaningful photograph (examples included family photos, life events, important places or contexts), and to explain its significance before inviting another group member to develop a further story based on what they learned about that person and their photograph. This exercise helped to achieve a number of important aims:

- it provided a way of learning by experience the process of eliciting and sharing photo-stories which they would use in the research;
- by collectively reflecting on their own stories and emotions across ethnic, linguistic, class, and national differences, the discussion facilitated understanding of intersectionality as a framework for the research;
- sharing stories facilitated the co-researchers' self- and other-awareness, communication skills, and a shared language for talking about experiences;
- as traditional distinctions between service providers and clients were broken down given that everyone (including co-researchers) was affected personally and professionally by the hurricane, the workshops provided space to speak about experiences of displacement and loss and thereby enhance individual resilience;

- it helped develop the capacity to name and interpret the relationships of power which shape how one lives and works (known as 'critical bifocality'; Weis & Fine, 2012).

As you can see, a significant amount of time, thought, and resources is put into building trust, working respectfully across differences, establishing a shared understanding of research processes, and democratising the research before engaging in more formal data-gathering within the broader community.

Identifying and clarifying the research focus

Building on this essential groundwork, the first task was to identify and clarify a shared research focus. A brain-storming exercise elicited a range of issues and concerns from co-researchers, including:

> the [lack of] health insurance, financial burdens, literacy and communication challenges, violent communities, flood-remediated housing, transportation, confronting pride of needy families who resist help, knowing what services had returned to the city, if and where records may have been saved, and finding ways to coordinate available services.
>
> (Lykes & Scheib, 2016, p. 746)

The co-researchers observed that the lack of basic services contributed to an increased reliance on themselves and other community-based health workers who were tasked with providing useful and sustainable responses to diverse community needs. Therefore, it was agreed to focus on their "roles and actions as women community health workers in greater New Orleans post-Katrina, seeking to explore how they were resources for both their own and their communities' recovery" (p. 746).

Gathering data

The community-based health promoters and co-researchers took more than a thousand photographs over a two-year period, recorded over a hundred individual stories and interviews, and wrote and re-wrote many collective stories about Hurricane Katrina's effects. These photos and narratives documented how communities respond to these challenges and evidenced the resilience in their responses as well as documenting local women's community-based health promotion.

The researchers outline three stages to their photoPAR method. Here, we briefly describe these three stages, illustrating them using images of underemployed men who were frequently depicted in the co-researchers' photographs.

1 *Individual storytelling*: the photographer explains what she has learned from taking a picture, both through observation and/or from interviewing those in her photograph. Individual stories about underemployed men included descriptions of the context (e.g. Latinos photographed in public

spaces waiting for opportunities to pick up a day's work, or pictures of African American men taken at a community centre) and stories shared by the men about the worry and uncertainty about finding reliable work.

2 *Creating phototexts*: the story and photograph are paired together in a phototext. Multiple phototexts are then clustered and re-clustered to generate ideas about what these texts have to say, and to examine the similarities and differences between the phototexts. Initially, similarities across the 'different' groups of underemployed men were categorised descriptively as 'under-utilised' and 'under-appreciated'. The purpose of clustering the photographs is to explore similarities and differences between them in order to *thicken* the description and analysis – especially by focusing on power. Through this process the co-researchers came to understand these experiences of underemployment as reflecting systemic inequalities that rendered these men as 'highly vulnerable to exploitation' and 'visible symbols of inequality and racism.' The researchers write a story which captures their newly emerging understanding of each cluster of photographs, and which explicitly centres exploitation as the problem for Latino and African American workers who are:

> being taken advantage of because they are undocumented or desperate. Their faces reflect the worry and uncertainly of not being able to find reliable work, of not knowing if they will have the luck to find someone who will give them work even for a couple of hours a day.
>
> (Lykes & Scheib, 2016, pp. 751–752)

3 *Creating photonarratives*: these are mini-theories reflecting the co-researchers' interpretations and critical analyses of the combined phototexts. Here co-researchers bring together different clusters of photographs to create a more holistic picture of what is happening in people's lives (for example, how communities are exploited in relation to insecure employment, but also poor housing, lack of access to banking, and how this is linked to alcohol abuse), as well as explicitly explaining these experiences in relation to power, marginalisation, and oppression within their communities.

Taking action

Putting research to work to create social change is an essential feature of PAR. So, the researchers had to think carefully about how best to share their research findings with organisational leaders, friends and families, and the wider New Orleans communities. They decided to use five 'movable banners' to display the photographs and stories. To give you an illustration, one of the banners was divided into two columns. One focused on the experiences of African Americans and included a photo of a housing development where many had lived before the hurricane. The federal government had condemned the building, despite some reports that it was habitable, and some people who tried to return to their homes were arrested. The second column focused on the experiences of Latinos and the problems of finding employment and accessing services for undocumented migrants. Positioned in relationship to one another on the banner, the images and stories reflect the particular challenges for each community, whilst clearly identifying exploitation as a shared source of suffering.

Reflecting and evaluating

The process of reflecting on and evaluating the impact of research is ongoing, but the authors offer their own reflections on the strengths of the project. These include:

- engaging new audiences to educate them about the potential contributions of cross-community collaborations in health promotion;
- exposing racist assumptions as underpinned by systems of exploitation;
- challenging media images by representing the lived experiences of African American men and Latinos through stories and photographs;
- advocating for these men as under-used and inaccurately represented in post-disaster planning and rebuilding systems;
- working together to strengthen the co-researchers' empathy, workplace solidarity, and resilience towards each other and their communities.

This project invites us to think very differently about helping in emergency situations by looking at caring labour that is exerted in the aftermath of a 'natural' disaster. It also invites us to look at experiences of helping in a very personal (given the shared experiences of loss and displacement) yet professional (helping is a core part of the health promoter's job) context. And, it invites us to explore the interconnections between individual (micro) helping behaviours, community-level caring responses, and institutional (macro) systems of care, such as national and international disaster responses. As the authors conclude, the co-researchers "cared for themselves and each other as survivors of and responders to this post-disaster context" and the process offered them opportunities to:

> make meaning of and perform their work as ethnically, racially, and linguistically diverse women community-based health promoters, and recover from some of the personal and social psychological losses experienced post-disaster.
>
> (Lykes & Scheib, 2016, p. 757)

Finally, this project also offered us a very different way of imagining what research methods in psychology might be. PAR has been described by some as a feminist response to conventional research practices (Fine & Torre, 2019), which is a form of praxis (putting theory and knowledge into action) rooted in concerns about politics, power, and participation. It is a rejection of knowledge produced by 'experts' from the top down, and instead works collaboratively and in partnership with those about whom knowledge is being created. In this sense, feminist research goes beyond simply adding another tool to the psychology researcher's toolkit. Rather, you are invited to consider different, ethically informed, democratic ways of working to produce contextually rich knowledge, enlivened by analyses of power, which seek to change the world for the better.

SECTION SUMMARY

- We have explored participatory action research as a very different model for doing research – one in which researchers are embedded within and work alongside communities to produce findings which are meaningful to communities and are put into practice immediately.
- We can see in this example the feminist lenses of location, power, place, reflexivity, intersectionality and representation, ethics, and social justice in action.

CHAPTER SUMMARY

- There are different ways of conceptualising what caring for and helping others might mean – from individual acts of heroism in emergency situations, to routine acts of care, to community-based responses to disasters.
- These different ways of understanding what helping is are not neutral – they are gendered (and racialised, classed, and structured by other intersecting forms of identity and inequality).
- 'Classic' social psychology experiments on bystander intervention (as a specific form of helping behaviour) have recently been applied by feminists to bystander intervention training designed to help people to intervene in risky sexual situations or domestic abuse.
- Qualitative research can use interviews to gain in-depth, contextually rich understandings of people's lived experience of helping.

9 Doing your own feminist research

Learning objectives

Study of this chapter should enable you to:

- Understand how you might use feminism to shape your own research and put into practice some of the exciting ideas that you have learned about when reading this book.
- Gain awareness of two areas of ongoing development in feminist research – the process of decolonising feminist research and the impact of new technologies on research.

As we near the end of our whistle-stop tour through research methods in psychology, we hope you've enjoyed riding alongside us and that we have been interesting, fun, and informative companions. Like travelling on a hop-on, hop-off bus, we have visited some of the iconic monuments (classic studies!) associated with the core areas of psychology, and some of the landscapes (methods and methodologies) in which these studies are located. Of course, and at the risk of pushing the metaphor too far, you can't see everything on just one trip. We couldn't hope to cover *every* type of data collection or analysis technique or to include *every* approach to research. We hope we have done enough to inspire you to travel further into feminist research, and to bring back with you wonderful 'thought mementoes' to help shape your own up-and-coming research endeavours. In this final chapter, then, we take a slightly different approach by looking to the future to think about how you might put some of the ideas in this book to use. Research is something that you *really* learn about by doing. This explains why practical research methods classes, in which you get hands-on experience of designing and conducting research, are a central part of BPS accredited courses in the UK. More than this, students are expected to be able to complete their own independent research project, often in their final year of study. You might find it interesting, if you haven't done so already, to look on your department's webpages to see what research is going on. Sometimes there are opportunities to get involved with an existing project.

Using a feminist lens to look at psychology, myself, and the world

One of the key messages in this book is that psychological knowledge is created by the questions we ask, the tools we use to do research, who we are as researchers, and the values we hold. Approaching psychology through a feminist lens also invites you to consider how research and activism have or could be connected. We have been encouraging you to think about taking up the position of scholar-activist – someone who uses research to create social change.

In Chapter 1, we talked about five reasons that we think you need a feminist Companion to research methods in psychology. Here we look back at these reasons and how we have addressed them within the book. We hope this book has helped you to:

- gain a more *comprehensive* picture of psychological research by demonstrating the range of different epistemologies (theories of knowledge) and varied methods and methodologies that psychologists use to produce knowledge;
- sharpen your *criticality* by foregrounding power and gender, helping you to question where psychological knowledge comes from, how it is produced and by whom, and to what effect;
- focus your attention on issues of *representation* by considering what or who is absent, silenced, or misrepresented in psychological theory and research;
- understand how to conduct research which is *inclusive* and addresses issues that are important to all peoples and communities – research in which people are actively involved in setting the agenda for research;
- to consider the *relevance* of research for people's lives and for making a difference in the world and especially for alleviating gender inequity.

We would encourage you to take the critical thinking skills that you have developed and honed as you have engaged with this book, and to apply them in your undergraduate psychology course (and in your everyday life!). To help you, we outline below some questions that we think it is useful to ask about psychological research/methods.

Thinking (like a feminist) critically

Are your critical senses sharpened and honed now as you approach the end of this book? We hope so! One of our aims in writing this book was to introduce you to some different ways of thinking about knowledge and research.

In Chapter 2, we invited you to explore research methods in psychology through the lenses of *place, power, social justice, ethics, representation and intersectionality*, and *reflexivity*. This final chapter presents a good opportunity to revisit these ideas with you (the researcher) in mind, and to think about how these lenses can shape your own research. To do this, we are going to start with the lens of reflexivity as this asks you to turn your gaze inwards to think about who you are.

The *lens of reflexivity* is about being mindful of your own role in the research, and acknowledging that the researcher's life experience will always shape how they see the world and their research. Rather than assuming that research can be truly objective, reflexivity is about making explicit the **subjectivity** of the researcher. Subjectivity refers to the personal values, feelings, and experiences that make you who you are, both in everyday life and as a researcher. It is these life experiences which often shape the research questions that we decide to pursue. We have discussed how historically one of the problems with research in psychology has been that it often fails to ask questions about women's lives, or about gender, in a way that is not skewed by assumptions and bias partly because the research has been undertaken primarily by men.

Of course, reflexivity is not only about understanding how the topics we are drawn to explore are linked to ourselves and our own life experiences. It is also about understanding and being explicit about the ways in which our own worldview – our values, assumptions, position in the world – shape the way that we conduct the research, who we recruit as participants, how we interpret our data, and how we share our research and with whom. The value of this approach is the insights that would otherwise not be possible.

In this book, we have noted that most psychological research is from Western, educated, industrialised, rich, and democratic (WEIRD) societies, which represent only about 12% of the world's population (Henrich et al., 2010). Looking at your own research through the *lens of place* invites you to consider how your research is shaped by your social location. This means not only the geographical location of the research (locally, nationally, or globally), but also the physical, social, cultural, and economic locatedness of the research.

The *lens of ethics* allows us to see that ethics is more than just filling in a form. It can be applied to every aspect of the research process, including the way we make sense of our findings. Values play an important part in what we believe to be ethical. What we understand to be right and wrong relies on what we think is important and what is less so. This is, of course, shaped by gender, culture, and other markers of difference. Looking at your research through this lens allows you to see how it is impacted by what we consider to be right and wrong, for instance, justice or care.

The *lens of representation and intersectionality* – throughout this book we have drawn attention to issues around representation and intersectionality. Thinking firstly about representation, who, or which voices or perspectives, are being represented in your research? As we've discussed, researchers tend to draw on their own experience to develop research questions and, given this, there is a danger that we will only represent people or experiences that are similar to our own. So, in your own research, as a starting point you might want to reflect on your own intersectional identities, and think about how to involve or work collaboratively with the people who are the focus of your research.

Looking through the *lens of power* can help you to critique existing studies, and to plan your own research. Thinking about who is most likely to benefit from a particular piece of research and who might be negatively impacted is a useful way to think about the way power differences play out. A good start to this is to take participants' experience seriously and see them as experts of the own experiences rather than imposing normative understandings.

The *lens of social justice* is about looking at how our research affects others. Psychology is, almost by definition, a discipline that aims to make the world better. While a worthy pursuit, it is a big commitment that requires that we consider how our research will impact different groups. Does your research properly take account of the broader societal implications of the process or outcomes of your project? The lens of social justice focuses on this aspect of research specifically.

The research process

Looking at your research through the different feminist lenses as we suggest should add both quality and rigour to your research project. In this section, we want to introduce a set of thinking tools to help you plan your research. We take you through each stage of the research process from your initial question through to presenting the findings from your research and provide some questions we hope you will find useful (see Figure 9.1 and Table 9.1).

We have included the questions in Table 9.1 not as a tick box exercise of questions that you need to provide a sure and quick answer to. Rather, we hope that you will use this as a tool for thinking. This thinking, as we have noted, can be *'sweaty work'*. There is no one right or perfect way to design and conduct a research study. Getting to a place where you have designed a project which feels comfortable for you (where you can clearly explain the choices you have made, and which meets your assessment criteria) is tough work and takes time.

Figure 9.1: The research process.

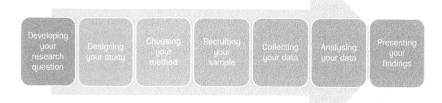

Table 9.1: Questions to ask about feminist psychological research and knowledge

Stage of research	Questions to consider	Things you can do
Developing your research question	What am I interested in? Why am I interested in this? Who else would be interested in it? Who will this question benefit? Who might be negatively affected? How does this question frame 'the problem'? Who is included/excluded in your research question? How is this question relevant to the lives of women and girls?	Spend some time just thinking about your topic and what initially captured your interest *See and hear for yourself* around the topic in: • academic literature • the media • social media • books, cinema and films Pay attention to the representation of different groups and who might be missing Look for how this topic has been understood by others Talk to other people about your ideas
Choosing your method	Will this method answer your question? What kind of information can this method give you? What information can it not give you? Who will find this method accessible, and who might be excluded? How does this method influence the relationship between the researchers and the participants? Does it give one the upper hand?	Look for examples of methods that have been used to answer similar questions, with similar groups of participants, or to achieve similar aims Get feedback on your research plan from other people (preferably people from your research population) or test out your research on one or two people before jumping in Imagine being a participant in your own research – what do you think it will feel like to complete these research tasks?

(Continued)

Table 9.1: *(Continued)*

Stage of research	Questions to consider	Things you can do
Recruiting your sample	Who (or what) will you include in this research, and why? Who (or what) will be excluded from the research, and why? Are there representatives or gatekeepers that you should be consulting? Are your recruitment materials accessible (e.g. are they clearly written)?	Look at examples of recruitment materials – maybe examples from research you have agreed to participate in yourself (or have decided that you definitely do not want to participate in) How are you addressed in this literature? What kind of a person are you assumed to be? Do you find yourself liking/trusting/respecting the person or team that have put this material together? Even undergraduate students are a very diverse bunch(!) so you want to make sure that your research addresses all this diversity
Collecting your data	How are you collecting your data? Are you collecting unnecessary data? Are you treating your participants and/or their data with respect? Are you being transparent and rigorous?	Try to make the space in which you are meeting your participants (be it physical or online) one that won't make them feel uncomfortable or out of place Make sure you brief them about the study and answer any questions before you begin Let them know they can withdraw at any time Be prepared and have procedures in place should your participant become upset Make sure you debrief and tell them how to reach you Tell them who they can contact if they want to make a complaint

(Continued)

Table 9.1: *(Continued)*

Stage of research	Questions to consider	Things you can do
Analysing your data	What concepts and theories are informing your analysis? What is your focus and why? What assumptions are embedded in these concepts? What might be lost in the process of analysing the data (i.e. when transcribing or using software)? What does your analysis capture, and what is left out?	Check whether you have been rigorous in your analysis of the data Have you thought carefully about what the consequences of excluding some data from your analysis might be? Check whether your analysis favours or ignores some aspects of your data (or perhaps some participants)
Reporting your findings	Who is your audience/readership? What impact might these findings have on the populations you are discussing or those who live and work with them? Could your findings be misinterpreted or used for different ends? How might others (e.g. the media) represent your findings? What impact might your research have, both positive and negative?	Find an example of a published paper which you enjoyed and can use as a model for your own writing Think about what you enjoyed about it, and how the authors managed this Imagine what the people who are implicated in the research might say about your findings (or ask them, share your findings with them) Think about what you have included/excluded and why? Will your audience be able to understand what you have written?

In the final part of this chapter, we want to focus on two ongoing areas of development in feminist research both within and beyond psychology: the continued influence of emerging technologies for shaping research practices and the process of **decolonising** feminist research. We've chosen these because we believe that they are the two current issues that will most impact the future practice of feminist research for those entering the field in the years to come.

Emerging technologies and feminist research

In recent years, technology has placed what is in practice a powerful microcomputer in the possession of over 80% of the world's population (O'Dea, 2022). This fact in itself has the potential to revolutionise research; however, the process has been hugely accelerated by the onset of a global pandemic and the resulting lockdowns. During this time it became impossible to do most psychological research face to face, so most of us had to get creative about our data collection. You've probably heard the saying 'with great challenges come great opportunities'. Well, this was definitely a great challenge, so what opportunities were there for rigorous, ethically informed, intersectional feminist research? Moving our research online definitely seemed the most obvious way forward.

There are lots of issues around online research. These include some that apply to more traditional forms of data collection, and which we've discussed throughout the book; however, there are others that are specific to the online environment. For the moment, let's focus on the ethics of this form of data collection because, as we have argued, all feminist research should be conscientiously ethical by design. So, let's start by considering the definition of internet-mediated research (IMR). For our purposes, we can consult the guidance produced by the British Psychological Society in its 2021 document *Ethics guidelines for internet-mediated research*. This document defines IMR as "any research involving the remote acquisition of data from or about human participants using the internet and its associated technologies" (2021c, p. 6). There are many benefits to IMR. We can consider these in relation to the stages of research we looked at above.

Developing your research question

While not all questions can be addressed through an online design, the digital environment does provide some flexibility and lends itself to statistical, text-based, visual, and creative methods. Having said that, most of us aren't computer programmers so the software can limit our options. Different computer programs have different **affordances** – that is, the properties of a thing that define how it can or should be used. There are things you can and can't do with them. When thinking about our research question, we need to consider what the technology does or does not allow. One of the things that the internet not only allows but facilitates is cheap and instantaneous communication across distances, allowing researchers to come together in ways they never could have before. So it becomes much easier to involve diverse populations in your study.

We can have participants from almost anywhere in the world. We can more easily create international research teams that bring very different backgrounds and experiences to a project. One of the studies discussed in Chapter 6, for instance, brought together over 30 researchers from eight countries and three continents to explore brain structure and activity – to ask questions together (Zhang et al., 2021).

Choosing your method

Some methods can require quite a lot of investment in terms of time and money. They can involve extensive travel, expensive laboratories and equipment, or large numbers of researchers and/or participants. While technology does not always make things easier, it often can. It can be flexible in lots of ways and allows us to use many different approaches. We are able to explore questions using *big data*, datasets that would be far too large to analyse with traditional methods. It gives us access to existing data from blogs, social media, websites, libraries, archives and, indeed, any data that can be found online. Many experiments can be conducted quite easily through carefully prepared programmes, and surveys have become so easy to conduct that you probably receive a request for one every time you book or purchase something online. For us, as primarily qualitative researchers, technology lends itself to online interviews, visual methods, and countless creative approaches to research.

Recruiting your sample

For internet-mediated research, anyone with access to the internet is a potential participant and any information stored digitally is a potential data source. In this sense, it has the potential to amplify hidden voices. Individuals who once felt alone and isolated now create online communities that researchers can engage with. For instance, research indicates that mothers of young children find support and comfort through social media and discussion groups where they can share their experience. The existence of these groups makes it much easier for researchers to find and focus on specific populations that they might be interested in studying. There are issues, of course. You can't really talk about IMR without being attentive to the *digital divide*. While access to the internet is widespread, there are still populations who are at the margins of this technology; for instance, older generations often struggle with the equipment, prisoners are allowed very limited use of digital technologies, and coverage does vary geographically. Also, the quality of access can vary. Some people may be connected 24/7, whereas others may only have a limited amount of time a day or a week. As we know, not everyone has a smartphone, a stable connection, or affordable data. So we do need to be very careful about who we are excluding when conducting research online. We have a similar concern, of course, around directly accessed data, as certain types of data may be more or less accessible on the internet, which may lead us to prioritise what's more available over what is more meaningful in terms of the research.

Collecting your data

Access to the internet can, in many cases, make it so much easier to access large amounts of high-quality data, which has, in some cases, revolutionised the way we conduct research. There are added benefits: it facilitates anonymity as you can avoid face-to-face contact; data is collected and held electronically so it can be easier to secure; fewer people handle the data; often the researchers have no access to personal details, which aids confidentiality; and in experimental contexts it can provide a consistent experience in terms of the interface. These are all welcome. However, each brings its own issues. Anonymity can have a detrimental impact on completion rates – it makes it much easier to walk away without explanation. Electronically held data is only as safe as the data management system and there are dangers that are particular to the digital environment such as viruses and hacking. While the researcher can control the interface so that it is consistent, we have no control over the conditions in which the participant is engaging – are they completely focused or are they trying to cook dinner at the same time?

Even if we have no participants *per se* and we are just collecting data from social media or chat rooms, we need to think carefully about the ethics of this process. What data can we consider to be publicly available (cf. Ravn et al., 2020)? What are the expectations of users (e.g. Williams et al., 2017)? Who owns the data? This has created a lot of discussion and debate amongst those conducting IMR. Opinions vary and they are in constant flux (Eynon et al., 2017).

The one concern that we can never get away from in IMR is the possibility, or more correctly probability, of running into technical problems. You know you'll have them, they seem unavoidable, but it is very difficult to know when and where they will strike. Even if the technical issues are the result of a failure of software or hardware, we need to keep an eye on the affordances of the tech, as we've said above. What is it making possible and what is it hindering?

Analysing your data

Conducting an interview using video conferencing means you can simply record the entire exchange, providing you with a full record that you can refer to and analyse. Often it will transcribe the data for you – though this is a developing technology. Similarly, software packages that support qualitative analysis, such as NVivo and Atlas.ti amongst others, which allow you to share files and work collaboratively have opened up the possibilities for feminist researchers. In fact, emerging technologies have made it possible to work much more easily with any kind of data across locations with geographically dispersed colleagues. This is most important because it facilitates the inclusion of different perspectives at every level of the research process, including that of analysing your data.

Reporting your findings

New technologies have made reporting of research findings much more accessible. No longer do you need to take yourself to the library to scan through the shelves of journals or books to find the study you are interested in. More and more academic publishing is happening online. This has made it possible to access feminist work from your computer. As we discussed in Chapter 6, the **Open Science** movement (also known as Open Research) aims to make the whole research process more transparent and accessible to everyone. Along with the standard publishing, research findings are often now reported in blogs and on pre-print sites where you can go and read up on the latest work happening in your area, including new work in feminist psychology. Pownall et al. (2021), in a paper on open science as early career feminist researchers, discuss the ways in which feminist epistemology can contribute to the movement by acting as grassroots changemakers. We agree that there is a lot of potential for feminists to contribute positively in this area. An example of this can be seen in the work of the Algorithmic Justice League, which aims to raise public awareness about the intersectional discrimination that can be perpetuated through badly design AI.

See and hear for yourself

Founded by Joy Buolamwini, a computer scientist and digital activist based at MIT, the Algorithmic Justice League (AJL) works to raise public awareness of the fact that AI systems can perpetuate all manners of discrimination. She first became aware of this when she discovered that face recognition software could not detect her because of her dark skin. The AJL applies the arguments we've made in this book about questions to the context of coding. The League argues that 'who codes matters, how we code matters'. The AJL believes we can code for a better future. These days Buolamwini defines herself as a poet of code who makes use of research and art to draw attention to the social implications of artificial intelligence.

If you would like to learn more about the AJL's activism, check out its website: https://www.ajl.org. The AJL has also produced an award-winning documentary on this topic titled 'Coded Bias', which can be found on a number of streaming services. We highly recommend it.

Decolonising feminist research

> For those who have been oppressed by colonization, research is a dirty word.
> (Thambinathan & Kinsella, 2021)

As we noted in Chapter 2, research in psychology is WEIRD. WEIRD because it reflects, maintains, and promotes the interests of a privileged minority of people in Western, Educated, Industrial, Rich, Democratic settings (Henrich et al., 2010). Psychology privileges research conducted by and with people located in the global North, thereby omitting non-White, non-Western, and peoples from the global South (or the 'Majority World'; Kağıtçıbaşı, 1996). When these researchers do turn their attention to marginalised and racialised communities, they do so "in the light of concepts, methods and beliefs about normality that are rooted in the WEIRD realities" (Adams et al., 2015, p. 213). Moreover, in the context of **globalisation**, these concepts, methods, and beliefs about what is normal are exported across national, cultural, religious, ethnic, and geographical boundaries as if they are equally applicable and meaningful. This also means that scholars from the global South face pressure to adopt these concepts and methods (and to write and publish in English), and to direct their work to debates circulating in the global North.

More than this, as we have alluded to in this book, psychology has had a long and troubling history of producing and using research in ways which are instrumental in **colonisation**. These include:

- assuming that knowledge produced in the global North represents universal truths about everyone;
- perpetuating inaccurate, harmful, and dehumanising stereotypes about people who are non-White or non-Western;
- contributing directly (e.g. its complicity with apartheid or more recently with torture) and indirectly (by claiming scientific objectivity) to the injustices;
- contributing to the dispossession, displacement, and exploitation of non-White and non-Western communities;
- contributing to the perpetuation of oppression, discrimination, and violence.

For further examples, see the American Psychological Association's apology regarding racism (see the *See and hear for yourself* box below).

Colonisation is not limited to the occupation of land, control over material resources, or exploitation of people, it also includes the occupation or domination of "*the total being of the colonized* – economically, culturally, socially, and psychologically" (Bulhan, 2015, p. 253). Research is a dirty word, then, because it has been used to enact **epistemic violence** – violence through knowledge rather than through weapons – against people of colour and those in the global South. Growing recognition of, and resistance to, the colonising practices of psychology has led to a burgeoning movement calling for the **decolonising** of psychology – including the decolonising of psychological research and research methods.

See and hear for yourself

Watch this video from Linda Tuhiwai Smith called *Decolonising Methodologies, 20 Years On*: https://www.youtube.com/watch?v=YSX_4FnqXwQ

See the American Psychological Society's *Apology to People of Color*: "The American Psychological Association failed in its role leading the discipline of psychology, was complicit in contributing to systemic inequities, and hurt many through racism, racial discrimination, and denigration of people of color, thereby falling short on its mission to benefit society and improve lives. APA is profoundly sorry, accepts responsibility for, and owns the actions and inactions of APA itself, the discipline of psychology, and individual psychologists who stood as leaders for the organization and field": https://www.apa.org/about/policy/racism-apology

You might also be interested in this set of webinars from the British Psychological Society on diversity and inclusion, including one on decolonising the curriculum:
https://www.bps.org.uk/about-us/diversity-and-inclusion/taskforce/webinars

So, what is meant by decolonising research?

According to Brendan Barnes, decolonising research

> ... raises questions about who we focus our research on, the types of questions that are asked, the relationship between researchers and participants, the values underpinning research, what can be inferred from the study, and the contributions to equality and justice. Decolonising methodologies also focus on the research enterprise itself, its pedagogies, systems, exclusions and power that privilege certain knowledges over others.
>
> (2018, p. 379)

As may be clear from the above description, attempts at decolonising research share much in common with feminist attempts to wrestle with **patriarchy** within psychology. You may not be surprised to learn that there is no one way of decolonising research, just as there is no one way of doing feminist research or feminist decolonising research. Having said this, it is possible to draw out some shared principles or values which underpin approaches to decolonising research methods. Catriona Ida Macleod, Sunil Bhatia, and Wen Liu (2020), for example, outline five principles guiding feminist decolonising psychology. These are:

- *Exposing the patriarchal colonialist legacy of mainstream psychological science* – this includes exposing the way that research has dehumanised racialised minorities, spread inaccurate stereotypes and discrimination, perpetuated hatred, and adopted a negative and pathologising lens through which to interpret and misrepresent people's lives.
- *Connecting gendered coloniality with other systems of power* – one such system of power is globalisation, and we can see how these different systems combine by looking at the example of mental health. Decolonising research might demonstrate how discrimination and oppression heighten experiences of mental distress for women and especially racialised minority women. At the same time, it might also illustrate how calls by organisations such as the Global Mental Health movement, the World Health Organisation

(WHO), and **Big Pharma** to 'scale up' access to psychological and psychiatric treatments globally, result in the export of culturally insensitive diagnoses and treatments from the global North.

- *Investigating topics that surface the intertwining of colonialist and gendered power relations* – writing about decolonising feminist psychology in an African context, for example, Shose Kessi and Floretta Boonzaier argue that psychology could attend to questions about the "afterlives of colonisation, slavery and apartheid" (2018, p. 305), including how African, gendered, and/or localised ways of conceptualising and understanding trauma (including violence and sexual violence) shape people's lives, identities, and experiences.

- *Using research methods that reflect the values of feminist decolonising psychology* – while innovative and creative research methods (including Photovoice, autoethnography, visual methods, storytelling, and participatory approaches) speak to the aim of democratising research and centring marginalised voices, like Barnes (2018) we do not assume that some methodologies are, by definition, more likely to contribute to decolonisation than others (however, we acknowledge that they lend themselves to different questions and produce different answers).

- *Focusing on transformative **praxis*** – this means putting research into practice as scholar-activists who use research to work towards creating more equitable societies.

Five things to do on your next project

And so, we've reached the end of our travels together – at least for now. In this chapter, we have considered how you can use all of the fabulous feminist perspectives on research methods in psychology to inform your own research practice. Now it's time for you to put this into action! We look forward to seeing all the wonderful knowledge you can create, and all the creative, innovative, and inspiring methods, tools, and techniques you incorporate into your own research. We can't wait to see, hear, and read about your research. In the meantime, we leave you with these five research 'rules' for feminist rebels:

- Do research that you care about, research that inspires and excites you!
- Use any and all methods that will best answer your questions.
- Look at your research through the six lenses as you design and plan your project.
- Consult, collaborate, and cooperate with communities to enrich your research.
- Become a scholar-activist to help change the world for the better (no pressure ☺).

Saying goodbye

Although it is time to draw this book to a close, this Feminist Companion will always be with you. Dip between the covers to revive your feminist consciousness and reignite your critical senses when you feel yourself flagging. We have both found feminist psychology a welcome refuge and much-needed source of inspiration when we have felt frustrated, infuriated, or despondent about psychology. We hope that you will treat this book as a springboard for learning more about how theory and research in feminist psychology can round out and expand your understanding of psychology and your identity as a psychologist.

Glossary

Acceptability – in the context of psychological interventions, whether people consider the intervention to be appropriate, how well the intervention is received, and their thoughts and feelings about undertaking the intervention

Activism – involves taking action (like campaigning or protesting) to achieve social or political change

Additive – where the effect of two independent things or variables in combination is equal to the sum of their individual effects

Affordances – the features or properties of a thing (like an app) which define what can (and cannot) be done with that thing

Altruistic – doing things out of a desire to help others rather than because of any benefit to the self

Analysis of variance (AnoVa) – a statistical test used to determine if all groups of participants in a study are affected by the same factors, and if they are affected to the same degree

Androgynous – having both masculine and feminine traits; also having an ambiguous appearance that is identifiable by others as neither obviously masculine nor feminine, but a combination of the two

Application or applied research – the use of *psychological* methods and knowledge to solve real world problems and alleviate human suffering

Attachment theory – the theory that humans are born with a need to form a close emotional bond with a caregiver

Attrition – the loss of participants from a research study over time

Autobiographical memory – memory of personal events which have taken place in a person's life

Aversion therapy – technique to try to change people's behaviour by learning to associate a negative consequence (such as an electric shock) with the unwanted behaviour

Benevolent sexism – harmful evaluations or representations of women that may appear to be positive but are actually damaging to people and gender equality more broadly (e.g. the idea that women need to be protected by men)

Big data – large complex data sets which are characterised by a variety of data or data from new sources, a large volume of data, and data which is generated very rapidly

Big Pharma – a term used to indicate the political and financial power of large multinational pharmaceutical companies and their influence in global health-care systems

Binary – having two parts or being composed of two things

Black boxing – used to describe something which seems to work, but nobody knows how it works; the inner workings are not visible or understood

Bogus pipeline – a fake lie detector used to encourage participants to truthfully respond to questions in a survey

Brain – the organ located in the skull which controls the body and is responsible for thoughts and mental processes

Brain organisation theory – the idea that men and women have different kinds of brains due to the influence of hormones during early development

Bystander intervention – intervention or intercession by someone who is present during an event but not taking part

Cannabinoid receptors – receptors are cells in the body which are designed to detect and respond to specific stimuli – in this case, cannabinoids, which are a type of chemical in marijuana plants that causes drug-like effects. These receptors are found throughout the body and are thought to play a key role in the regulation of mood, appetite, pain, and other physiological processes

Causal inference – the process of reasoning to determine whether an observed change indicates a cause-and-effect relationship

Chromosomes – thread-like structures found within cells which carry genetic information and play an important role in the passing on of characteristics between generations and for variability between people

Coding scheme – predetermined framework for observing and recording the frequency with which a prescribed set of behaviours occurs

Cognitive psychology – the scientific study of mental processes

Cohen's d – a measure of effect size which describes the extent to which the distribution of scores between different samples of participants overlap

Colonialism – domination of one people, territory, or country by another for the purposes of economic, political, or cultural exploitation

Community-level intervention – intervention designed to promote wellbeing within a whole population or community rather than being targeted at individuals

Computer tomography (CT) – a technique for producing three-dimensional images of the brain or other soft tissues

Context stripping – the positivist approach is associated with the search for universal, context-free laws to explain human behaviour, and associated methodological approaches attempt to study variables in isolation; often referred to within positivist approaches as objectivity

Control group – a group of participants who, for the purposes of comparison, are not exposed to the thing of interest which is manipulated or altered by the researcher (the independent variable)

Co-researchers – a term used to describe involving participants as active and equal partners in designing, implementing, and disseminating research

Correlation – the relationship between two variables or the extent to which two variables change in relationship to one another

Credibility – presenting an interpretation of an experience in such a way that it is immediately recognisable to other people who share that experience

Decolonising – the process of recognising the ways in which knowledges that do not originate from the West have been marginalised or oppressed in the context of imperialism, colonialism, and power and to seek to change this

Deduction – a process of reasoning used to reach a conclusion in which the researcher starts out with a general statement, or **hypothesis**, and examines different possibilities to reach a specific, logical conclusion

Deductive method – a method designed to test a theory

Demand characteristics – participants' beliefs or guesses about whether a particular outcome or behaviour is expected in research settings or tasks

Dependent variable – a thing-of-interest which is monitored by researchers during experiments to see if there is a change which can be attributed to another variable that the research has altered or manipulated (the **independent variable**)

Dichotomy – a contrast drawn between two things in which they are represented as opposed or very different

Diffusion of responsibility – the lessening of personal responsibility to take action experienced in the presence of other people who could also potentially take action

Digital divide – term used to describe the gap between those who have access to technologies and those who do not

Dimorphic – the existence of two distinct forms of a species

Disciplinary reflexivity – reflecting on how the norms and practices within the discipline shape research (for example, norms about the value of science and objectivity)

Discourse analysis – a method for studying the language used in talk and texts to reveal how reality is constructed and to reveal the ideological work that language does

Ecological validity – the extent to which the results from a study can predict or be applied to the real world

Effect size – a measure describing how small or large a difference between groups (say between men and women) might be, or how much of a change in behaviour or attitudes is observed

Electroencephalography (EEG) – a method of measuring electrical activity in the brain

Epistemic violence – violence exerted against or through knowledge

Epistemology – this is the theory of knowledge and is concerned with the origins, nature, and scope of knowledge including what we know and how we know it

Essentialism – the view that certain categories of people (e.g. women, racial groups) have an underlying reality or true nature – e.g. women are inherently, or by their nature, nurturing (see also *context stripping*)

Ethical guidelines – the standards and principles set out by professional bodies such as the British Psychological Society which govern how psychologists should behave when conducting research, especially with a concern to protect participants from harm

Ethics – beliefs about how research should be conducted, including the responsibilities of researchers to protect participants from harm

Ethnography – a research method to study culture through close observation and active participation

Experiment – a scientific method designed to test a hypothesis

Experimental conditions – discrete contexts for the controlled observation of one variable on another

Experimenter expectancy effects – the unintended effect of the expectations held by the researcher has on the findings (including, for example, expectations about what the researcher thinks they will find)

False memories – the idea that people can come to believe that they possess memories of events that did not actually occur (see also *recovered memories*)

Falsification – the act of disproving a hypothesis

Feasibility – an investigation conducted prior to the research study to establish the suitability of the design and the sensitivity of the measures

Field experiment – experiment conducted in a real-world setting

Functional magnetic resonance imaging (fMRI) – functional magnetic resonance imaging measures the small changes in blood flow that occur with brain activity

Functional reflexivity – reflecting on the process of conducting the research and your own practices within this, including the decisions that you made at different points in the research process

Gender differences – differences between men and women thought to be the result of environmental factors such as social and cultural norms about expected differences between men and women (see also **sex differences**)

Gender roles – social expectations about how people are supposed to behave, their characteristics and capabilities based on their assigned sex

Generalisability – the extent to which research findings based on one sample or context can be applied to another

Genes – a basic biological unit which determines which traits or characteristics are inherited by children from their biological parents

Globalisation – refers to the interdependence of economies and cultures across the world and the, often unequal, ways in which cultures influence and change each other through trade, migration, and communication

Grey matter – a type of brain tissue which processes information from sensory organs

Hawthorne effect – the tendency for some individuals to change their behaviour when they believe that they are noticed, watched, and paid attention to by researchers

Hormones – chemical messages in the body

Hypothesis – a precise, testable statement of what the researcher predicts will be the outcome of the study, based on the hypothetico-deductive approach associated with the scientific method (see also **research question**)

Hypothetico-deduction – a form of logic which consists of posing a hypothesis and testing it against experience to see if it can be falsified (i.e. proven to be incorrect)

Ideographic – a focus on the individual and their unique experience

Ideology – a system of ideas or ideals; ideological work is action which builds and maintains the coherence of a specific system of beliefs that privileges a particular worldview or set of interests

Independent variable – a thing-of-interest which the research manipulates or alters during experiences to see whether this causes a change in another thing-of-interest (the **dependent variable**)

Individual differences (sometimes called *differential psychology*) – the study of how people are both similar and different to each other in how they behave, how they think, or how they feel

Individualising – a term used in critical psychology to indicate that a particular concept, description, or theory is distorting because it focuses solely on what goes on in individuals' minds, largely ignoring the way that much of human life and experience is affected by the social and collective

Inductive method – a method which aims to develop a theory from the data

Inferential statistics – statistics that allow you to make predictions about a population on the basis of collecting data from a smaller sample of that population, unlike descriptive statistics, which simply describe data from the sample (for example, giving the percentage of people in a sample who strongly agreed with a given statement)

Intensive parenting – a type of parenting involving the devotion of attention and resources to children's free time, emotions, and behaviours

Internal reliability (or *internal consistency*) – assesses whether all the elements of a test or all the individual items are measuring the same underlying construct

Intersectionality – a term which derives from Black feminist ideas and describes how our identities exist within 'interlocking systems of oppression' and structures of (in)equalities (Crenshaw, 1991). It highlights how intersecting oppressed identities carry with them certain social expectations and norms. Importantly, intersectionality is rooted in a concern for social justice, stigma, and structural oppression, all of which are cornerstones of feminist psychology

Interview – a conversation with a purpose between the researcher and participant

Intrapersonal – refers to factors or constructs occurring *within* the individual

Longitudinal – researchers study the same group of people or phenomena over an extended period, repeatedly collecting data at different time points

Matched pair study – a type of experimental design in which participants are matched on the basis of key characteristics (like reading speed) so as to compare the impact of one variable (say, caffeine) given to some of the group on the performance (finishing a book) of both groups. By matching participants the researchers can be confident that the matched characteristic (in this case, reading speed) has not influenced performance and that any difference in the performance of the groups is likely due to the manipulated variable (in this case, caffeine)

Maternal sensitivity – the extent to which mothers respond to their infants in a timely and appropriate manner

Meta-analysis – a statistical analysis which combines the results of multiple studies

Multimorphic – having multiple forms simultaneously

Naturalistic observation – studies which observe people in natural or everyday settings rather than in a laboratory or other setting which is specifically designed for research purposes

Neoliberalism – an ideology or set of beliefs which emphasises economic prosperity, competition, and the minimisation of state intervention in economic and social activities, and where citizens are depicted as consumers who are responsible for buying, selling, or trading their own skills to continually improve their lives and wellbeing

Neuroanatomy – the study of the structures and organisation of the nervous systems of humans and animals

Neuroendocrinology – the study of the relationships between the nervous system (including the brain) and the endocrine system

Neurofeminism – the practice and critique of neuroscience informed by feminist theory

Nomothetic – concerned with studying similarities between people in order to establish laws or make generalisations

Objectification – degrading act of seeing and/or treating women as an object or thing rather than as a person

Objectivity – the idea that research should be free from all bias and independent of the researcher's own beliefs, personal feelings, and influence

Oestrogen – hormone found in males and females but often referred to as a female sex hormone due to the higher levels found in females and the role they play in the development of female secondary sex characteristics and the regulation of the reproductive system

Open science/Open research – a movement to make research more accessible to the public and to encourage the sharing of knowledge and data between researchers

Oppression – unjust treatment or exercise of power, prevention of opportunities or freedoms

Paradigm – a philosophy or set of beliefs about how research should be produced

Participant observation – observational studies in which the researcher enters into the setting and takes part in the everyday activities of the people under observation

Participatory action research – an approach to research which emphasises collaboration between researchers and local communities to produce knowledge of use to the community with the intention to create social change

Pathologisation – regarding a behaviour, trait, person, or way of being in the world as psychologically abnormal, problematic, a disease or illness which needs to be treated, cured, or solved

Patriarchy – a system of society or government in which men hold the power and women are largely excluded from it

Peer review – the review and critical evaluation of research by other researchers which forms an integral part of the process of academic research and publishing

Personal reflexivity – examining your own beliefs, values, judgements, life experiences, and identity and how these shape your research

Personality – the qualities or characteristics which are typical of the individual or characteristic patterns of behaviours, thoughts, and emotions

Phrenology – study of the bumps on the skull as a measure of characteristics or abilities of the individual

Pluralism – recognition and acceptance of a diversity of different approaches and positions in relation to, in this case, research methods

Polygraph – a device or procedure for detecting lies by measuring and recording physiological indicators such as blood pressure, pulse, respiration, or skin conductivity

Positivism – a philosophy in which the goal is to describe what people experience through observation and that knowledge should be open to verification through empirical research

Positron emission tomography (PET) – a technique using radioactive glucose to help study activity and locate structures in the body

Poststructuralism – a style of critical reasoning which rejects the idea of a single unitary truth

Praxis – the process by which a theory, lesson, or skill is enacted or embodied; putting theory into practice

Predictability – the likelihood that a specific event will occur

Progesterone – a hormone which plays a significant role in maintaining the early stages of pregnancy

Prosocial – acts of kindness, compassion, and helping behaviours undertaken for the benefit of others

Qualitative methods – methods of collecting data which result in non-numerical data

Quantitative measures – tools which produce data in numerical form

Reactivity – changes in people's behaviour which result from knowing that they are being observed; for example, during psychology experiments or research

Reciprocity – the idea that both researchers *and* those who participate in research should experience some benefit from the study

Recovered memories – belief that people can forget, repress, or not be able to access memories of events that happened in their lives, often for some time, but can later remember or recover these memories

Reductionism – reducing complex phenomena to their most basic parts

Reflexivity – the process of deeply engaging in self-reflection about who we are as researchers, how our biases guide and inform the research process, and how our worldview is shaped by the research we do (Wilkinson, 1988)

Reification – treating a concept or idea as if it were a concrete object or real thing

Relational – the interconnectedness of phenomena, how people or things are connected to one another

Reliability – the extent to which all the items (questions or statements) on a questionnaire/test measure the same underlying construct (aspect of personality, for example), and the extent to which the test elicits the same outcome for individuals over time

Repeated measures design – studies in which the same individuals complete the same measures at (a minimum of two) different points in time to measure change over time

Replicability – the extent one study can be repeated exactly and produce the same results

Representation – a concept which draws attention to issues around describing, speaking, or acting on behalf of someone, or a group of people, especially when representing through research people who are different to the researcher

Research question (see also **hypothesis**) – a question that a research project sets out to answer; the term research question is preferred over hypothesis in qualitative research to reflect the different underlying philosophy

Rigour – a way to establish confidence in the findings of qualitative research focusing on explicit decision-making and consistency in the implementation of methods

Self-fulfilling prophecy – when one person's false expectations about how another will behave eventually result in that person behaving in ways which confirm this expectation

Sex differences – differences between males and females thought to be driven by biological differences (see **gender differences**)

Sex/gender binary – the idea that there are two (and only two) distinct forms of human being: male and female

Significance – the probability that the result from a statistical test has occurred by chance

Social desirability – the tendency for people to present themselves in a favourable way or in accordance with social norms or conventions

Social justice – a belief in fairness and equality in terms of wealth, opportunities, privileges, healthcare, housing, civil rights, education, and all other aspects of society

Social psychology – the study of how individual or group behaviour is influenced by the presence and behaviour of others

Social role theory – the idea that gender differences arise out of the roles that men and women are expected to undertake in society (as wife, mother, breadwinner, etc.)

Spinal fluid – the fluid that flows in and around the hollow spaces of the brain and spinal cord and which acts as a watery cushion or buffer

Standardised – consistent and uniform set of research procedures; a standardised test or measure is one which is administered and scored in the same way for every participant, thus allowing scores for different individuals to be compared

Standardised mean difference – a measure of effect size often in a meta-analysis in order to combine the results of a number of studies that all assess the same outcome (e.g. depression), but measure it in a variety of ways (i.e. using different psychometric scales)

Statistical difference – a way of evaluating whether any observed difference is likely to be due to chance

Statistical probability – a measure of how likely an event is to occur

Structured observation – a systematic method of collecting data within a controlled environment in which observations are made regarding a predetermined set of behaviours

Subjectivity or subjective experience – a person's perspective or opinion, particular feelings, beliefs, and desires

Sustainability – maintaining or supporting a process or practice continuously over time and considering the most effective use of resources to ensure that they remain available for the long term

Sweaty work – term to describe the intellectual or conceptual work involved in trying to illuminate processes that power obscures

Taken-for-granted – knowledge which is assumed to be accurate and collectively shared

Test of difference – a statistical test which is used to compare two sets of data to determine if they differ

Testosterone – a hormone affecting development which is present in males and females but often described as a 'sex hormone' or 'male hormone' due to typically being present in larger quantities in men and being linked to the development of male sex organs

Test-retest reliability – a measure of the consistency of a test over time established by administering the test at two different time points and comparing how the same individuals score on this test on the two occasions. If the scores are similar, the test is said to reliably or consistently measure the construct

Transparency – being open about, and carefully recording, decisions taken about how the research has been conducted

Triangulation – when researchers use more than one method or data source to study the same issue, and then compare and contrast the results from each data source and/or synthesise what is learned from each

Trustworthiness – a way of describing how to establish the quality of qualitative research by asking the question: Can we trust the research findings?

t-test – a statistical test used to determine whether there is a significant difference between the mean or average scores of two groups

Universalised – describes how research which is conducted with one group of people (like white, middle-class, able-bodied men) is assumed to reflect the experiences of everyone

Validity – the extent to which a questionnaire or test actually measures what it sets out to measure

Variability hypothesis – the idea that males generally display greater variability in traits than females do

Variables – special name given to things-of-interest in psychology which can be altered, manipulated, or measured by researchers when conducting experiments

Victim-blaming – when the victim of crime or unjust treatment is held partly or wholly responsible for the harm they have experienced

White matter – a type of brain tissue which transmits information to different parts of the brain

References

Adams, G., Dobles, I., Gómez, L. H., Kurtiş, T., & Molina, L. E. (2015). Decolonizing psychological science: Introduction to the special thematic section. *Journal of Social and Political Psychology, 3*(1), 213–238. https://doi.org/10.5964/jspp.v3i1.564

Ahmed, S. (2016). *Living a feminist life*. Duke University Press.

Ainsworth, M. D. S., Blehar, M. C., Waters, E., & Wall, S. N. (1978/2015). *Patterns of attachment: A psychological study of the strange situation* (Classic Edition). Psychology Press.

Ainsworth, M. D. S., & Bowlby, J. (1991). An ethological approach to personality development. *American Psychologist, 46*(4), 333–341. https://doi.org/10.1037/0003-066X.46.4.333

Alexander, M. G., & Fisher, T. D. (2003). Truth and consequences: Using the bogus pipeline to examine sex differences in self reported sexuality. *Journal of Sex Research, 40*(1), 27–35. https://doi.org/10.1080/00224490309552164

Alvarez, L. D. C., Leach, J. L., Rodriguez, J. L., & Jones, K. N. (2020). Unsung psychology pioneers: A content analysis of who makes history (and who doesn't). *American Journal of Psychology, 133*(2), 241–262. https://doi.org/10.5406/amerjpsyc.133.2.0241

American Psychological Association (APA) (n.d.). Experiment. In *APA dictionary of psychology*. Retrieved July 7, 2021 from https://dictionary.apa.org/experiment

Angrosino, M. V. (2005). Recontextualizing observation: Ethnography, pedagogy, and the prospects for a progressive political agenda. In N. K. Denzin & Y. S. Lincoln (Eds.), *The Sage handbook of qualitative research* (3rd ed., pp. 729–745). Sage.

Aune, K., & Holyoak, R. (2018). Navigating the third wave: Contemporary UK feminist activists and 'third-wave feminism'. *Feminist Theory, 19*(2), 183–203. https://doi.org/10.1177/1464700117723593

Babcock, L., & Laschever, S. (2003). *Women don't ask: Negotiation and the gender divide*. Princeton University Press.

Barnes, B. R. (2018). Decolonising research methodologies: Opportunity and caution. *South African Journal of Psychology, 48*(3), 379–387. https://doi.org/10.1177/0081246318798294

Baron-Cohen, S. (2003). *The essential difference: Men, women and the extreme male brain*. Allen Lane.

Baron-Cohen, S., Knickmeyer, R. C., & Belmonte, M. K. (2005). Sex differences in the brain: Implications for explaining autism. *Science, 310*(5749), 819–823. https://doi.org/10.1126/science.1115455

Beck, A. T., Ward, C. M., Mendelson, M., Mock, J. E., & Erbaugh, J. K. (1961). An inventory for measuring depression. *Archives of General Psychiatry, 4*(6), 561–571. https://doi.org/10.1001/archpsyc.1961.01710120031004

Bem, S. L. (1974). The measurement of psychological androgyny. *Journal of Consulting and Clinical Psychology, 42*(2), 155–162. https://doi.org/10.1037/h0036215

Bijsterbosch, J., Harrison, S. J., Jbabdi, S., Woolrich, M., Beckmann, C., Smith, S., & Duff, E. P. (2020). Challenges and future directions for representations of functional brain organization. *Nature Neuroscience, 23*(12), 1484–1495. https://doi.org/10.1038/s41593-020-00726-z

Bongiorno, R., Bain, P. G., & David, B. (2014). If you're going to be a leader, at least act like it! Prejudice towards women who are tentative in leader roles. *British Journal of Social Psychology, 53*(2), 217–234. https://doi.org/10.1111/bjso.12032

Bowlby, J. (1958). The nature of the child's tie to his mother. *International Journal of Psychoanalysis, 39*(5), 350–371. http://www.psychology.sunysb.edu/attachment/online/nature%20of%20the%20childs%20tie%20bowlby.pdf

Brabeck, M. M., & Ting, K. (2000). Feminist ethics: Lenses for examining ethical psychological practice. In M. M. Brabeck (Ed.), *Practicing feminist ethics in psychology* (pp. 17–35). American Psychological Association.

Brescoll, V., & Lafrance, M. (2004). The correlates and consequences of newspaper reports of research on sex differences. *Psychological Science, 15*(8), 515–520. https://doi.org/10.1111/j.0956-7976.2004.00712.x

Brewin, C. R., & Andrews, B. (2017). Creating memories for false autobiographical events in childhood: A systematic review. *Applied Cognitive Psychology, 31*(1), 2–23. https://doi.org/10.1002/acp.3220

British Psychological Society (BPS) (2021a). *BPS Code of Human Research Ethics.* https://www.bps.org.uk/sites/www.bps.org.uk/files/Policy/Policy%20-%20Files/BPS%20Code%20of%20Human%20Research%20Ethics.pdf

British Psychological Society (BPS) (2021b). *Code of Ethics and Conduct.* https://www.bps.org.uk/sites/www.bps.org.uk/files/Policy/Policy%20-%20Files/BPS%20Code%20of%20Ethics%20and%20Conduct.pdf

British Psychological Society (2021c). *Ethics guidelines for internet-mediated research.* https://www.bps.org.uk/sites/www.bps.org.uk/files/Policy/Policy%20-%20Files/Ethics%20Guidelines%20for%20Internet-mediated%20Research.pdf

Budds, K. (2021). Validating social support and prioritizing maternal wellbeing: Beyond intensive mothering and maternal responsibility. *Philosophical Transactions of the Royal Society B, 376*(1827). https://doi.org/10.1098/rstb.2020.0029

Bulhan, H. A. (2015). Stages of colonialism in Africa: From occupation of land to occupation of being. *Journal of Social and Political Psychology, 3*(1), 239–256. https://doi.org/10.5964/jspp.v3i1.143

Burman, E. (1991). Power, gender and developmental psychology. *Feminism & Psychology, 1*(1), 141–153. https://doi.org/10.1177/0959353591011018

Burman, E. (1995). What is it? Masculinity and femininity in cultural representations of childhood. In S. Wilkinson & C. Kitzinger (Eds.), *Feminism and discourse: Psychological perspectives* (pp. 49–67). Sage.

Burman, E. (2010). Therapy as memory-work: Dilemmas of discovery, recovery and construction. In J. Haaken & P. Reavey (Eds.), *Memory matters: Contexts for understanding sexual abuse recollections* (pp. 196–215). Routledge.

Burman, E. (2011). Psychology, women, and political practice in Britain. In A. Rutherford, R. Capdevila, V. Undurti, & I. Palmary (Eds.), *Handbook of international feminisms: Perspectives on psychology, women, culture, and rights* (pp. 219–243). Springer.

Burman, E. (2017). *Deconstructing developmental psychology* (3rd ed.). Routledge.

Burr, V. (2003). *Social constructionism.* Routledge.

Burt, M. R. (1980). Cultural myths and supports for rape. *Journal of Personality and Social Psychology, 38*(2), 217–230. https://doi.org/10.1037/0022-3514.38.2.217

Calado, B., Luke, T. J., Connolly, D. A., & Landström, S. (2020, April 6). Implanting false autobiographical memories for repeated events. https://doi.org/10.31234/osf.io/5yw6z

Calkins, M. W. (1896) Community of ideas of men and women. *Psychological Review, 3*(4), 426–430. https://doi.org/10.1037/h0064618

Campbell, R., & Schram, P. J. (1995). Feminist research methods: A content analysis of psychology and social science textbooks. *Psychology of Women Quarterly, 19*(1), 85–106. https://doi-org.surrey.idm.oclc.org/10.1111/j.1471-6402.1995.tb00280.x

Corsaro, W. A. (2020). Big ideas from little people: What research with children contributes to social psychology. *Social Psychology Quarterly, 83*(1), 5–25. https://doi.org/10.1177/0190272520906412

Costa, P. T., & McCrae, R. R. (1992). *Revised NEO Personality Inventory (NEO-PI-R) and NEO Five-Factor Inventory (NEO-FFI) professional manual.* Psychological Assessment Resources.

Crafter, S. (2015). Cultural psychology and deconstructing developmental psychology. *Feminism & Psychology, 25*(3), 388–401. https://doi.org/10.1177/0959353515572703

Crenshaw, K. (1989). Demarginalizing the intersection of race and sex: A black feminist critique of antidiscrimination doctrine, feminist theory and antiracist politics. *University of Chicago Legal Forum, 1989*(1), 139–167.

Criado Perez, C. (2019). *Invisible women: Exposing data bias in a world designed for men.* Random House.

Crowne, D. P., & Marlowe, D. (1960). A new scale of social desirability independent of psychopathology. *Journal of Consulting Psychology, 24*(4), 349–354. https://doi.org/10.1037/h0047358

Darley, J. M., & Latané, B. (1968). Bystander intervention in emergencies: Diffusion of responsibility. *Journal of Personality and Social Psychology,* 8(4, Pt. 1), 377–383. https://doi.org/10.1037/h0025589

Deese, J. (1959). On the prediction of occurrence of particular verbal instructions in immediate recall. *Journal of Experimental Psychology, 58*(1), 17–22. https://doi.org/10.1037/h0046671

Defrancisco, V. P., Kuderer, J., & Chatham-Carpenter, A. (2007). I. Autoethnography and women's self-esteem: Learning through a living method. *Feminism & Psychology, 17*(2), 237–243. https://doi.org/10.1177/0959353507076557

Del Giudice, M., Puts, D. A., Geary, D. C., & Schmitt, D. P. (2019). Sex differences in brain and behavior: Eight counterpoints. *Psychology Today,* 8 April. https://www.psychologytoday.com/gb/blog/sexual-personalities/201904/sex-differences-in-brain-and-behavior-eight-counterpoints

DePrince, A. P., Allard, C. B., Oh, H., & Freyd, J. J. (2004). What's in a name for memory errors? Implications and ethical issues arising from the use of the term 'false memory' for errors in memory for details. *Ethics & Behavior, 14*(3), 201–233. https://doi.org/10.1207/s15327019eb1403_1

De Wolff, M. S., & Van IJzendoorn, M. H. (1997). Sensitivity and attachment: A meta analysis on parental antecedents of infant attachment. *Child Development, 68*(4), 571–591. https://doi.org/10.1111/j.1467-8624.1997.tb04218.x

Döring, N., Reif, A., & Poeschl, S. (2016). How gender-stereotypical are selfies? A content analysis and comparison with magazine adverts. *Computers in Human Behavior,* 55(Pt. B), 955–962. https://doi.org/10.1016/j.chb.2015.10.001

Duchesne, A., & Kaiser Trujillo, A. (2021). Reflections on neurofeminism and intersectionality using insights from psychology. *Frontiers in Human Neuroscience,* 475. https://doi.org/10.3389/fnhum.2021.684412

Eagly, A. H. (1995). The science and politics of comparing women and men. *American Psychologist, 50*(3), 145–158. https://doi.org/10.1037/0003-066X.50.3.145

Eagly, A. H., & Crowley, M. (1986). Gender and helping behavior: A meta-analytic review of the social psychological literature. *Psychological Bulletin, 100*(3), 283–308. http://dx.doi.org/10.1037/0033-2909.100.3.283

Eagly, A. H., Eaton, A., Rose, S., Riger, S., & McHugh, M. (2012). Feminism and psychology: Analysis of a half-century of research. *American Psychologist, 67*(3), 211–230. https://doi.org/10.1037/a0027260

Eagly, A. H., & Karau, S. J. (2002). Role congruity theory of prejudice toward female leaders. *Psychological Review, 109*(3), 573–598. https://doi.org/10.1037/0033-295X.109.3.573

Eagly, A. H., & Riger, S. (2014). Feminism and psychology: Critiques of methods and epistemology. *American Psychologist, 69*(7), 685–702. https://doi.org/10.1037/a0037372

Eynon, R., Fry, J., & Schroeder, R. (2017). The ethics of online research. In N. G. Fielding, R. M. Lee, & G. Blank (Eds.), *The SAGE handbook of online research methods* (2nd ed., pp. 19–37). Sage.

Fausto-Sterling, A. (2019). Gender/sex, sexual orientation, and identity are in the body: How did they get there? *Journal of Sex Research, 56*(4/5), 529–555. https://doi.org/10.1080/00224499.2019.1581883

Fausto-Sterling, A. (2000). *Sexing the body: Gender politics and the construction of sexuality.* Basic Books.

Fenton, R. A., & Mott, H. L. (2018). Evaluation of the intervention initiative: A bystander intervention program to prevent violence against women in universities. *Violence and Victims, 33*(4), 645–662. https://doi.org/10.1891/0886-6708.VV-D-16-00074

Fine, C. (2010). *Delusions of gender: The real science behind sex differences.* Icon Books.

Fine, C. (2017). *Testosterone Rex.* Icon Books.

Fine, C., Joel, D., & Rippon, G. (2019a). Eight things you need to know about sex, gender, brains, and behavior: A guide for academics, journalists, parents, gender diversity advocates, social justice warriors, tweeters, facebookers, and everyone else. *Scholar & Feminist Online, 15.* https://sfonline.barnard.edu/neurogenderings/eight-things-you-need-to-know-about-sex-gender-brains-and-behavior-a-guide-for-academics-journalists-parents-gender-diversity-advocates-social-justice-warriors-tweeters-face-bookers-and-ever/

Fine, C., Joel, D., & Rippon, G. (2019b). Responding to ideas on sex differences in brain and behavior: Agreements, ghost disagreements, and points for continued debate. *Psychology Today, 17 July.* https://www.psychologytoday.com/gb/blog/sexual-personalities/201907/responding-ideas-sex-differences-in-brain-and-behavior

Fine, M., & Torre, M. E. (2019). Critical participatory action research: A feminist project for validity and solidarity. *Psychology of Women Quarterly, 43*(4), 433–444. https://journals.sagepub.com/doi/10.1177/0361684319865255

Flood, M. (2011). Involving men in efforts to end violence against women. *Men and Masculinities, 14*(3), 358–377. https://doi.org/10.1177/1097184X10363995

Foucault, M. (1980). *Power/knowledge: Selected interviews and other writings, 1972–1977.* Pantheon.

Foucault, M. (1981). Truth and power. In M. Lemert (Ed.), *French sociology: Rupture and renewal since 1968* (pp. 293–307). Columbia University Press.

Franzblau, S. H. (1999). II. Historicizing attachment theory: Binding the ties that bind. *Feminism & Psychology, 9*(1), 22–31. https://doi.org/10.1177/0959353599009001003

Fredrickson, B. L., Roberts, T.-A., Noll, S. M., Quinn, D. M., & Twenge, J. M. (1998). That swimsuit becomes you: Sex differences in self-objectification, restrained eating, and math performance. *Journal of Personality and Social Psychology, 75*(1), 269–284. https://doi.org/10.1037/0022-3514.75.1.269

Gaskins, S. (2013). The puzzle of attachment: Unscrambling maturational and cultural contributions to the development of early emotional bonds. In N. Quinn & J. Mageo (Eds.), *Attachment reconsidered* (pp. 33–64). Palgrave Macmillan.

Guthrie, R. V. (1976/2004). *Even the rat was white: A historical view of psychology* (2nd ed.). Allyn & Bacon Classics Edition.

Haaken, J., & Reavey. P. (Eds.) (2010). *Memory matters: Contexts for understanding sexual abuse recollections.* Routledge.

Haldeman, D. C. (1994). The practice and ethics of sexual orientation conversion therapy. *Journal of Consulting and Clinical Psychology, 62*(2), 221–227. https://doi.org/10.1037/0022-006X.62.2.221

Hanisch, C. (1969). *The personal is political.* Accessed October 2021. http://www.carolhanisch.org/CHwritings/PIP.html

Happel, A. A. (2012). *Practicing gender: A feminist ethnography of an all girls' afterschool club.* Dissertation, Georgia State University, 2012. https://scholarworks.gsu.edu/eps_diss/91

Hathaway, S. R., & McKinley, J. C. (1940). A multiphasic personality schedule (Minnesota): 1. Construction of the schedule. *Journal of Psychology, 10*(2), 249–254. https://doi.org/10.1080/00223980.1940.9917000

Hays, S. (1996). *The cultural contradictions of motherhood.* Yale University Press.

Hays, S. (1998). The fallacious assumptions and unrealistic prescriptions of attachment theory: A comment on 'Parents' Socioemotional Investment in Children'. *Journal of Marriage and Family, 60*(3), 782–790. https://doi.org/10.2307/353546

Henrich, J. (2020). *The WEIRDest people in the world: How the West became psychologically peculiar and particularly prosperous.* Penguin.

Henrich, J., Heine, S. J., & Norenzayan, A. (2010). The weirdest people in the world? *Behavioral and Brain Sciences, 33*(2/3), 61–83. https://doi.org/10.1017/S0140525X0999152X

Hines, M. (2020). Neuroscience and sex/gender: Looking back and forward. *Journal of Neuroscience, 40*(1), 37–43. https://doi.org/10.1523/JNEUROSCI.0750-19.2019

Hochschild, A. (2012). *The second shift: Working families and the revolution at home.* Penguin.

Hollingworth, L. S. (1914). Variability as related to sex differences in achievement: A critique. *American Journal of Sociology, 19*(4), 510–530. https://www.jstor.org/stable/2762962

hooks, b. (1984). *Feminist theory: From margin to center.* Routledge.

hooks, b. (2000). *Feminism is for everybody: Passionate politics.* South End Press.

Hopkins-Doyle, A., Sutton, R. M., Douglas, K. M., & Calogero, R. M. (2019). Flattering to deceive: Why people misunderstand benevolent sexism. *Journal of Personality and Social Psychology, 116*(2), 167–192. https://doi.org/10.1037/pspa0000135

Hyde, J. S. (2005). The gender similarities hypothesis. *American Psychologist, 60*(6), 581–592. http://dx.doi.org/10.1037/0003-066X.60.6.581

Hyde, J. S., Bigler, R. S., Joel, D., Tate, C. C., & van Anders, S. M. (2019). The future of sex and gender in psychology: Five challenges to the gender binary. *American Psychologist, 74*(2), 171–193. https://doi.org/10.1037/amp0000307

International Labour Organization (ILO) (2018a). *Care work and care jobs: For the future of decent work.* ILO.

International Labour Organization (ILO) (2018b). *Domestic workers across the world: Global and regional statistics and the extent of legal protection.* ILO.

International Labour Organization (ILO) (2020). *ILO Monitor: COVID-19 and the world of work* (6th ed.). ILO.

Joel, D. (2012). Genetic-gonadal-genitals sex (3G-sex) and the misconception of brain and gender, or, why 3G-males and 3G-females have intersex brain and intersex gender. *Biology of Sex Differences, 3*(27). https://doi.org/10.1186/2042-6410-3-27

Joel, D., Berman, Z., Tavor, I., Wexler, N., Gaber, O., Stein, Y., Shefi, N., Pool, J., Urchs, S., Margulies, D. S., Liem, F., Hänggi, J., Jäncke, L., & Assaf, Y. (2015). Sex beyond the genitalia: The human brain mosaic. *Proceedings of the National Academy of Sciences of the United States of America, 112*(50), 15468–15473. https://doi.org/10.1073/pnas.1509654112

Joel, D., & Vikhanski, L. (2019). *Gender mosaic: Beyond the myth of the male and female brain*. Endeavour.

Jordan-Young, R. M. (2010). *Brain storm: The flaws in the science of sex differences*. Harvard University Press.

Kağıtçıbaşı, Ç. (1996). *Family and human development across cultures: A view from the other side*. Erlbaum.

Keener, E. and Mehta, C. M. (2017) The past, present, and future of masculinity, femininity and gender: Honoring feminist scholar Sandra L. Bem (1944–2014), Part 1. *Sex Roles*, 76 (9/10).

Kessi, S., & Boonzaier, F. (2018). Centre/ing decolonial feminist psychology in Africa. *South African Journal of Psychology*, 48(3), 299–309. https://doi.org/10.1177/0081246318784507

Kirkman, M., Harrison, L., Hillier, L., & Pyett, P. (2001). 'I know I'm doing a good job': Canonical and autobiographical narratives of teenage mothers. *Culture, Health & Sexuality*, 3(3), 279–294. https://doi.org/10.1080/13691050010026097

Kitzinger, C. (1987). *The social construction of lesbianism*. Sage.

Kitzinger, C. (1991). Feminism, psychology and the paradox of power. *Feminism & Psychology*, 1(1), 111–129. https://doi.org/10.1177/0959353591011016

Kitzinger, C. (1994). Should psychologists study sex differences? *Feminism & Psychology*, 4(4), 501–506. https://doi.org/10.1177/0959353594044003

Kitzinger, C., & Wilkinson, S. (1997). Validating women's experience? Dilemmas in feminist research. *Feminism & Psychology*, 7(4), 566–574. https://doi.org/10.1177/0959353597074012

Kitzinger, J. (2003). Creating discourses of 'false memory': Media coverage and production dynamics. In P. Reavey & S. Warner (Eds.), *New Feminist Stories of Child Sexual Abuse* (pp. 106–119). Routledge.

Koss, M. P. (1985). The hidden rape victim: Personality, attitudinal, and situational characteristics. *Psychology of Women Quarterly*, 9(2), 193–212. https://doi.org/10.1111/j.1471-6402.1985.tb00872.x

Koss, M. P., Gidycz, C. A., & Wisniewski, N. (1987). The scope of rape: Incidence and prevalence of sexual aggression and victimization in a national sample of higher education students. *Journal of Consulting and Clinical Psychology*, 55(2) 162–170. https://doi.org/10.1037/0022-006X.55.2.162

Kuhn, T. S. (1962). *The structure of scientific revolutions*. University of Chicago Press.

Lafrance, M. N., & Wigginton, B. (2019). Doing critical feminist research: A *Feminism & Psychology* reader. *Feminism & Psychology*, 29(4), 534–552. https://doi.org/10.1177/0959353519863075

Latané, B., & Darley, J. M. (1970). *The unresponsive bystander: Why doesn't he help?* Appleton-Century-Crofts.

Latour, B., & Woolgar, S. (1979). *Laboratory life: The construction of scientific facts*. Sage.

Lazard, L. (2017, November 24). Here's the truth about false accusations of sexual violence. *The Conversation*. https://theconversation.com/uk

Lazard, L. (2020). *Sexual harassment, psychology and feminism: #MeToo, victim politics and predators in neoliberal times*. Palgrave Macmillan.

Lazard, L., & Capdevila, R. (2021). She's so vain? A Q study of selfies and the curation of an online self. *New Media & Society*, 23(6), 1642–1659. https://doi.org/10.1177/1461444820919335

Lazard, L., & McAvoy, J. (2020). Doing reflexivity in psychological research: What's the point? What's the practice? *Qualitative Research in Psychology*, 17(2), 159–177. https://doi.org/10.1080/14780887.2017.1400144

Leadbitter, K., Buckle, K. L., Ellis, C., & Dekker, M. (2021). Autistic self-advocacy and the neurodiversity movement: Implications for autism early intervention research and practice. *Frontiers in Psychology, 12*, 782–788. https://doi.org/10.3389/fpsyg.2021.635690

Leavy, P., & Harris, A. (2019). *Contemporary feminist research from theory to practice.* Guilford Press.

Lewis, R., Rowe, M., & Wiper, C. (2017). Online abuse of feminists as an emerging form of violence against women and girls. *British Journal of Criminology, 57*(6), 1462–1481. https://doi.org/10.1093/bjc/azw073

Loftus, E. F., & Ketcham, K. (1994). *The myth of repressed memory: False memories and allegations of sexual abuse.* St. Martin's Griffin.

Loftus, E. F., & Palmer, J. C. (1974). Reconstruction of automobile destruction: An example of the interaction between language and memory. *Journal of Verbal Learning and Verbal Behavior, 13*(5), 585–589. https://doi.org/10.1016/S0022-5371(74)80011-3

Loftus, E. F., & Pickrell, J. E. (1995). The formation of false memories. *Psychiatric Annals, 25*(12), 720–725. https://doi.org/10.3928/0048-5713-19951201-07

Logan, L. S. (2015). Street harassment: Current and promising avenues for researchers and activists. *Sociology Compass, 9*(3), 196–211. https://doi.org/10.1111/soc4.12248

Logothetis, N. K. (2008). What we can do and what we cannot do with fMRI. *Nature, 453*(7197), 869–878. https://doi.org/10.1038/nature06976

Lonsway, K. A., & Fitzgerald, L. F. (1994). Rape myths: In review. *Psychology of Women Quarterly, 18*(2), 133–164. https://doi.org/10.1111/j.1471-6402.1994.tb00448.x

Lykes, M. B. (2017). Community-based and participatory action research: Community psychology collaborations within and across borders. In M. A. Bond, I. Serrano-García, C. B. Keys, & M. Shinn (Eds.), *APA handbook of community psychology: Methods for community research and action for diverse groups and issues* (Vol. 2, pp. 43–58). American Psychological Association.

Lykes, M. B., & Scheib, H. (2016). Visual methodologies and participatory action research: Performing women's community-based health promotion in post-Katrina New Orleans. *Global Public Health, 11*(5/6), 742–761. https://doi.org/10.1080/17441692.2016.1170180

Maccoby, E. E., & Jacklin, C. N. (1974). *The psychology of sex differences.* Stanford University Press.

Macleod, C. I., Bhatia, S., & Liu, W. (2020). Feminisms and decolonising psychology: Possibilities and challenges. *Feminism & Psychology, 30*(3), 287–305. https://doi.org/10.1177/0959353520932810

Magnusson, K. (2022). Interpreting Cohen's d effect size: An interactive visualization (v. 2.5.2) [Web App]. *R Psychologist.* https://rpsychologist.com/cohend/

Main, M., & Solomon, J. (1990). Procedures for identifying infants as disorganized/disoriented during the Ainsworth Strange Situation. In M. T. Greenberg, D. Cicchetti, & E. M. Cummings (Eds.), *Attachment in the preschool years: Theory, research, and intervention* (pp. 121–160). University of Chicago Press.

Mamlouk, G. M., Dorris, D. M., Barrett, L. R., & Meitzen, J. (2020). Sex bias and omission in neuroscience research is influenced by research model and journal, but not reported NIH funding. *Frontiers in Neuroendocrinology, 57*, 100835. https://doi.org/10.1016/j.yfrne.2020.100835

Marecek, J. (1993). Disappearances, silences, and anxious rhetoric: Gender in abnormal psychology textbooks. *Journal of Theoretical and Philosophical Psychology, 13*(2), 114–123. http://dx.doi.org/10.1037/h0091108

Masuda, T., Batdorj, B., & Senzaki, S. (2020). Culture and attention: Future directions to expand research beyond the geographical regions of WEIRD cultures. *Frontiers in Psychology, 11*, 1394. https://doi.org/10.3389/fpsyg.2020.01394

Mattis, J. S., Grayman, N. A., Cowie, S.-A., Winston, C., Watson, C., & Jackson, D. (2008). Intersectional identities and the politics of altruistic care in a low-income, urban community. *Sex Roles, 59*(5/6), 418–428. https://doi.org/10.1007/s11199-008-9426-2

McClelland, S. I. (2011). Who is the 'self' in self reports of sexual satisfaction? Research and policy implications. *Sexuality Research and Social Policy, 8*(4), 304–320. https://doi.org/10.1007/s13178-011-0067-9

McClelland, S. I. (2017). Conceptual disruption: The self-anchored ladder in critical feminist research. *Psychology of Women Quarterly, 41*(4), 451–464. https://doi.org/10.1177/0361684317725985

McKinley, N. M., & Hyde, J. S. (1996). The objectified body consciousness scale: Development and validation. *Psychology of Women Quarterly, 20*(2), 181–215. https://doi.org/10.1111/j.1471-6402.1996.tb00467.x

Milchman, M. S. (2012). From traumatic memory to traumatized remembering: Beyond the memory wars, Part 1: Agreement. *Psychological Injury and Law, 5*, 37–50. https://doi.org/10.1007/s12207-012-9122-y

Milgram, S. (1974). *Obedience to authority: An experimental view*. Harper & Row.

Moane, G. (2014). Liberation psychology, feminism, and social justice psychology. In C. V. Johnson & H. L. Friedman (Eds.), *Praeger handbook of social justice and psychology* (Vol. 1, pp. 115–132). Praeger.

Morawski, J. G., & Agronick, G. (1991). A restive legacy: The history of feminist work in experimental and cognitive psychology. *Psychology of Women Quarterly, 15*(4), 567–579. https://doi.org/10.1111/j.1471-6402.1991.tb00431.x

Mukherjee, S. (2018). *Indian suffragettes: Female identities and transnational networks*. Oxford University Press.

Neto, F. (2012). The Satisfaction with Sex Life Scale. *Measurement and Evaluation in Counseling and Development, 45*(1), 18–31. https://doi.org/10.1177/0748175611422898

National Union of Students (NUS) (2010). *Hidden marks: A study of women students' experiences of harassment, stalking, violence and sexual assault*. NUS. https://itstopsnow.org/sites/default/files/2018-02/Hidden%20Marks-A%20study%20of%20women%20students%27%20experiences%20of%20harassment%2C%20stalking%2C%20violence%20%26%20sexual%20assault%20%28NUS%29.pdf

O'Dea, S. (2022, February 23). *Smartphone subscriptions worldwide 2016–2027*. Statista. https://www.statista.com

Office for National Statistics (ONS) (2018). *Household satellite account, UK: 2015 and 2016*. https://www.ons.gov.uk/economy/nationalaccounts/satelliteaccounts/articles/householdsatelliteaccounts/2015and2016estimates

Orne, M. T. (1962). On the social psychology of the psychological experiment: With particular reference to demand characteristics and their implications. *American Psychologist, 17*(11), 776–783. https://doi.org/10.1037/h0043424

Otgaar, H., Howe, M. L., & Patihis, L. (2021). What science tells us about false and repressed memories. *Memory, 30*(1), 16–21. https://doi.org/10.1080/09658211.2020.1870699

Oxford English Dictionary (n.d.). Social Justice. Retrieved October 26, 2021 from https://www.oed.com/

Parratt, K. A., & Pina, A. (2017). From 'real rape' to real justice: A systematic review of police officers' rape myth beliefs. *Aggression and Violent Behavior, 34*, 68–83. https://doi.org/10.1016/j.avb.2017.03.005

Persson, S., & Pownall, M. (2021). Can open science be a tool to dismantle claims of hardwired brain sex differences? Opportunities and challenges for feminist researchers. *Psychology of Women Quarterly, 45*(4), 493–504. https://doi.org/10.1177/03616843211037613

Peters, M., Laeng, B., Latham, K., Azyyouna, R., & Richardson, C. (1995). A redrawn Vandenberg and Kuse mental rotations test: Different versions and factors that affect performance. *Brain and Cognition, 28*(1), 39–58. https://doi.org/10.1006/brcg.1995.1032

Pireddu, S., Bongiorno, R., Ryan, M. K., Rubini, M., & Menegatti, M. (2022). The deficit bias: Candidate gender differences in the relative importance of facial stereotypic qualities to leadership hiring. *British Journal of Social Psychology, 61*(2), 644–671. https://doi.org/10.1111/bjso.12501

Pownall, M., Talbot, C. V., Henschel, A., Lautarescu, A., Lloyd, K. E., Hartmann, H., Darda, K. M., Tang, K. T., Carmichael-Murphy, P., & Siegel, J. A. (2021). Navigating open science as early career feminist researchers. *Psychology of Women Quarterly, 45*(4), 526–539. https://journals.sagepub.com/doi/10.1177/03616843211029255

Pynchon, T. (1973). *Gravity's rainbow*. Viking Press.

Quinn, N., & Mageo, J. (2013). Attachment and culture: An introduction. In N. Quinn & J. Mageo (Eds.), *Attachment reconsidered: Cultural perspectives on a Western theory* (pp. 3–32). Springer.

Ravn, S., Barnwell, A., & Barbosa Neves, B. (2020). What is 'publicly available data'? Exploring blurred public–private boundaries and ethical practices through a case study on Instagram. *Journal of Empirical Research on Human Research Ethics, 15*(1/2), 40–45. https://doi.org/10.1177/1556264619850736

Reason, P. E. (1994). *Participation in human inquiry*. Sage.

Reavey, P., & Warner, S. (2003). *New feminist stories of child sexual abuse: Sexual scripts and dangerous dialogues*. Routledge.

Riley, S., Evans, A., & Robson, M. (2018). *Postfeminism and health: Critical psychology and media perspectives*. Routledge.

Rippon, G. (2019). *The gendered brain: The new neuroscience that shatters the myth of the female brain*. Random House.

Rippon, G., Eliot, L., Genon, S., & Joel, D. (2021). How hype and hyperbole distort the neuroscience of sex differences. *PLoS Biology, 19*(5), e3001253. https://doi.org/10.1371/journal.pbio.3001253

Rippon, G., Jordan-Young, R., Kaiser, A., & Fine, C. (2014). Recommendations for sex/gender neuroimaging research: Key principles and implications for research design, analysis, and interpretation. *Frontiers in Human Neuroscience, 8*, 650. https://doi.org/10.3389/fnhum.2014.00650

Rivers, N. (2017). *Postfeminism (s) and the arrival of the fourth wave: Turning tides*. Springer.

Roediger, H. L., & McDermott, K. B. (1995). Creating false memories: Remembering words not presented in lists. *Journal of Experimental Psychology: Learning, Memory, & Cognition, 21*(4), 803–814. https://doi.org/10.1037/0278-7393.21.4.803

Rose, N. S. (1985). *The psychological complex: Psychology, politics, and society in England, 1869–1939*. Routledge & Kegan Paul.

Rosenberg, M. (1965). Rosenberg Self-Esteem scale (RSE). *Acceptance and Commitment Therapy. Measures Package, 61*(52), 18.

Rosenthal, R. (1967). Covert communication in the psychological experiment. *Psychological Bulletin, 67*(5), 356–367. https://doi.org/10.1037/h0024529

Rutherford, A. (2018). Feminism, psychology, and the gendering of neoliberal subjectivity: From critique to disruption. *Theory & Psychology, 28*(5), 619–644. https://doi.org/10.1177/0959354318797194

Ryan, M. K., Haslam, S. A., Morgenroth, T., Rink, F., Stoker, J., & Peters, K. (2016). Getting on top of the glass cliff: Reviewing a decade of evidence, explanations, and impact. *Leadership Quarterly, 27*(3), 446–455. https://doi.org/10.1016/j.leaqua.2015.10.008

Segall, M. H., Campbell, D. T., & Herskovits, M. J. (1966). *The influence of culture on visual perception* (pp. 174–184). Bobbs-Merrill.

Senft, T. M., & Baym, N. K. (2015). What does the selfie say? Investigating a global phenomenon. *International Journal of Communication, 9*, 1588–1606.

Shields, S. A. (1975). Functionalism, Darwinism and psychology of women: A study of social myth. *American Psychologist, 30*(7), 739–754. https://doi.org/10.1037/h0076948

Slater, J., & Jones, C. (2018). Around the Toilet: A research project report about what makes a safe and accessible toilet space (April 2015–February 2018). Sheffield Hallam University.

Smith, J. A., Harré, R., & Van Langenhove, L. (Eds.) (1995). *Rethinking methods in psychology.* Sage.

Spence, J. T., & Helmreich, R. (1972). The Attitudes Towards Women Scale: An objective instrument to measure attitudes towards the rights and roles of women in contemporary society. *Catalogue of Selective Documents in Psychology, 2*, No. 66.

Tariq, M., & Syed, J. (2017). Intersectionality at work: South Asian Muslim women's experiences of employment and leadership in the United Kingdom. *Sex Roles, 77*(7), 510–522. https://doi.org/10.1007/s11199-017-0741-3

Thambinathan, V., & Kinsella, E. A. (2021). Decolonizing methodologies in qualitative research: Creating spaces for transformative praxis. *International Journal of Qualitative Methods, 20.* https://doi.org/10.1177/16094069211014766

Thompson, H. B. (1903). *The mental traits of sex.* University of Chicago Press.

Thompson, J. (2017). 'Who expects death threats for asking for a woman on a banknote?' Caroline Criado-Perez campaigns to give women greater visibility in society. *Financial Times,* 10 November. https://www.ft.com/content/1d250ebe-bf1b-11e7-b8a3-38a6e068f464

Triandafilidis, Z., Ussher, J. M., Perz, J., & Huppatz, K. (2017). An intersectional analysis of women's experiences of smoking-related stigma. *Qualitative Health Research, 27*(10), 1445–1460. https://doi.org/10.1177/1049732316672645

Turley, E., & Fisher, J. (2018). Tweeting back while shouting back: Social media and feminist activism. *Feminism&Psychology,28*(1),128–132.https://doi.org/10.1177/0959353517715875

Unger, R. K. (1979). Toward a redefinition of sex and gender. *American Psychologist, 34*(11), 1085–1094. https://doi.org/10.1037/0003-066X.34.11.1085

van Anders, S. M. (2013). Beyond masculinity: Testosterone, gender/sex, and human social behavior in a comparative context. *Frontiers in Neuroendocrinology, 34*(3), 198–210. https://doi.org/10.1016/j.yfrne.2013.07.001

van der Zee, T., & Reich, J. (2018). Open Education Science. *AERA Open.* https://doi.org/10.1177/2332858418787466

Van IJzendoorn, M. H., & Kroonenberg, P. M. (1988). Cross-cultural patterns of attachment: A meta-analysis of the strange situation. *Child Development, 59*(1), 147–156. https://doi.org/10.2307/1130396

Vasquez, M. J. (2012). Psychology and social justice: Why we do what we do. *American Psychologist, 67*(5), 337–346. https://doi.org/10.1037/a0029232

Warfield, K. (2014, October 29–30). *Making selfies/making self: Digital subjectivities in the selfie.* Fifth International Conference on the Image, Berlin, Germany. https://kora.kpu.ca/islandora/object/kora:39/datastream/PDF

Waters, E., Bretherton, I., & Vaughn, B. E. (2015). Preface. In M. D. S. Ainsworth, M. C. Blehar, E. Waters, & S. N. Wall, *Patterns of attachment: A psychological study of the strange situation* (Classic Edition). Psychology Press.

Watson, S. (2019, November 6). Analysis shows horrifying extent of abuse sent to women MPs via Twitter. *The Conversation.* https://theconversation.com/analysis-shows-horrifying-extent-of-abuse-sent-to-women-mps-via-twitter-126166

Wechsler, D. (1955). *Manual for the Wechsler Adult Intelligence Scale (WAIS).* Psychological Corporation.

Weis, L., & Fine, M. (2012). Critical bifocality and circuits of privilege: Expanding critical ethnographic theory and design. *Harvard Educational Review, 82*(2), 173–201. https://doi.org/10.17763/haer.82.2.v1jx34n441532242

Weisner, T. S. (Ed.). (2005). *Discovering successful pathways in children's development: Mixed methods in the study of childhood and family life.* University of Chicago Press.

Weisstein, N. (1971). Psychology constructs the female. *Journal of Social Education, 35,* 362–373.

Whitaker, K., & Guest, O. (2020). #bropenscience is broken science. *The Psychologist, 33,* 34–37.

Whitley, B. E. (1984). Sex role orientation and psychological well-being: Two meta-analyses. *Sex Roles, 12,* 207–225. https://doi.org/10.1007/BF00288048

Whitley, B. E. (1988). Masculinity, femininity and self-esteem: A multitrait-multimethod analysis. *Sex Roles, 18,* 419–431. https://doi.org/10.1007/BF00288393

Wigginton, B., & Lafrance, M. N. (2019). Learning critical feminist research: A brief introduction to feminist epistemologies and methodologies. *Feminism & Psychology.* https://journals.sagepub.com/doi/10.1177/0959353519866058

Wilkinson, S. (1988). The role of reflexivity in feminist psychology. *Women's Studies International Forum, 11*(5), 493–502. https://doi.org/10.1016/0277-5395(88)90024-6

Wilkinson, S., & Burns, J. (1990). Women organising within psychology. In E. Burman (Ed.), *Feminists and psychological practice* (pp. 140–162). Sage.

Williams, M. L., Burnap, P., & Sloan, L. (2017). Towards an ethical framework for publishing Twitter data in social research: Taking into account users' views, online context and algorithmic estimation. *Sociology, 51*(6), 1149–1168. https://doi.org/10.1177/0038038517708140

Willig, C., & Rogers, W. S. (Eds.) (2017). *The SAGE handbook of qualitative research in psychology.* Sage.

Wilson, E. A. (2015). *Gut feminism.* Duke University Press.

WIN – Wellcome Centre for Integrative Neuroimaging (2021, August 26). *What is FMRI?* https://www.ndcn.ox.ac.uk/divisions/fmrib/what-is-fmri

Wolf, N. (1990). *The beauty myth: How images of beauty are used against women.* Chatto & Windus.

Woolley, H. T. (1914). The psychology of sex. *Psychological Bulletin, 11*(10), 353–379. https://doi.org/10.1037/h0070064

Worrell, M. (2003). Working at being survivors: Identity, gender and participation in self-help groups. In P. Reavey & S. Warner (Eds.), *New feminist stories of child sexual abuse* (pp. 222–237). Routledge.

Xue, B., & McMunn, A. (2021). Gender differences in unpaid care work and psychological distress in the UK Covid-19 lockdown. *PLoS One, 16*(3), e0247959. https://doi.org/10.1371/journal.pone.0247959

Yapp, E. J., & Quayle, E. (2018). A systematic review of the association between rape myth acceptance and male-on-female sexual violence. *Aggression and Violent Behavior, 41*, 1–19. https://doi.org/10.1016/j.avb.2018.05.002

Yardley, E. (2008). Teenage mothers' experiences of stigma. *Journal of Youth Studies, 11*(6), 671–684. https://doi.org/10.1080/13676260802392940

Zhang, Y., Luo, Q., Huang, C. C., Lo, C. Y. Z., Langley, C., Desrivières, S. & IMAGEN Consortium. (2021). The human brain is best described as being on a female/male continuum: Evidence from a neuroimaging connectivity study. *Cerebral Cortex, 31*(6), 3021–3033. https://doi.org/10.1093/cercor/bhaa408

Subject Index

violence
  abuse 17–18, 45, 50, 121
  against women and girls 17, 30–31
  child/childhood sexual abuse 54–68
  domestic abuse/violence 13–14,
    123–125
  rape 14, 31, 78–79, 124
  sexual abuse 123

sexual assault 16, 30–31, 67, 78–79,
  121–124
sexual harassment 16, 26, 120–121
sexual violence 19, 79, 120–124

WEIRD: White, Educated, Industrialised,
  Rich and Democratic 26–27, 139,
  147–148

Author Index